PRAISE FOR
THE WRITER'S WORLD

"A brilliant publishing enterprise. One of the best elements in American culture is a genuine, welcoming interest in writing from other languages. Beginning with essential writers from Ireland, Mexico, and Poland, the series fills a vital need. Edward Hirsch is absolutely the right general editor to guide the series. In a time of clouds, anxieties, disasters, and blunders regarding our place among the nations, here is a beacon."
— ROBERT PINSKY

"These handsome, beautifully written, and thoughtfully edited volumes could not come at a more opportune moment. Even as our political borders are growing more rigid and fiercely defended, these welcome books remind us of the ways in which literature will always cross the most seemingly impermeable barrier and leap the highest wall."
— FRANCINE PROSE

"What an inspired way to engage other cultures: through the meditations of writers on the subject that they know best—writing. And what we discover in the essays collected in The Writer's World is that for all of our seeming differences and genuine divisions, we are bound by words, which in every language offer windows through which to glimpse the heart of the matter: what it means to be alive."
— CHRISTOPHER MERRILL

"The Writer's World is a wonderfully intriguing and exciting series. Each book is like a conference of great writers and thinkers brought together to consider matters essential to culture and society. There's nothing like it."
— C. K. WILLIAMS

ROMANIAN WRITERS
on Writing

Vanity doubled by vitality, vulnerability mixed in with force, and the fear of dissolution intimately linked with the desperate pride of defeating historical time confer upon Romanian literature a special tension, born from wandering and threat. The eighty writers gathered in *Romanian Writers on Writing* explore this unsettling tension and exemplify the powerful, polyphonic voice of their country's complex literature.

CONTRIBUTORS

Gabriela Adameşteanu
Ştefan Agopian
Tudor Arghezi
George Bacovia
George Bălăiţă
Cezar Baltag
Ion Barbu
Lucian Blaga
Ana Blandiana
Max Blecher
Nicolae Breban
Emil Brumaru
Matei Călinescu
Ion Luca Caragiale
Mateiu I. Caragiale
Ion Caraion
Magda Cârneci
Mircea Cărtărescu
Nina Cassian
Paul Celan
Ruxandra Cesereanu
E. M. Cioran
Andrei Codrescu
Radu Cosaşu
Gheorghe Crăciun
Ioan Petru Culianu
Leonid Dimov
Virgil Duda

Petru Dumitriu
Mircea Eliade
Mihai Eminescu
Carmen Firan
Filip Florian
Benjamin Fundoianu /
    Benjamin Fondane
Bogdan Ghiu
Paul Goma
Vintilă Horia
Florina Ilis
Doina Ioanid
Eugène Ionesco /
    Eugen Ionescu
Panait Istrati
Nora Iuga
Mircea Ivănescu
Florin Lăzărescu
Gherasim Luca
Dan Lungu
Mariana Marin
Virgil Mazilescu
Gabriela Melinescu
Florin Mugur
Ion Mureşan
Alexandru Muşina
Gellu Naum
Mircea Nedelciu

Octavian Paler
Hortensia Papadat-
    Bengescu
Camil Petrescu
Radu Petrescu
Răzvan Petrescu
Marta Petreu
Cristian Popescu
Simona Popescu
Marin Preda
Liviu Rebreanu
Ana Maria Sandu
Mihail Sebastian
Alexandru Sever
Mircea Horia Simionescu
Ion D. Sîrbu
Marin Sorescu
Nichita Stănescu
Bogdan Suceavă
Octav Şuluţiu
Lucian Dan Teodorovici
Dumitru Ţepeneag
Constantin Ţoiu
Floarea Ţuţuianu
Tristan Tzara
Matei Vişniec
Alexandru Vlad

THE WRITER'S WORLD
Edward Hirsch, SERIES EDITOR

The Writer's World features writers from around the globe discussing what it means to write, and to be a writer, in many different parts of the world. The series collects a broad range of material and provides access for the first time to a body of work never before gathered in English. Edward Hirsch, the series editor, is internationally acclaimed as a poet and critic. He is the president of the John Simon Guggenheim Memorial Foundation.

Chinese Writers on Writing (2010)
EDITED BY Arthur Sze

Hebrew Writers on Writing (2008)
EDITED BY Peter Cole

Irish Writers on Writing (2007)
EDITED BY Eavan Boland

Mexican Writers on Writing (2007)
EDITED BY Margaret Sayers Peden

Nineteenth-Century American Writers on Writing (2010)
EDITED BY Brenda Wineapple

Polish Writers on Writing (2007)
EDITED BY Adam Zagajewski

Romanian Writers on Writing (2011)
EDITED BY Norman Manea and Sanda Cordoş

Trinity University Press gratefully acknowledges the following Patrons of The Writer's World:

Sarah Harte and John Gutzler
Mach Family Fund, Joella and Steve Mach

The press also thanks Bard College for its generous support of this book.

ROMANIAN WRITERS

On Writing

Norman Manea,
EDITOR

Sanda Cordoş,
CO-EDITOR

Raluca Manea and Carla Baricz,
ASSISTANT EDITORS

TRANSLATORS

TRINITY UNIVERSITY PRESS
San Antonio, Texas

Published by Trinity University Press
San Antonio, Texas 78212

Copyright © 2011 by Norman Manea and Sanda Cordoş

Complete copyright information continues on page 297.

Cover design by Kristina Kachele Design, LLC
Book design by BookMatters, Berkeley
Cover illustration: *1st of December (Romania)*, by Roman Tolici, 2006

The paper used in this publication meets the minimum requirements of the American National Standard for Information Sciences—Permanence of Paper for Printed Library Materials, ANSI Z39.48-1992.

Trinity University Press strives to produce its books using methods and materials in an environmentally sensitive manner. We favor working with manufacturers that practice sustainable management of all natural resources, produce paper using recycled stock, and manage forests with the best possible practices for people, biodiversity, and sustainability.

Library of Congress Cataloging-in-Publication Data

Romanian writers on writing / Norman Manea, editor ; Sanda Cordos, co-editor.
    p. cm. — (The writer's world)
Includes bibliographical references and index.

Summary: "The eighty writers collected here explore the special tensions found in Romanian literature, conferred by vanity doubled by vitality, vulnerability mixed in with force, and the fear of dissolution linked with the desperate pride of defeating historical time. The contributors exemplify the powerful, polyphonic voice of their country's complex literature"—Provided by publisher.

ISBN 978-1-59534-082-5 (pbk. : alk. paper)
  1. Romanian literature—History and criticism.   2. Authorship—Literary collections.
  3. Romania—In literature. I. Manea, Norman. II. Cordos, Sanda.

PC803.R66 2011
859.08—dc22
                                                            2011004947

15 14 13 12 11   5 4 3 2 1

Contents

Preface

By strict definition, an anthology is eclectic when—as in this case—it does not focus on a certain theme, but on an entire literature. If selection of texts necessarily implies the taste and skill of the anthologist—self-defining qualities in the context of an anthology—the criteria and particular circumstances of this selection must be, I believe, clearly stated in the preliminaries of the volume.

For me, the essential criteria of literary affiliation is and has always been language. Therefore, we chose to omit from our collection certain important writers who were born in Romania or whose literary careers were influenced, at least partially, by their Romanian heritage, but who wrote in other languages. I am referring to German writers of Romanian origin (Gregor von Rezorri, Oskar Pastior, Paul Schuster, Dieter Schlesak, Franz Hodjak, Herta Müller, Ernest Wichner, et al.), to writers who wrote in Hebrew (Aharon Appelfeld, Dan Pagis, Yoel Hoffmann) or in Yiddish (Itik Manger, Alexander Spiegelblat), as well as to the entire community of Hungarian writers that developed in Romania and continues to thrive there.

This anthology is also limited to prose writers and poets, even if, or precisely because, the number of Romanian critics and essayists who have contributed in a profound and stimulating way to the discussion on writing and the writer's task is not at all marginal. This ample and interesting secondary material could easily justify a separate anthology. In connection with the aforesaid omissions, I must mention, even in such a brief note, the conspicuous absence of Lucian Raicu, who in everything he has written about books and authors, both foreign and Romanian, classic and modern, remains an acute and original thinker of uncommon expressivity and artistic creativity.

Fortunately, this anthology does include great names of Romanian exile, writers who at some point in their lives wrote in Romanian, even if they later embraced other cultures, world culture. I am referring to Eugen Ionescu (Eugène Ionesco), B. Fundoianu (Benjamin Fondane), Paul Celan, Tristan Tzara, Mircea Eliade, and E. M. Cioran.

Addressing itself primarily to the American reading public and readers of English at large, the present anthology is the inevitable result of a confrontation with the difficult problem of translation. Though we benefited from the skill of two excellent and perfectly bilingual translators, there were, predictably enough, cases when the finesse and plurality of meanings in the original were diminished or drastically deformed in the foreign linguistic and cultural context. Not only did the linguistic transport from a Romance language deriving from an Eastern and Central European culture with a large degree of Slavic and Balkan sedimentation into a Germanic language prove challenging, but one was also faced with the difficulties arising from changes in literary taste of the modern and postmodern *Anschaung* of the new generation, not only of American but of global readers. We have preferred, therefore, to avoid ambiguous, if not repelling, situations as much as possible.

It's useless to say that the present anthologists hope that in spite of, or perhaps precisely because of, the previously mentioned limitations, the reader will find that this selection offers a revealing and inviting window into the originality and profundity of Romanian literature. A Romanian saying ("We don't have saints, only poets"), often used to refer derogatorily to the country, could perhaps gain, in this manner, a more fitting use.

I could not end these laconic statements without thanking my collaborators: Sanda Cordoş, associate professor of Romanian literature at the prestigious trilingual university Babes-Bolyai in Cluj-Napoca, the capital of Transylvania, for her meticulous and assiduous research and selection of texts in Romania's libraries, and the young and wonderfully gifted translators and editors, Carla Baricz and Raluca Manea. This book would not have been possible without their competence and patient devotion. (*Translated by Carla Baricz*)

Norman Manea
Bard College, July 2010

Introduction

SANDA CORDOŞ

> I accuse you and your historical circumstances . . . for all my
> insufficiencies of intelligence, culture, intellectual life and
> genius. If I had been French, I might have been a genius.

To a large extent, this sentence, which Eugène Ionesco wrote when he was twenty-five in an incendiary book entitled *No*—at a time when his name was Eugen Ionescu and he was still living in Romania—is emblematic for the profile of the Romanian writer. The latter feels exasperated by the peripheral character of the culture and language in which he creates, derides his inability to detach himself from the historical circumstances in which he is forced or decides to become involved with, and projects, in a compensatory manner, the phantasm of evading and becoming, one day, the chosen one. Several events made Ionescu's despair into the equivalent, in his case, of a prophecy.

In 1934, when the pamphlet *No* was published, Romanian literature in an artistic sense was relatively recent, no older than a century, much like the national history of the country in a modern sense. But since, as historian Lucian Boia points out, "Romania first took form in consciousnesses" and "one could say that it is a country created by scholars: writers, historians, men of learning,"[1] writers have lived with the pressing urgency of a country that must be constantly (re)made. This often meant that artistic pursuits had to be abandoned in favor of national projects and that those involved in journalism had to become involved in the shaping of governments, parliaments, universities, civic organizations, and others. Practically, with the exception of the first

Romania: Borderland of Europe (London: Reaktion Books, 2001); *România: Ţară de frontieră a Europei* (Bucureşti: Humanitas, 2002), 221.

I

generation engaged in this twofold project (national and literary), the so-called '48 generation, which shared the messianic ideology of the 1848 Revolutions in Europe and in which enthusiasm and faith in the future prevailed (despite the fact that quite a few of its representatives were exiled), all other literary generations dramatically felt the pressure of *historical circumstances*. The tremendous energy invested in building the country was always accompanied both by a feeling of futility and an awareness of its provisional endurance. This ambivalent attitude is to be found in the testimonies of the writers who were members of the so-called generation of great classics in the second half of the nineteenth century, Mihai Eminescu and I. L. Caragiale, those who forged the trails deemed paradigmatic for Romanian literature. The former, situated in a post-Romantic tradition, presides over a solemn orientation, with metaphysical openings and abyssal experiences; the latter is the initiator of an orientation that valorizes—with humor and dramatic touches—street talk and everyday life along with its aberrations; he is a precursor to Ionesco, who translated him into French. Swamped in his journalistic work, Eminescu acknowledges the following in a letter from 1882: "In the eight years since I have returned to Romania [from studies in Berlin and Vienna], one disappointment followed another and I feel so old, so tired that in vain do I reach for my pen to try and write something. I feel that I can no longer do that, I feel depleted from a moral perspective and that I would need a long, a very long break to recover. And, in spite of all this, like the common factory workers, I can't have such a break anywhere, with anybody. I am crushed, I cannot find myself, and no longer recognize myself."

A few years later, Caragiale, who, exasperated by the atmosphere of political intrigues and corruption in the country, spent the last years of his life in voluntary exile in Berlin, expounds similar views: "I do not hold my pen dear, quite the contrary. It is a tool with which I have never made anything useful for my world, but with which I have caused myself a lot of trouble and great disservice. If I could, I would exchange it at any point for a tool more honorable, more useful to me and others. Let my enemies have this one blessing from me: for all generations to come, may at least one out of three children become Romanian literati, and nothing but Romanian literati."

Emil Cioran, Ionescu's coeval, also speaks of the "aggressive void of the sorrowful motherland and the emptiness that rages through her sons' souls," because, he continues, when living in Romania "you automatically become Job" and "a prisoner of time" (*The Passionate Handbook*). Mircea Eliade, a member of the same generation, writes, decades later, at the end of his *Memoirs:* "I belong to the most fortunate generation that Romanian history has ever known. Neither prior to nor following our generation did Romania enjoy the freedom, the wealth and the availability that we, who wrote between 1925 and 1940, enjoyed . . . We were the first among Romanians who could work on something other than national history, Romanian philology and cultural prophesying—without having the feeling that we would betray the cause of the people." But, the writer goes on to concede, "we had intuited for a while that *we would not have time*, that the freedom that we enjoyed was provisional, and our safety illusory, that, very soon, *History* would detain us again." Under the pressure of this fleeting chance, but also because of a renewed energy of production, the interwar period (which did not lack, otherwise, in political problems—in particular the emergence in the 1930s of a right-wing, pro-fascist movement that was supported by some writers) is one of exceptional literary effervescence. Literary reviews and circles that encourage ideological debates and an ongoing dialogue with Western culture (which serves as a catalyst) appear. As E. Lovinescu, the most influential literary critic of the moment, put it: "In our day and age, the light shines from the West: *ex occidente lux!* Progress can only mean the fecundation of the national element by the creative element of Western ideology" (*The History of Modern Romanian Civilization*). In fact, the great directions of European modernism are to be found in Romania in the remarkable works of fiction writers Hortensia Papadat-Bengescu, Camil Petrescu, Liviu Rebreanu, Max Blecher, Mateiu I. Caragiale, Mihail Sebastian, Mircea Eliade and of poets Benjamin Fundoianu, Tristan Tzara, Tudor Arghezi, Ion Barbu, Lucian Blaga, Gherasim Luca, Gellu Naum, et al. As Tudor Vianu, another important critic, shows, "a very scrupulous aesthetic consciousness" as well as the sacrificial conception of the act of creation come into being. "The creation of culture sometimes asks for exceptional sacrifices: it kills and ravages. Creation has its own fire . . . Creation often crushes the creator," writes Lucian Blaga, poet and, at the same time, author of an original work on the philosophy of culture.

The two traits are also to be found in the postwar period, the most difficult for Romanian literature as it takes place—from 1947 to 1989—under a Communist, dictatorial regime. Political power turns literature (as well as all other arts) into a form of propaganda. For over a decade, with rare and miraculous exceptions, only those books that follow political directives, serving *the formation of communist consciousness* (to use a frequent expression from the documents of the Communist Party) get published. Gradually, however, and more determinedly from the mid-1960s onward, a significant part of literature—the one truly important from an aesthetic perspective—manages to gain a certain autonomy in relation to political power and thus to disseminate alternative values to the official ones. Shielded by its aesthetic and fictional status, literature plays the role of a free press for decades and reveals communal traumas: it engages religious themes under an atheistic regime that banned the circulation of the Bible, and the rich problematic of the individual *I* where the ideology of the collective *we* reigned and where the individual was considered subversive. Literature speaks of unhappiness, despair, and anguish in a world condemned to happiness in the name of official optimism. Despite the intervention of censure, which eliminates from manuscripts those pages or chapters thought of as hostile, literary works of superior quality, well received by the reading public, are published. One could evoke here the following poets: Geo Dumitrescu, Ion Caraion, Radu Stanca, Ştefan Aug. Doinaş, A. E. Baconsky, Mircea Ivănescu, Florin Mugur, Nichita Stănescu, Leonid Dimov, Cezar Baltag, Gabriela Melinescu, Nora Iuga, Ana Blandiana, Emil Brumaru, Virgil Mazilescu, Mircea Cărtărescu, Marta Petreu, Ion Mureşan, Alexandru Muşina, Mariana Marin, Magda Cârneci, Matei Vişniec. Among fiction writers, one notes Marin Preda, Radu Cosaşu, Constantin Ţoiu, Radu Petrescu, Mircea Horia Simionescu, George Bălăiţă, Nicolae Breban, Norman Manea, Dumitru Ţepeneag, Gabriela Adameşteanu, Augustin Buzura, Gheorghe Crăciun, Mircea Nedelciu, Alexandru Vlad, Ioan Groşan, Adina Kereneş, et al.

Faced with ongoing political pressure and ever more precarious living conditions, the writers of this period conferred a major existential investment upon the act of writing, practicing what Gabriela Adameşteanu, the fiction writer, calls the "artistic deontology of a religious type," a "schizophrenic or monastic" condition, intensified by totalitarian seclusion, "of the artist who 'sacrifices' . . . every lived moment, exposing it to a foreign gaze." This sacrificial conception (albeit blurred by irony and sarcasm) is common to a majority of the writers of the time who have been collected in the present volume, from Ion Caraion and Marin Preda to Mircea Cărtărescu and Cristian Popescu. It was also put forth in seminal books by literary critic Lucian Raicu (particularly in *Reflections on the Creative Spirit*, 1979) as well as in works by Norman Manea. The latter is one of the writers who has reflected in a constant and acute manner on the act of literary creation, both in his fiction and in the essays from the volumes *The Apprenticeship Years of Augustus the Fool* (1979) and *On the Edge* (1984). This problematic is also found in the books written in exile, particularly *On Clowns: the Dictator and the Artist* (1992) and *The Hooligan's Return* (2003), in which the theme of nomadic language emerges. Unfortunately, the author excluded himself from the present selection, preferring to play host to his Romanian colleagues.

After the fall of communism in December 1989, a new cycle of desperate reconstruction began in Romania. Writers became involved in journalism, academia, politics, to a lesser degree, and various groups and organizations that dealt with the onerous task of rebuilding civil society. Since the decades spent under dictatorial rule had intensified "the sense of perpetual threat and of a provisional state" (as Mircea Martin, the critic, would argue) as well as the feeling of captivity, after 1990 literature developed, in a compensatory manner, a powerful vision of the country as a cursed land. Since "we live here as emigrants" (Petre Barbu, *God Blesses America*, 1995), it is here that the "metastasis of hope" (Adrian Oțoiu, *Hot Keys for Soft Windows*, 1998) takes place, here that "everybody dreams of no longer being Romanian, and rather of becoming American, Canadian, Australian, European" (Florina Ilis, *The Children's Crusade*, 2005). Radu Pavel Gheo's book *Farewell, Farewell My Land, with î from i, with â from a*, a confession about the author's one-year immigration to the U.S. and his subsequent return to Romania, also tells of a country that drives you away and calls you back at the same time. In an interview from 2004, Matei Călinescu, the Romanian writer and American professor, speaks of the Romania of recent years as a fascinating "center of vanity, the place where you can have a concrete experience of vanity, an experience religious and metaphysical at the same time, which the Ecclesiast describes well: everything is vanity and a striving after wind . . ."

Vanity doubled by vitality, vulnerability mixed in with force, and the fear of dissolution intimately linked with the desperate pride of defeating historical time confers upon Romanian literature a special tension, born from wandering and threat, which is proper, otherwise, to true literature of all ages. As Mircea Cărtărescu, one of the most important Romanian writers of the moment, puts it: "Romanian literature is a *normal* European literature, with authors who are hyperconscious of their craft, extremely technical, complex and yet easy to understand and love. Nothing so exotic it can no longer be understood; on the other hand, there is something unsettling and nostalgic coming out of Romanian." A language which Herta Müller, a German writer of Romanian origins (who emigrated in 1987), says is, like all Romance languages, lithe and delicate. Comparing it to German, she writes: "Its spontaneity is greater, I believe it is more alive and has more levels, especially in the realm of feelings, of relations. In German, for instance, if you have a lover and want to address him lovingly, you call him *Schatz*—*Schatz* means treasure. Whereas in Romanian there are so many words for the same thing, there is more tenderness and that is why it is more difficult to translate."

I would be happy if American readers discovered something of the powerful, polyphonic voice of Romanian literature through the present anthology, which has the inevitable limits of any endeavor of its kind, but strives to offer a selection representative of Romanian literary craft.

(Translated by Raluca Manea)

Mihai Eminescu

(1850–1889)

Born in 1850, as the seventh of eleven children of a family of small-time boyars, Mihai Eminescu had a tumultuous life, which began with his escape from the German high school he attended. During his adolescence, he worked as a copyist for the law courts and as a line prompter for a traveling theater. He began university studies in philosophy—never completed—in Vienna and Berlin, cities from which he returned in 1874 to work as a professor, librarian, school inspector, and newspaper man. In 1883 he began experiencing psychological disturbances, which led to fewer and fewer moments of lucidity. Eminescu died in 1889, in a psychiatric clinic.

Recognized by his contemporaries as an exceptional poet, Eminescu published only one volume of poetry during his lifetime—*Poems* (1883). However, the posthumous editions of his *Works* is made up of twenty volumes containing mostly poetry but also prose, theater, journalistic writings, essays, translations (among others, from Kant), and correspondence. An encyclopedic and tormented soul, Eminescu cultivated different species and forms of literature, crystallizing the modern Romanian literary terminology (still valid today) and exploring both Romantic motifs—such as the titan, the genius, cosmogony, the national mission—as well as post-Romantic damnation, alienation, impossibility of communication, absurdity of living, and the death of God. Due to his great talent and to the force of his literature, but also because of the vulnerability of his life (marked by illness, deprivations, and an unhappy liaison with the poet

Veronica Micle) in which thousands of readers have recognized themselves, Eminescu benefits both from high critical acclaim and a cult following. He is considered by many, if not by most, the national poet. (*Translated by Carla Baricz*)

THE PERSONALITY OF THE CREATOR

[. . .] Rather than pseudo-talent in literature, better talent in humaneness. Better to be first in the village than second in Rome. There have been thousands upon thousands of men such as you in the world and there will continue to be. None of you—it shouldn't cross any of your minds that you are geniuses. For, my children, our earth is poorer in geniuses than the universe is in fixed stars; and it is easier for a new solar system to be birthed in the immeasurable valleys of chaos, than for a genius to be born on Earth. Homer and Shakespeare, Raphael, the geniuses of art are born once every three, four thousand years. Newton and Galileo, Kant or Darwin, the geniuses of science, once every thousand years, so that I really do not know if from Adam to Pope Leo IX there have been more than a dozen. As for the rest, we are all some wretched souls to whom these kings of thought give work for generations to come. If we have talent, meaning a few centigrams of brains more than the *semen communis*, we can value it for our time by conscientious work; if we do not work, we remain much like our brothers, the beasts. [. . .]

As an artist or a man of letters, it is good that your person remains unknown to your readers—and the more talent you will have, the more this is necessary. Distance makes it seem that the author of this or that interesting piece must be a very special man—in fact, however, whatever your powers of imagination or judgment may be, you still remain man, with all the defects and weaknesses attributed to this word. If you could taste, unknown and in secret, the praises of those people, how you would love them—and well, if you can't, don't show yourself to them. [. . .]

How long has it been since someone (whoever this may be) read the biography of a genius and attempted to find, to encipher even, the likeliness of his individuality into those large features of a great man? For, truly, in each human organism there are, potentially, the chords of the whole of humanity.

We do not speak of the steps—these are infinite. Perhaps it is from there that we draw the pleasure that people find in the works of the poets—and from there the oftentimes startling similarity of passages, even of organic thoughts of those great authors. It is the *same* man who lives in all—and inferior natures think that those [those great men] have all plagiarized each other, when in reality perhaps they have not even read one another.

And because each one finds anew the pith of his individuality in those great ones, he thinks it his duty to reissue in commentaries and individual ramifications that pith; thus are then born the different glossarists and explicators, all of them poets of "the great authors."

Translated by Carla Baricz

To My Critics

Many as they be, few flowers
Bear some fruit for the next year;
At life's gate now are all knocking;
Many, fruitless, disappear.

It is easy to write poems
When you have nothing to say,
Stringing empty words on patterns
That impress as mere word-play.

When, however, fiery yearnings
And mad passions tear your heart,
And your heart is bound to listen
To them all, to each in part,

At the gate of thought, like flowers
At life's doorway, they beseech
Entrance to the world and covet
The appropriate garb of speech.

Of your troublesome existence,
Of your passions, groans and sighs,

Where are the relentless judges,
Where the evil-minded eyes?

Ah! at such most trying moments
One feels covered up with shame:
Where can one for truth discover
The best suited word and name?

Critics, you bear fruitless flowers,
Though you strive as best you may;
It is easy to write poems
When you have nothing to say.

Translated by Leon Levițchi

Ion Luca Caragiale

(1852–1912)

Born in 1852 in a family that produced a number of actors, Ion Luca Caragiale attended the Conservatory in Bucharest, taking classes in declamation and mimicking. He worked as a functionary, line prompter, beer seller, general director of theaters, and newspaper man. He also edited a number of literary magazines. Disliking the atmosphere of corruption and intrigue present in the country, he immigrated with his family to Berlin in 1905, where he continued to live until his death in 1912.

He is considered, along with Mihai Eminescu, the creator of "Romanian literature" in the modern sense, since his works, like those of his poetic counterpart, combine classical concision with realism and character studies. As a playwright, he published a volume of *Theater* (1889) containing comedies and drama. He also wrote prose, and was known as the author of sketches (most of them comical) that were published first in serial form and then in the volumes *Light Sketches* (1896), *Sketches* (1897), *Moments* (1901), *Mitică* (1902)—and of novellas: *Sin, A Torch for Easter, Lucky Man* (1892), and *Two Lost Tickets* (1901). From his many articles, he is known for "The Wings of the National Question" (1896) and "1907 from Spring to Autumn" (1907).

His works combine the genius of classic comedy (of situations, manners, language) of the Molière type with the investigation of psychological anxieties and foreign situations. Considering him "the greatest of unknown playwrights," Eugène Ionesco writes of him in a sketch dedicated to Caragiale in *Notes and Counternotes:* "The distance between a language as obscure as it is elevated and the petty cunning of his characters, deriving from their ceremonious politeness and their fundamental knavishness, the grotesque adulteries mixed in all of this, cause this theater at long last to pass beyond naturalism into the realm of the absurdo-fantastic. Never dominated by a feeling of culpability, nor by the idea of some sacrifice, nor by any other idea ('As long as we have a head, why would intelligence be necessary?' Caragiale ironically asks himself), these characters with their consciences strangely at ease are the crassest in all of universal literature. Thus, the critique of society gains an unprecedented ferocity in Caragiale."

FROM "SOME OPINIONS"

1896

A work of art is a being, whose life giver is not, cannot be anything but talent. Without this flame of life, flame more mysterious and more uncertain than even Roentgen's rays, you can obtain artificial things but not artistic works, and nothing is more other, compared to the artistic, than the artificial.

Between the artistic and the artificial lies the same difference as between the dame who notes at the entrance of a panorama the fee of fifty bani and the figures of wax inside. [. . .]

In order to make a work of art, a viable work, talent is needed, talent and more talent. I purposefully said viable, so as to eliminate from the start the idea of durability from this discussion, an idea so foreign to discussion. Often the literati make the mistake (after our great opinion) of mixing in their research regarding intellectual creations, the question: Will this work last? How long will it last? Such questions are entirely beside the point. Our question, when faced with an artistic piece, can only be this: Is this work *viable*? For, again, if it has life—albeit only for today, tomorrow, or for centuries—it will have lived, and this is the condition of being, life, not the length of life.

Very well, what is the most salient difference between an insect that lives only for a day in the shadow of an Egyptian pyramid and that pyramid? The dimensions? The density and the solidity of the material structure? Its durability in time? Of course not. The deepest difference between them is that the insect is alive and the pyramid is not.

The pyramid is of granite, the insect of some mucous tissues; the insect can barely be seen while the pyramid is pyramidal; the pyramid is an ancient knowledge of the sun, and perhaps it will remain unmoving and cold on its foundation long after the sun will have ceased in its capacity of sending it even one ray of warmth and light. Yes, but the pyramid stands and will stand; and the insect will die, but lives.

So it is with a work of art. It must live, it must be viable, and like all beings, it too will have a duration in time. Nevertheless, we could not take this comparison too far because we would run up against a greater difference that exists between the being-in-itself and being-as-work-of-art.

It is a strange difference!

Talent has given the work of art the breath of life. This life, however, is only latent; in order for it to become brevetted, it requires the concord of an intelligence, of a skill and judgment of another.

Life stays hidden within a kernel for a long time, lying in wait, with a patience greater than many attempts, for the propitious exterior condition in which it may spring into light, germinate, grow, bear fruit and other seeds for further life. What are warmth, light, and moisture for a seed are skill and human judgment for the work of human talent.

Just like a grain of wheat found after five thousand years in the sarcophagus of an Egyptian mummy is reborn like the grain picked last year, if planted in good earth, similarly, a viable work of art, after an abandonment and a forgetting of centuries, is reborn again in the warmth of skilled eyes. Under the spade of the shoddy worker, who digs to make himself a path, fly shards of marble; he would proceed with his destructive action if someone else did not check his hand; for the being into which he hits with his spade slumbers hidden, it does not yet have the voice to shout. It fell asleep when the last pair of skilled eyes turned their gaze aside; however, at the first gaze of other skilled eyes, it will certainly awake and, with a new and whole strength of life, it will call to itself a world.

How long have masterpieces not slumbered, hung in a corner on the wall of some tavern, drowned in the smoke of proletarian pipes! A pair of skilled eyes reawakened them to life. It is understood that the cases of complete material dissolution are not considered in this discussion. The sole copies of books from the Library of Alexandria, the marvelous temple at Ephesus, and others are gone for good without any hope of restoration, much like the grains of wheat from a field given up to the flames.

FROM *LETTER TO MIHAIL DRAGOMIRESCU*

1909

It is not about filling the wide world with a work of art, but about filling a narrow work of art with the world; for a work of art must live long, not wide, as a ray which penetrates straight ahead, not as a hot air balloon which fills out at the sides. Otherwise, both world and work are—I cannot find a more appropriate word—*poor.*

Translated by Carla Baricz

Hortensia Papadat-Bengescu

(1876–1955)

Born in the family of an officer and married to one shortly after receiving her baccalau-
reate, Hortensia Papadat-Bengescu was the mother of five children, whose education
and upbringing were her main concern, though during the First World War, she also
worked as a nurse. She began publishing late, around the age of forty, but she was
encouraged by the more prominent literary critics of her day, who recognized in her
a modern and profound Romanian prose writer. She was the author of short stories—
Deep Waters (1918), *The Sphinx* (1920), *The Woman Before the Mirror* (1921), *Provincial
Romance* (1925), *Tragic Drawings* (1927)—as well as plays (*The Old Man*, 1920) and novels.
Along with *The Dragon* (1923), a novel exploring the realities of war, Papadat-Bengescu
created what is considered to be the most original Romanian saga, the epic cycle of
the Hallipa family, containing the novels *The Disheveled Maidens* (1926), *Concert of Bach
Music* (1927), *The Hidden Path* (1932), *The Fiancé* (1935), and *Roots* (1938). Submitted for
publication in 1947, at a time when the press came under the control of the government, *The Stranger*, the last novel of the cycle, was mysteriously lost.

Combining her interest in urban life with her interest in human psychology, the
writer investigated the layers of neuroses and obsessions generated by the distortions
and perversions that sometimes occur in family life: incest, adultery, and maladaptive
attractions. Papadat-Bengescu confessed that she always desired to reconstitute the
soulful body of characters which, often being in contradiction with the *physical body*,
creates insurmountable dramatic tensions.

FROM "AUTOBIOGRAPHY"

[. . .] I write, and I publish. I write with passion in the thread of becoming. Then again, I would like to *find out*. The artist needs—a double medal—thrill and quiet. Quiet that nevertheless permits a permanent listening to the thrill; self-conscience, necessary so that he is not stopped in his tracks by the questions of conscience. And behold, I find out. I sign up for the decisive value of a critical opinion. I can, from now on, bend joyfully to the anointment of any gift, and can patiently stand any pressure. My literary physiognomy is configured. Unfinished, I can reconstruct my enigma.

[. . .] "And so it came," any writer subscribing to the same law—of inspiration—will say with conviction, about the phenomenon of creation. So, one day, at some hour, *something* will rise up in him already armed.

The pollen from all the ambit, borne by all the winds, has fallen in a furrow—that one. Behold the plant. Now you are its clime and its gardener . . . or the child that you will keep alive and raise as best you can. Born in toil—for a quaking, a breaking has accompanied the miracle. Raised with fatigue: the care of weeding out that which adheres to the fruit without touching any part of the essential substance, no mercy, so as to save its breath, so as to save the tiniest of signs of the authentic; a tension of energies, a fear of responses . . . The literary fact will necessarily have to enter into the domain of the aesthetic, but, whatever the risks may be, it will have to attempt to never lose any part of the truth. Here is the passion and here the toil . . . If an asperity will accompany a roughness of the facts, if the syncope of a word will keep in itself a disharmony between the soul and the fact of a dream, they will be synchronicities, necessities, but not precepts. Where the object will allow for ornaments or where it will demand them, you will be glad to ornament, for you have in your fingers the silk and the bead; the aesthetic is a temptation to which you will not yield on purpose—for in doing so you will steal from yourself something even more profound, which does not merit sacrificing.

For this *passion* I will be understood and rewarded. Even in condemnation, I will sometimes encounter the testimony of the operating suggestion.

Translated by Carla Baricz

Tudor Arghezi

(1880–1967)

Following an unhappy childhood and a few years during which he worked in a sugar plant, the future writer (whose real name was Ion Theodorescu) joined a monastic order. Between 1900 and 1905, he served as deacon at the Orthodox Metropolitan Seat in Bucharest. For the next five years he lived in Geneva, where he attended university courses and enrolled in a vocational school. He published widely in Romania (and even edited a journal), becoming involved in philogermanic publications during World War I, which led to his arrest at the end of the war. Paradoxically, during World War II, he published a virulent pamphlet against the German occupation, for which he was again arrested and interned in a camp. After the instauration of the Communist regime, he become critical of dogmatic attitudes and of censorship; consequently, his public activity (including the circulation of books) was banned from 1948 to 1954. He made a comeback, with great honors, in 1955, and from that point onward dedicated himself to two kinds of texts: propagandistic and subversively ambiguous.

A strong personality, effulgent and insubordinate to literary doctrine, Arghezi was one of the greatest Romanian poets. He made a late debut in book form yet went on to publish prodigiously. His most important volumes are *Suitable Words* (1927), *Flowers of Mildew* (1931), *Evening Booklet* (1935), *Hore* (1939), *One Hundred and One Poems* (1947), *Song to Man* (1956), *Leaves* (1961), and *Litanies* (1967). The poet mastered like no other the most diverse registers of language, from imprecation and malediction to prayer and suavity, while addressing several obsessive themes: the argument with God (the psalm being the privileged form of revolt), death, nascent as well as violently erotic love, and the grotesque degradation of the human being. The same obsessive themes are to be found in his novels: *Our Lord's Mother's Eyes* (1934), *Lina* (1942), *The Annunciation Cemetery* (1936). He was also a translator (of poetry in particular) and a formidable journalist. Part of his texts were published in the media (tablets, prose poetry, pamphlets) and were later collected in the volumes *Wooden Icons* (1929), *The Black Gate* (1930), *The Toy-Laden Book* (1931), *Tablets from the Land of Kuty* (1933), and *What Have You Against Me, Wind?* (1937).

Cuts on the Arm of the Pen

A writer's studio must be provided with a fireplace. In it you throw at least three quarters of your manuscripts. What comes out of a flame must be consumed in a flame.

Only after you put out a book do you realize—in case you would rather not deceive yourself—how bad it is.

The level you have tried to reach remains generally below the transformation of the written word in a leaden text. Can you content yourself with little?

But, after any kind of book there is some consolation. Hope—that you can't abdicate from. A book to come, a better one.

Writing is not entertainment. Martyrdom, patience, abnegation, and many sacrifices.

Duty. You have to be rigorous, strict, demanding with yourself and not allow yourself concessions. A single concession to the banal can do you in. To an artist, who is not a monger of words and titles, the benefit of arrogance and pride is prohibited.

If literature had not become industrialized, a single book would have sufficed to a writer for a lifetime, provided that it were as dense as rock and crystal. Crystal in particular stays in the forge longer; ashes. The job of the chimney sweeper–critic is to tell the difference.

A manuscript is of interest to you as long as you work on it. For the sake of the effort, neither for its sake, nor yours.

The writer's responsibility is not easy. He is responsible to the honor of the language, which is not his. He is responsible to vocation in particular, which is not his either. It is a curse: he who has played with the impalpable and the diaphanous and has tempted them is bound to decompose.

You have to know how to displease, not only how to please. Always saying yes and never no is stupefying.

When you start soiling pure paper, think hard about what you are doing. You get involved for life.

Do not rest. Do not fall asleep. You have to be always other and incandescent.

The sun does not set toward your sloth.

There is talent and there is pseudotalent. There are strong characters, and there are mutts. You do what you see others do and you are satisfied. Your notoriety can thrive on trifles and sometimes even more so than when you have an honest reputation. Satire tells us that generally this is the case.

Plagiarism has its nuances. The press welcomes many literary merits.

Be daring. Let yourself go with the flow of your voice, like the blackbird, like the thistle finch, like the swallow, like the titmouse.

Whether or not you are successful in finishing your page, that is one thing. But it is a different thing altogether that you have attempted to succeed regardless of the result.

A writer is lucky. Another one is not. It is like a spell; you are not responsible for it.

Translated by Raluca Manea

George Bacovia

(1881–1957)

Though he completed law studies at the University in Iaşi, Bacovia never practiced law. Instead, he worked as a clerk, accountant, and librarian until 1932, when because of a worsening neurosis, he retired to an isolated life. This neurosis became the substance of his volumes of poetry: *Lead* (1916), *Yellow Sparks* (1926), *Pieces of Night* (1926), *With You . . .* (1930), *Comedies, After All* (1936), and *Bourgeoisie Stanzas* (1946). If the first three books display a symbolist dimension, evident in the poet's preference for the artificial, for musicality, and for the cultivation of a refined chromatics corresponding to internal states, these preferences fade in favor of direct appellations in the later volumes. Bacovia's themes, however, remain constant. The poet often seeks to express nothingness, emptiness, monotony, and the claustrophobic provinces, as well as a vision that combines the feeling of uselessness with (self) irony.

GLOSS

1946

Behold savant
With a drunken heart
Love.
Nature is static.
Lovemaking reborn
   With summer fire,
   With diamonds
Of winter.
   Metempsychosis.
   Metamorphosis,
   And how much more.
Fare well
By and by
Behold savant.
   If there is not
Someone to speak to,
   It is writable.

ENOUGH

1926

When at peace, I will write a verse
In which you will see that I am abandoned?
Wanting to decipher what was dispersed,
   It is almost as if I did not know what I wanted . . .

Weeping, I told myself to weep not?
I had, could . . .
Who knows, I too, what I thought,
   Another time, in the wood!

I will write a verse, when at peace . . .

Translated by Carla Baricz

Panait Istrati

(1884–1935)

Born to a laundress who raised him as a single parent (his father was a Greek contra-
bandist), Istrati only attended primary school; an autodidact, he developed a consuming passion for reading. Early on he traveled around the Balkans, and then to Egypt,
supporting himself by taking temporary jobs; he worked as a dockworker, shop assistant, baker, painter. He published articles on social themes but also literary pieces in
the journals of the workers' movement. In 1916 he headed west, journeying thorough
Switzerland and France, continuing to make a living on improvised means. In 1921 he
attempted to commit suicide; the police found a letter on his person addressed to the
French writer Romain Rolland, who responded by encouraging him to live and, most
importantly, to overcome his despair through writing. The same Rolland, reading the
manuscript of *Kyra Kyralina*, Istrati's first work, called him "a Balkan Gorki."

Istrati wrote in French and then translated his work into Romanian. He produced
a cycle of autofictional short stories, whose protagonist, Adrian Zografi, a nomad,
undergoes dramatic and sensational experiences but who, above all, has "a persistent
need to scrutinize the pits of the human soul," which he does in *Kyra Kyralina* (1925),
Uncle Anghel (1925), *The Bandits* (1930), *The Thüringer House* (1933), *Kodin* (1935), and
others. Istrati also wrote several books of fiction—*The Perlmutter Family* (1927), *The
Thistles of the Bărăgan* (1928)—as well as some explicitly biographic volumes: *Past and
Future* (1925), *My Departures* (1928), *To the Other Flame* (1929). Translated into Romanian

that same year, under the title *The Confession of a Loser,* this book spoke of the great disappointment caused by false social equity in the USSR. In 1930 Istrati returned to Romania, where he continued to publish fervently and led a life of very intense experiences, as a man—according to his own definition—"in revolt since birth."

PREFACE TO *ADRIAN ZOGRAFI,* OR *THE CONFESSIONS OF A WRITER OF OUR TIMES*

If to write constitutes a drama for he who transforms his vocation into a cult, even when he juggles with his native tongue, what is that to me, who, in a haphazard French, still need to open *Larousse* a hundred times a day, to ask it to reveal—for instance—when one writes *amener* and when *emmener*? But this is infernal torment! I advance like a mole forced to climb an incandescent staircase. And I suffer immensely not knowing (ever) whether I am improving or worsening my text.

Unhappy are those who share my fate! Before becoming a writer, I was well acquainted with the most difficult labors, but I did not suspect that I had yet to discover the most inhuman of all: that which is practiced under people's admiring gaze and which, when completed, leaves your body and soul drained to death. Yes, this soul that I protected so much from the yoke of my immediate needs and which was my principal joy! Today it leaves me little by little, without my being able—as in the time when I was a mere worker—to rescue it from a sinful death. *Condemned to write*—this is my heroism turned inside out.

Did I want it ever so slightly? No! Contrary to what Martin Eden did,[1] I never sent a manuscript to an editor or a literatus, and those who today send me theirs, reminding me of my "great chance," do not know that Romain Rolland fought with me from January 1921 to May 1922 to convince me to write. It is the first proof of heroism that I knew in him: "Work," he would shout to the man who had left the hospital in Nice. "I owe my salvation to work!"

Before that moment, I had abandoned my literary attempts at page thirty,

1. Martin Eden—protagonist in Jack London's eponymous novel (1909).

forty at the most. And these writings in Romanian were spaced out every few years. I was terrified of literary work, which *would not come on its own!* I imagined that novelists write just as the nightingale sings. It was, otherwise, a comfortable mode of thinking, which went along with my *dolce far niente.* I was not fond of effort.

The voice in Villeneuve impressed me with its special accent: when you have something to say and the gift of expressing it, giving it up is a crime, and laziness shameful.

I obeyed then, with great zeal. Yet, not knowing the language deprived me, from the beginning, of the joy of writing, *of writing in French.* I felt my chest like it was a furnace full of metals in fusion, which were looking for a way out and would not find casts ready to receive them. I would dam, at every step, the incandescent matter, to check whether I needed *two ll*'s or a *stressed e, two pp*'s or only one, a masculine or a feminine ending. I do not know how I did not go mad at the time. And how much beautiful gold, squandered on the ground!

I wrote all my books and my entire correspondence in this manner. Has there ever been, in history, a writer more cramped than me? [. . .]

Well, all throughout my life—one of the most painful one can find—the only behavior carried out as perfectly as possible was that of having defeated the difficulty of behaving like a generous man. Yes, today, when our life finds itself at the whim of the common cold, I can shout to all: rummage through my existence, you will find in it all that you want against me, but you will not find any trace of that flaw that plagues humankind: egotism, the terrible egotism that makes people indifferent to their neighbor's hardship.

This is where my *Adrian Zografi* stands entirely.

Adrian will prove, with the example of his own life, that it is not absolutely necessary to have a stoic or virtuous soul in order to be able to and have to live a generous life. This is so, simply because generosity offers more satisfactions to the soul than egotism.

Life is beautiful only when you are sheltered from misery at the center of universal suffering; or when you live in a grand villa, surrounded by beautiful women, fawning friends, elegant cars, and cute dogs, as most artists and moralizing wolves of our apocalyptic century do.

Life can be more beautiful while dying on a plank bed without resentment, with a consciousness free of any shameful burden—*despite the fact that you had the occasion and even the desire, at times, to do like everybody else.*

Humankind can survive without roads, without electricity, and even without physical hygiene; it perishes, however, if it does not have pure souls. [. . .]

Once having believed in all democracies—in all dictatorships and all sciences—and having been disappointed everywhere, I directed my last hope for social justice toward the arts and artists. Given their great influence upon the masses, I was expecting, thinking of what springs forth from their books, books of revolted giants, that they would all come down into the streets to be at the helm of the crusade against bestial civilization, unmasking all democratic, dictatorial, religious, scientific, pacifist, or moralizing hypocrisies.

None of this was seen, as you know. Art is a fraud, just like all other so-called values. I made art myself and I figured it out pretty well, so I have every right to say: just another fraud. The artist does what the man of the cloth does: he preaches the sublime, but gathers as much loot as possible; he abandons you to the wolves and retreats in order to feed off his "fortune," perfectly protected by the same machine guns that he is asking you to destroy.

This is what the arts and artists that rummage through your entrails are. Crooks!

For that reason, when, from their lair, they urge you to adhere to one thing or another, shedding tears for your suffering, you should not adhere to anything!

Not even to those "international homelands" which are so fashionable in our times.

Long live the man who does not adhere to anything!

Translated by Raluca Manea

Mateiu I. Caragiale

(1885–1936)

The son of the writer I. L. Caragiale, Mateiu Caragiale studied law in Bucharest and Berlin. He never completed his studies, and after a few years of working as a governmental clerk, he married an aristocrat and retired to a country house, where he dedicated himself passionately to the study of heraldry (resulting in a number of articles) and literary creation. An exigent writer, he published only the novella *Remember* (1924) and the novel *The Kings of the Old-Court* (1929) during the course of his life; his volume of poems, *Eagles*, appeared a few months after his death, in 1936. Considered a last representative of the fin-de-siècle period, Mateiu Caragiale was a refined prose writer, an aesthete, and the creator of crepuscular universes and enigmatic nocturnal characters (of the dandy sort), which his texts consistently veil in obscurity.

In the course of the 2001 literary conference "The Romanian Novel in the Twentieth Century," *The Kings of the Old-Court* was designated as the most important Romanian novel of the modern era.

FROM "REMEMBER"

[. . .] I had been delayed on bad weather in an evening establishment in Bucharest and had been found out by an acquaintance from school; I had also glimpsed him, from afar, in Berlin; he studied something around there it seems. Garrulous to an extreme and droll in his way, he filled my head with a thousand nothings, gazette histories, girls, and maids in boarding houses—all uplifting things after the exemplar of Haşdeu's *The Little One*.[1] What a disparity between my view of Berlin and this man's, who sat before me, congratulating himself with his own cheap shamelessness! Yet why was the memory of Sir Aubrey awakened,[2] alive as never before, why did the phantom of Berlin nights with their bizarre meetings arise so strongly before me? Had it been, perhaps, the bitter fumes of the spirit of piths that came from the ancient and renowned distillery? No, it was something else. More intoxicating than any drink, a quick and powerful miasma of carnation, which loosed itself from a little missus sitting at the next table over, enveloped me—the miasma that the youth with blue stones had spread, the miasma that once, toward midnight, the woman with red hair had left behind her in a deserted alley in Tiergarten. And I saw again both her and him and the window with the turbid greenish light, all real, as by the strength of some spell. I did not oppose an impelling thrust, untried until that moment, to narrate to someone the history of Sir Aubrey de Vere.

I was heeded with the greatest consideration. I only noted how from time to time a smile played quietly over the lips of my acquaintance. When I finished, with the fishing out of the cadaver, he asked me if this was the whole story? I answered yes, it was. "Let me tell you the end then," he began again, "there was a great to-do. It's true, it was hushed up at once, but the breath of truth could not be suppressed. You will hear mind-boggling things, just you wait . . ."

I cut him off: "I do not wish to know anything." And since he stared at me with amazement, not knowing what to understand, I stressed the last word,

1. Allusion to the satirical novella *The Little One* (1864) written by B. P. Hasdeu, which led to a famous press trial in Iaşi.

2. Sir Aubrey de Vere is the main character of the novella *Remember*; he disappears in a mysterious manner.

repeating it several times. "It will seem strange to you," I continued, "but, as I see it, the beauty of a story rests only in its mysterious part; if you reveal it, I find that it loses all of its charm. Circumstances have allowed me to encounter in life a smidgen of novels that would fulfill my requirement for a mystery without end. Why should I let you ruin it for me?" Speaking thus, I wasn't quite lying; rather, on the flip side of this manner of looking at things, somewhat careless, more literary than not, something loftier hid, a noble thinking that convinced me to seal the lips of my acquaintance and which, had I told him about it, I doubt he would have been able to understand. Much as I did not want to see the mutilated likeness of that poor youth so as not to deprecate in my mind the serene icon of his outer person, I did not permit myself to find out anything about him, fearing something that could smear his soulful memory. Let this too remain beautiful, without blemish in its mysterious and haughty shadow, let Sir Aubrey de Vere remain just as I liked to see him, only so—what do I care what he was really like? I have vanquished the only proof that I knew him in person. I burned the letter in whose seal the sphinx smiled, encircled by the inscription: *Remember. Remember?*—yes, of course I will not forget, but how the years blur some of my older memories, making them float cloudily at the border between reality and the imagined; if fate will consecrate me a long life, at the very end perhaps it will seem to me that all of these lived circumstances were only a dream or some history read or heard somewhere, a long time ago.

Translated by Carla Baricz

Liviu Rebreanu

(1885–1944)

Born to a country teacher in Transylvania (which was at the time part of the Austro-Hungarian Empire) as the eldest of thirteen children, Rebreanu attended classes at the Military Academy in Budapest and was, for a few years, second lieutenant in the imperial army. He crossed the border clandestinely into Romania and settled in Bucharest, where he worked in journalism. Later on, having become a respected writer, he went on to found journals, became the director of the National Theater and, for many years, led the Society of Romanian Writers. Having made modest attempts in theater, Rebreanu published notable volumes of short fiction (including some exceptional pieces)—*Worries* (1912), *The Gamins* (1916), *Confession* (1916), *Resentfulness* (1919)—but only acceded to true artistic maturity and public recognition with the publication of his novels: *Ion* (1920), *Forest of the Hanged* (1922; which was made into a film by Liviu Ciulei and which won the Palme d'Or at the Cannes Film Festival in 1965), *Adam and Eve* (1925), *Ciuleandra* (1927), *The Young King* (1929), *The Revolt* (1932), *Embers* (1934), *The Gorilla* (1938), and *Both* (1940). Convinced that "art is the creation of real people and real life, not so much a matter of stylistic craft but of the pulse of life," Rebreanu followed the precepts of traditional realism and an austere stylistics, through which he managed to create epic worlds of great vitality. His most important novels, *Ion*, *Forest of the Hanged*, and *The Revolt*, deemed masterpieces, are great, polyphonic constructions, Tolstoyan in character, and multilayered in terms of narrative structure and theme.

They bring to the fore the life of nuanced and individualized characters who are often emblematic of major problems or national dilemmas. The epic breadth is doubled by a tragic dimension and great psychological depth.

FROM "CONFESSIONS"

The *Forest of the Hanged* was born out of a photograph that a friend of mine showed me, at the end of 1918.[1] The photograph depicted a forest full of hanged Czechs, behind the Austrian-Italian front. My friend was going to the Peace Conference where the photo was going to be used as evidence of how the Czechs had been treated by the leaders of the Austrian monarchy.

The photograph made a strong impression on me and haunted me for a long time. I had heard that many Romanians had suffered similar executions. I had been told that in Bistrița, that is, in my own country, many Romanian-Bukovinian priests and peasants had been hanged.

I had a new short story, "The Catastrophe," whose protagonist—a Romanian officer in the Austrian army—was led by circumstances to fight against the Romanian armies. Under the impression of the photograph of the hanged Czechs, I decided to use the protagonist in "The Catastrophe" for a novel, which was to be called *The Forest of the Hanged*. The plot of the novel came together fast and on its own: I will make such a forest with hanged men in Bukovina, where the executed people will all be Romanian. My protagonist, after seeing so many Romanians murdered by the very leaders of the country for which he fights and puts his life in danger, rebels and is eventually hanged, in the same forest, after trying, in vain, to cross over to the other side, to the Romanians.

Around the same time I was transcribing *Ion* for the press. The plan of the new novel was on my mind constantly, although more so from the point of view of the anecdote. It was a cerebral subject, in which the entire action was based on equally cerebral data. . . .

Several months later, I learned that a brother of mine—my family thought

1. *Forest of the Hanged* (1922)—psychological novel based on a World War I tale.

he was a prisoner somewhere in Russia—this brother of mine—a student turned artillery officer in the Austrian army, brought to fight on the Romanian front against Romanians—tried to cross over to the Romanians; he was captured, sentenced, and executed by hanging, as early as May 1917. Neither the place of his execution, nor its circumstances and details, were known. During that turbulent time, when the hostilities on our side had not completely ceased, one had no way of gathering such information.

Several months went by before I could discover, roughly, the area where the tragedy of this twenty-two-year-old took place. Meanwhile, I had completed the transcription of *Ion*, and then, every night, at my desk, I would struggle with *The Forest of the Hanged*. I began the novel about four times, thirty to fifty pages each time. I felt as though I had found neither the pace, nor the atmosphere. I would stubbornly persevere every night, and my toil would be in vain. On the other hand, as I was writing, in the heavy silence, I began to perceive slight knocks on my window, delicate as those of immaterial fingers. I opened the window and scrutinized the dark. There was no one, nothing . . . However, when these mysterious knocks kept recurring night after night, insistently—because I am, I repeat, pious and superstitious—I told myself that it could only be my brother's soul that sought the Christian care which had obviously not been granted to him.

Then I set out to find at all costs the grave of my hanged brother. And, after much research and a series of adventures, I discovered it in the end at Ghimeş, in an orchard, on the margins of the old border. The place was not even marked. Only with the help of the gravedigger in the village was I able to establish where he had been executed and buried. I went to the mayor's old house, where my brother had been tried and sentenced. I went into the little room where he spent his last hours and from where he left for his martyrdom. I went into the next village, in Făget, where he had stayed beforehand. I met the Romanian priest who had been his friend, but who was not allowed to accompany him on his final journey. I spoke with a peasant girl—spry, pretty—with whom I found several letters of his. The mayor gave me his brimless cap, which he had to exchange for a civilian hat when he embarked on his final journey . . . I had him unburied and his bones relocated on the other side of the rivulet that had been the border, in old Romanian earth, as he had wished during his final moments and as it had not been granted to him.

And, ever since that time, I was able to write *The Forest of the Hanged* in peace. The mysterious knocks on the window ceased, I found a beginning with which I was content and a meaning for the protagonist of my novel. . . .

Apostol Bologa bears almost no resemblance to my brother.[2] A few exterior traits at most and perhaps certain moments of exaltation. My brother's tragedy provided me with the context in which the novel is set and a few local characters: the priest, the gravedigger, Ilona, etc. For the portrayal of the soldiers, I used my knowledge of and acquaintance with our officers. Klapka, for instance, bears many resemblances with a Romanian officer, who is a colonel today.

With Apostol I meant to synthesize the prototype of my own generation. Apostol Bologa's hesitations are ours, all of ours, just as his tribulations . . . Only such an individual could be the protagonist of a novel in which the struggle between duty and feelings constantly threatened to degenerate into empty, jingoistic rhetoric.

The subject of *The Forest of the Hanged*, a cerebral construction in the beginning, was humanized only when the contact with real life and with the land intervened. Without my brother's tragedy, *The Forest of the Hanged* would either have not come out at all, or would have had an anemic, scholarly build, like all the books that are concocted in the head, deprived of the living and refreshing sieve born out of life experience in the soul of their creator. . . .

Translated by Raluca Manea

2. Apostol Bologa is the protagonist of *The Forest of the Hanged*.

Camil Petrescu

(1894–1957)

Born in 1894, to the family of an officer who passed away before his son came into the world, Petrescu was brought up by adoptive parents. He studied philosophy at the University of Bucharest. He enlisted in the Romanian army during World War I and was wounded, taken prisoner, and lost his hearing as a result. He later worked as a journalist and editor of literary journals. The Communist regime adopted him with great honors, and he produced a number of books during this controversial period, though he felt his conception of social justice to be increasingly betrayed. After the fall of the Communist regime, the stenograph version (*Comrade Camil's Trial*) of a session during which political activists dictated to him the manner in which to rewrite a play was made public.

His most important and influential books were released in the interwar period. Although he made his debut with *Lyrics* (1923), he contributed remarkable work in theater—*Valiant Souls* (1925), *Theater: Mioara* and *Venetian Act* (1929), and *Theater (1946–47)*; essays—*Theses and Antitheses* (1936), *The Esthetic Modality of Theater* (1937), and the posthumous work *The Doctrine of the Substance* (1988); and especially the novels *The Last Night of Love, First Night of War* (1930) and *Procrustes' Bed* (1933). Striving to render the authenticity of life and convinced that "true works possess something that makes one shiver," Petrescu creates a type of vulnerable character (somewhat similar to those of T. Williams) with a predisposition to suffering and unhappiness, who mixes sensorial acuity with feverishness of thought and finds himself in possession of a repressed personality.

The anthologized excerpts are footnotes to *Procrustes' Bed*, considered to be the most beautiful and enigmatic romance novel in Romanian literature.

FROM *PROCRUSTES' BED*

Much later, on several occasions, after long conversations that took place in the afternoon between three and five, in that refuge with geometric and finished furniture from "The Decorative Art," I had the feeling that through this woman's refusal to express herself—she preferred only to read or "live" quietly, for herself, in her free time—an ensemble of experience and beauty, so useless in its intentional ineffability, was lost. I urged her then to write and offered to facilitate the publication of any attempt she might make since it just so happened that I was in a position to do so.

She was looking at me surprised, with a veil of distrust in her warm, blue eyes:

—But it's impossible, what are you saying . . . you're kidding.

—Why do you say that?

And, bursting into a smile, for she almost never burst into laughter, even though her smile, no matter how cheerful, always retained a trace of sadness:

—But I do not know how to write . . . I wonder if I wouldn't even make spelling errors.

—Art has nothing to do with orthography . . . Error-free writing is the keep that Romanian language teachers earn. It is not mandatory except for those who are not writers. Great creators are more prolific in spelling errors than bankers. Eminescu wrote less orthographically than any of the poets who came after and imitated him . . . His work is tidied up, when published, by his editors. A student in fifth grade can master orthography.

She was playing, caressing the suede of the cubic armchair.

—No, really, how am I going to write?

I felt the need to become categorical.

—Pen in hand, in front of a notebook and by being honest with yourself to the point of confession.

She thought for a second and, as if she couldn't conceive of this idea, rejected it:

—I can't . . . How am I going to write? . . . I have no inclination for it.

—If I wanted to make a cheap joke I would say: precisely because you don't . . . But I am telling you, seriously: none of the great writers had talent.

—!? . . .

—It's the sheer truth . . . Let's say that there were exceptions. Flaubert. Maupassant, perhaps. Let's add Anatole France, without a doubt. But they are not among the best.

It seemed that I had blurred the clarity of her conviction to an extent. She was hesitating.

—A writer with no beautiful style . . . with nothing?

—Beautiful style, madam, is the opposite of art . . . It is like diction in theater, like calligraphy in science.

At this point she was outraged. The warm, blue hue in her gaze turned to platinum, fixing itself on me.

—Then what is a writer?

—A writer is an individual who expresses in writing with preliminary sincerity that which he felt, which he thought, which he experienced in his life and in the lives of those he knew or of inanimate objects. Without orthography, without composition, without style, without calligraphy.

She smiled, arranging her navy blue sweater, with bluish geometric patterns.

—So, if I understand correctly, anyone who is sincere can be a writer?

In a grave voice:

—No, but you can.

Her eyes were shining in an ironic and coquettish manner:

—You probably said this to other women, no?

—Yes, to some . . .

—Whose noses or shoes you fancied?

—Noses or shoes such as theirs, or even more beautiful, I had already encountered . . . I fancied their noses and their shoes, otherwise acceptable, but that followed from my belief that these women could express an inner richness, a blossoming of their sensitivity. Madam, only those who have something to say must write.

Her gaze darkened, all her gestures became immobilized, and later she said in that deep and unsettling voice, with a kind of closing of the iris over everything that is interior. Clearly, in sadness:

—I have nothing to say.

Not even the brutality with which I later published in a small-distribution magazine, without her knowledge or permission—making small changes— these letters, which otherwise had a strictly personal destination and which I had received a few months before, not even the good reception that some critics gave them were able to change her mind about it. Her horror of exhibitionism, even of a psychological kind, was more powerful.

Translated by Raluca Manea

Lucian Blaga

(1895–1961)

Born in the family of a priest, in a Transylvanian village which he would consider a haven for the rest of his life, Blaga received his bachelor's and doctoral degrees in philosophy in Vienna. He was a press attaché and adviser to the Romanian embassies in Warsaw, Prague, Bern, Vienna, and Lisbon. From 1939 onward, he taught courses in the philosophy of culture at the University of Cluj. He was blacklisted in 1948 by the Communist regime, which began harassing him for the views he held as an idealist philosopher. Blaga's philosophic works include *The Dogmatic Aeon* (1931), *Luciferian Knowledge* (1933), *Horizon and Style* (1936), *The Genesis of Metaphor and the Meaning of Culture* (1937), *The Trilogy of Culture* (1946), and *The Trilogy of Values* (1946). He was also an important poet, author of several volumes superlatively acclaimed by critics and influential to generations that followed: *Poems of Light* (1919), *The Prophet's Footsteps* (1921), *In the Great Passage* (1924), *In Praise of Sleep* (1929), *At the Courtyard of Yearning* (1938), *Unsuspected Steps* (1943). As a playwright, his important works include *The Whirling of Waters* (1923), *Daria* (1925), *Manole the Craftsman* (1927), and *The Children's Crusade* (1930). In these writings, which are born out of a cosmic and apocalyptic expressionism, Blaga managed an original synthesis between the negative, anxiety-ridden states of the modernist spirit and the magic, plenary experiences that originate in Romanian folk mythology. He translated abundantly from world poetry and is famous for his translation of Goethe's *Faust*. His memoir, *The Chronicle and Song of Ages* (1965), as well as the autobiographical novel *Charon's Ferry* (1990), which could not be edited until after the fall of the Commu-

nist regime, were published posthumously. (*Translated by Carla Baricz*)

To My Readers

This is my house. Across from it
the sun and the garden with beehives.
You pass on the road,
look through the slats of the gate,
waiting for me to speak.
Where do I begin? Believe me,
one can speak about anything any time:
about fate, about the good snake,
about the archangels who plow men's gardens,
about the sky we grow toward,
about hate and silence, sadness and crucifixions,
but most of all about the great passing.
But words are the tears of those who wanted
very much to cry and could not.
Bitter are all words,
so let me walk silently among you,
meet you on the road with my eyes closed.

Self-Portrait

Lucian Blaga is mute like a swan.
In his country
the snow of being fills the place of the word.
Since the beginning
his soul has been searching,
mutely searching
to the last frontiers of the world.

He is searching for the water the rainbow drinks from.
He is searching for the water
from which the rainbow drinks
its nonbeing and its beauty.

BIOGRAPHY

Where and when I sprouted into the light I do not know.
From my side of the shadow, I'm tempted to believe
that the world is a song.
A smiling stranger in it, under a spell,
I trace my outline with astonishment.
I sometimes say words that don't fit me,
and sometimes love things that don't love me back.
My eyes are full of wind and imagined victories.
As for walking, I walk like everyone else:
when guiltily, on hell's roofs;
when guileless, on orchid mountain.

Locked in the circle of the ancestral fire
I trade secrets with the old ones,
the kinfolk washed by waters under the rocks.
On an evening I listen in peace
to the forgotten tales of blood
turning back their course to spill in me.
I bless the bread and the moon.
By day I live scattered in the storm.

With words about to extinguish themselves
in my mouth, I sing—
I praise and sing the great passing,
the world's sleep, the wax angels.
I pass the burden of my star
from one shoulder to another.

Translated by Andrei Codrescu

Ion Barbu

(1895–1961)

Under his real name, Dan Barbilian received a diploma in mathematics, a discipline which he taught at the University of Bucharest and to which he made a number of contributions of international standing. As a poet, he published only two volumes of work during his life, both received superlatively by critics. These volumes (*After Snails*, 1921, and *Short Game*, 1930) became an important point of reference for subsequent writers and were a turning point in Romanian lyricism. Hoping to "challenge the demiurge in the imagining of possible worlds," Barbu sublimates allusions (to Greek mythology, Balkan folklore, mathematical topographies, Nietzsche, Poe, and many other thinkers and writers) into a hermetic, spiritual, solar, nonfigurative poetry. Due in part to this strange alchemy, his creative trajectory is comparable, in the words of Ioana E. Petrescu, an important critic of his work, "to that made in sculpture by Constantin Brâncuşi."

Notes from a Literary Confession

The preliminary question: Can and must the poet explain his work? The answer: He does not *have* to, but he can explain it. A physics analogy. Poetry, much like a physical phenomenon, participates in the mysteriousness of life. And, much like a physical phenomenon, it allows for a mechanical model. Poetry's states of rarity and dream can be reduced to a rational model.

An exegesis cannot, in any case, be absolute. I could, using the easy manner of judgment through comparison, enunciate further. If a poem permits an explanation, then rationally it also permits an infinity.

A poet possessing a certain mathematics can give not one, not two, but a great number of explanations for a more allusive poem. And, precisely because of this, because of this great liberty in the constitution of an explanation, it would be best for our preference to be guided by a *choice*. In the present case, we will make a choice while keeping in mind the widest spiritual boundaries.

Before passing to this exegesis, however, I would like to examine another point. How can it be that a poem that is not a fraud can be or can be seen as hermetic?

A first cause can be observed in the point of contention found at the intersection of the following two categories: experience and notation. It is quite possible that a series of operations, of mental disassociations of one's spiritual events, can find themselves well chronicled in a permutation of syntax (a permutation that, of course, does not intervene in the maintaining of that permanence, which is a certain genre of language). This inscribing of a part of the event within the special nature of the syntax is sufficient from the point of view of lyrical enunciation. Any commentaries, within the actual poetical text, would be a scholarly proceeding, oratorical, or in any case, antipoetic.

In mathematics, for example, the physiognomy of a page would become wild and repelling if the smallest joints of rationality would reestablish themselves in view of an overall clarity. Nevertheless, it is true that, in mathematics, the key can always be found through *gnosis*, through analysis. The gaining of a hermetical poem's sense is more due to happenstance.

A second cause that might legitimize hermetic poetry is of a more mysterious nature. Thomas de Quincey, the great moralist, dreamer, and English critic, observes somewhere that the symbols of our future sentiments can very well be preexistent to these states and so remain, for the less divinatory consciences, hermetic. In a similar manner, the ancients did not inscribe the feeling of fragility and timeliness in emotional values. The association of these sentiments to the poetic corpus is the late masterpiece of Christendom.

Imagine, in Rome (even in decadent Rome) one of those grammarians, those men of letters of that epoch, at work before some passages of Shakespeare, where he gives us, for example, this unforgettable image of passing beauty in which the countenance of flowers is likened to a cloud that is slowly effaced (in the process of being erased): "dislimmed cloud." The association would have seemed to that grammarian as an arbitrary one, incomprehensible, batty. The region corresponding to the domain of these symbols did not exist in his conscience: the flowers and everything are resolved in obscurity, in the hermetic.

It is likely that in the more complex times in which we live, in which different durations exist side by side, the conscience of a poet will have the misfortune of encountering the more backward consciences of his contemporaries (without the word "backward" carrying any pejorative here)—consciences engaged in their particular times. The misunderstanding occurs at this point.

Translated by Carla Baricz

Tristan Tzara

(1896–1963)

The pseudonym Tristan Tzara was adopted by Samuel Rosentock in 1915, at a time when he was assiduously submitting work to a number of literary magazines and had begun studying mathematics and philosophy at the University of Bucharest. In November of the same year he launched the Dada movement at the Cabaret Voltaire in Zurich. By 1920 he had established himself in Paris, where he helped found the surrealist movement. During the Second World War, Tzara took part in the antifascist resistance. Until 1948 (the year when the Communist regime took full control of the presses) he continued to publish his works in Romania, where his volume of poems, *First Poems, Followed by the Zurich Insurrection,* appeared in 1934. In France, he wrote and published volumes of poetry, theater, and Dada manifestos, among which: *La Première Aventure Céleste de M. Antipyrine* (1916), *Vingt-cinq Poèmes* (1918), *De Nos Oiseaux* (1923), *Sept Manifestes Dada* (1924), *L'Homme Approximatif* (1931), *Grains et Issues* (1935), *Midis Gagnés* (1939), and *Parler Seul* (1956).

Tzara's works depart from symbolism and pass through a poetry of irony, self-persecution, and absurdity arriving at a total and violent break with tradition, a break that cultivates automatic writing and pure chance. The writer confessed that through these extreme means he sought the moral betterment of a sick and lying world.

(Translated by Carla Baricz)

It Evenings

The fishermen return with the waters' stars
They dole out portions to the poor, string beads for the blind
The emperors go to the park at this hour which appears like
the old age of an engraving
And the servants bathe the hunting dogs
The light dresses up with gloves
Open your window therefore
And come out of the room you night like the pit out of the peach
Like the priest out of the church
God: teasel the wool of obedient lovers
Ink the birds, change the picture on the moon
—Let's go catch bugs
To put 'em in a box
—Let's go to the creek
To make clay pots
—Let's go to the fountain
So I can kiss you
—Let's go to the park
And stay up till the rooster sings
To scandalize the town
—Or let's sleep in the stables
So the hay pricks you and you hear the cows chew
Afterwards they'll yearn for their calves
Hey Mamia let's get out of here let's get out of here

Translated by Julian Semilian & Sanda Agalidi

Introduction to Don Quixote

Flight of a nimble hasty horse was my life
I knew to scour the entire world
Only one girl was dear to me
And I slept till late in the morning

The old horse split up into sections
Which will turn into hands of worms chewed by mice
My love: see the learning you don't find in books
Sit quietly by the table and sew

I'll tell you what awaits you down the road
Sew my thought on a silk dress
Until your pupils hurt and you'll be a bride
Until my thought will be a book

Translated by Julian Semilian

Benjamin Fundoianu /
Benjamin Fondane

(1898–1944)

The pseudonym of Benjamin Wexler, Fundoianu began but never finished law studies. He submitted his work to a number of modernist and avant-garde literary reviews, some of these texts having been reunited in the volume *Images and Books from France* (1922). He is known for having established the first avant-garde theater in Romania. In 1923 he settled in Paris, changing his pseudonym and continuing to submit works for publication at home. From France he also edited his volume of poems *Views* (1930), a work that proposes the depoetization of nature and the projection of an interior, nightmarish, and anguished landscape upon reality. Under the name Benjamin Fondane, the writer produced a number of collections; especially famous are his collections of essays *La conscience malhereuse* (1936) and *Rimbaud, le voyou* (1933) and the verse collection *Ulysses* (1933). In 1944 he was arrested by the Gestapo, deported, and murdered at Auschwitz. (*Translated by Carla Baricz*)

FROM "A FEW WILD WORDS"

To Claude Serret

PARIS, 1929

This volume is the work of a poet who died at age twenty-four in 1923 or so. Since then his trace has been lost on the Continent. Those who recognized him in a movie "studio," or in the office of an insurance company, met a cold man, with scant enthusiasm for carrying out his assigned activity, a man not shedding any tears for a past in which he has spent the energy that a significant matter deserves. Dead? No, killed in accordance to all the rules of the art, after a long moral uremia, in which his will *to accomplish* and his will *to exist* grimly fought, stripping each other of feathers and blood, as in the celebrated rooster fights of Flanders. The one fallen, his mouth in the dust, was survived by me. It is not yet the moment to decide if I was the victim, or if I was the killer.

This poem was born in 1917, during the war, in a Moldavia that was small like a walnut, in a fever of growth and destruction. Nothing of what constituted the *raw material* of lyricism still existed in reality. The poet was looking while, behind the windowpanes, the gray armies were flowing while striking death drums; he was inventing a peaceful universe in which he was creating, *inventing*, tilling landscapes today, the mystical exaltation of death in bread tomorrow. The excuse for his descriptive poetry consists in the first place in the fact that his description did not have a model in reality, being born from the haze of his mind, as an intimate protest against the mechanical landscapes of blood, barbed wire, tanks. Nature, in his poems, appeared raised at a higher potentiality than its normal image, as an escape valve through the firewall, while the true escape valve was fire itself. A symptom of neurosis? Romanticism? Earth was mixed with iron, fire, and glass splinters; tilling was a lost custom, oxen an obsolete myth, dung an unknown vegetation . . . While Dada was exploding elsewhere and the civil massacre was starting on the street, the poet was reflecting the world with his head turned backward in disgust. On the great people's graveyard, for one person who untimely left the lyceum, *vacation* was starting.

What a joy to discover day after day, covered in death by the city's hood, the *lost paradise*! This poetry, which on the surface was confessing a scant kinship with the rural world of Francis James, as it was proven at the working table, was aspiring toward the mystical power of Baudelaire. Beyond anecdote, the equivalency, the polyvalence, the correspondence were being sought. It was put together neither from images, nor from emotions, but from volumes, harmonized surfaces, matched equilibria, precise contacts, and measurable weights. Not even in one single case was reality, whatever it was, taking precedence in the inspiration or the technique used for the poem. The latter was conceived as an autonomous universe with its arbitrary laws, with its foreseen hazards. A kind of Morse alphabet was establishing in nature aerial border customs. The identity principle was rejected. With Goethe, appearance was considered a symbol. One should not make here a confusion with the symbolist poetry that in Romania has existed only as a flag and a pretext for revolution. Arghezi, Minulescu, Bacovia were not symbolists. Maybe only St. Petică, D. Iacobescu; partially Ion Vinea, and Maniu.

The spiritual state being given (once forever), the work was starting only then, to give the verse a density, by creating it as a measuring tool, milestone, and to give it a kind of autonomy that must be preserved in the ear but lost in the intellect. What ascetic joy in formulating the laws of this cosmos; for the first time the alexandrine was to be still-stoned in the Romanian language. Of course the too rhetorical alexandrine had to be unstitched, broken, liberated from its purely formal music; the pairing of male and female rhymes, its breath, its respiratory organs alone had to be preserved. Conversely, the assonance was surreptitiously but progressively taking the place of the rhyme; to rhyme *sud* with *surd, seacă* and *calcă, semne-ren*, and *trup-sărut* in a full verse correct and massive, had to give the poem a singular interior force, increased by the vocation of giving the language a kind of deaf and abrupt sonority, an echo of metal and of gun bullet, instead of the laugh of a pearl gravel licked by a crystal goblet. The priority of the Slavic vocabulary was to be affirmed and cultivated in spite of the Latin one considered inadequate for poetry. Static by choice, this aesthetics of the poem, in which the raw material of inspiration was selected to be static, the psychic principles belonging to the dynamic order, love, hate, speed, chance, had to be forcefully eliminated. A system like many others, of course; legitimate as everything there is, and fertile with one single condition: that of getting out of it.

Poetry! How much hope I invested in you, how much blind certitude, how much messianism. I believed that indeed you can liberate and give an answer where metaphysics and ethics have long ago closed shop. I believed you were the only valid method of obtaining knowledge, the only reason for a being to persevere in being. In the poem, with a magnifying glass in my eye. I was figuring out the thousands of stellar revolutions and aberrations. Only in the poem did the unreal world through which we pass as ghosts seem to take shape, to become living matter. Only in the poem, a slow product of calculation and chance, was the latter resorbed like a thread in a wound. Man undressed of the aleatory, the capricious, the spontaneous generation, and projected outside him a world seen *sub specie aeterni*. The terrestrial paradise was in an idea. The idea was the center and the kernel of the poem. At that time I was naked but I was unaware of it. The snake did not yet show me, with his gingerly finger, in what corner of the scenery shop there is the recently painted Tree of Good and Evil.

I ate the fruit of the forbidden tree. And I immediately saw that I was naked. That Beauty was not less of a liar than the Truth and Goodness, than Progress and Civilization. Suddenly words abandoned me. I started to cry through the night without words. I became blind with a lamp in my hands. Lies, Hugo, Goethe. A seraphic lie, Eminescu. With Baudelaire and Rimbaud only a sliver of truth was starting. Against a few laws that circumcise us at birth, against the blindfolded evidence, against destiny. The poem was bringing only an *alibi*. To God's question: "What did you do on this Earth?" the poet was replying: "The Latin kin is queen . . ." etc. The poet considered life as an America already discovered, as a world map utterly known by heart, on which the fixed points, the only ones considered to be human, and not the prairies, the virgin horses, the Amazons, the pampas, the poles, had to be sung. Life's ethics and therefore that of the poem were prudence, malice, the eggnest . . . One single attribute of Beauty: to be useless. The poem was nothing but a mask, the most beautiful, on an ugly and pockmarked face, that of the ultimate ideal. Ideal, idea, balderdash!

I spat left and right, equally nauseated by Truth and Absurdity, Law and Chance. For about four years I kept silent like a 100 percent war-mutilated soldier. I thought that poetry has been exhausted in me by a hand bringing instead the seven lean cows. On the day when it came back by itself, like an

artesian well, sprinkling my muscles with a rainbow, without knocking at the
door, I understood from what a profound misery I was getting my head out,
what mysteriously fertile friend was throwing me a life-buoy. I understood
that you could neither repudiate poetry nor catch it by lasso when you feel
like it. It opened the door and cried out: "Tut-tut!" From that moment I
understood that a poem is something else . . . What? . . . I did not figure this
out too well . . . and I still can't . . . Something that modifies reality? No . . .
Something that modifies me? . . . Myself? But who? And who am I?

If to be a poet meant to believe in the lie of poetry, then my current poetry
is worth less as remedy than kitchen physics. The poetry of those times is
there, with its light of those times, with its wisdom, punishes me, points its
finger at me. Such a verse as:

And—in spite of he who sows fire and sand in the desert

could make me remorseful if I was not already fully so of not sowing namely
sand and fire, of rejecting the desert in which nothing but manna grows, that
leads nowhere but to the promised land, that does not know any joy except
the broken one of the Tables of the Law. From this poem *that found what it
was seeking* I am separated by so many things that I can see all its faults in
transparency, as through X-rays. So why do I print it today? To kill it for the
second time, to finish with a past of which I would like to be more ashamed. I
should have burned it, or at least left it intact, not involving my hand of today
in a mechanism that is foreign to me. If nevertheless I repaired here and there
a verse or a strophe out of a moral imperative of a honest craftsman who cannot market a watch that doesn't work, it was a huge effort to do this using my
memory, having the old model in front of me, without wanting to contaminate
a precise state of mind with another one, mobile and morbid, with which it
has nothing in common.

Of course, all the things I told here, from afar, seem to me—why?—completely useless. I know that nobody seeks the poem with the risk of breaking
it, or God with the danger of losing Him. I know that we still are in the
reign of words and that the boys, at the newspapers, for one verse, a single
one, that reminds more or less of Mallarmé, Baudelaire, or Apollinaire, still
debate the originality of Arghezi here, and the young fauna of Ilarie Voronca
there. Nobody wants to understand that the poet is born in a moral environ-

ment, in a cultural broth, and that he preserves on his face the tattoo of a few vanquished obstacles. To what extent a poet lies, to what extent he says the truth; to what extent he imitates or modifies reality—that's what nobody asks himself.

Poetry is not a social function, it is an obscure force that precedes man, that follows him. From all sides its gaze smiles at us, gauges us, throws confetti and artillery shells at us. The evening dress is therefore compulsory. Some elegance, some decency, gentlemen. The whole *positive* future depends upon the attitude you might have on the cord, during the horror dance. One flower, a single one, thrown from a treacherous box and, in the glance of the acrobat that hangs on to it, the equilibrium faints, the air breaks up like a bottle. Keep on walking gentlemen, panic is a bad joke, here is the next number. *The show goes on.* The tickets are not reimbursable. Nothing is reversible. Nothing that has been will ever be again. At the last judgment only poetry will judge mankind. It alone did not lose man for even one second from its sharp sight. Who dares to raise up his head and set on the words? Man is an animal that poetry carves out from clay or blows up with dynamite.

Translated by Dan Solomon

Mircea Eliade

(1907–1986)

A precocious talent, endowed with great will and an unusual drive for work, Eliade
began to write and publish (fiction and popular scientific articles) as a teenager. He
earned his bachelor's and doctoral degrees in philosophy at the University of Bucharest, where he began teaching in 1933. As the recipient of a fellowship, he lived in India
for four years (1928–32). A leader of his generation, he maintained an effervescent and
influential voice in the press, encouraging his contemporaries, with pathos and despair,
to deliver a great cultural performance and "to irrupt in history." Some of these articles
as well as several other essays from this period were collected in the following volumes:
Oceanography (1934), *Soliloquies* (1932), *India* (1934), *Fragmentarium* (1939), *Euthanasius's
Island* (1943). At the end of the 1930s, his press publications became infused with political themes originating in a nationalist, pre-legionary discourse (the Legion being a type
of fascist group).

An advocate of the Romanian version of existentialism in literature (*trăirismul*) that
stands for authenticity, sincerity, and the quest for extreme experiences, whose themes
are despair, love, and revolt against a conventional world, Eliade published several
novels that were favorably received by audiences and critics alike: *Isabel and the Devil's
Waters* (1930), *Maitreyi* (1933), *The Return from Paradise* (1934), *The Failing Light* (1934),
Work in Progress (1935), *The Hooligans* (1935), *Mademoiselle Christina* (1936), *The Serpent*
(1937), and *Wedding in Heaven* (1938).

During World War II, he worked as a cultural attaché in London and as a cultural adviser in Lisbon. Starting in 1945, he settled in Paris, where he continued his research in the philosophy and history of religions, which he pursued even after settling in the United States in 1956, as a professor at the University of Chicago. While conducting his research in English and in French, Eliade continued to write articles in Romanian (especially in the years following the war), which he published in magazines founded by Romanian immigrants, as well as literary works. He wrote fantasy short stories in which both themes and characters are treated as signs or camouflages of the sacred: *Short Stories* (1963), *The Old Men and the Bureaucrats* (1968), *With the Gypsy Girls and Other Stories* (1969), *In Dionysus' Court* (1977), *Youth without Youth* (1980), and *Nineteen Roses* (1980). A similar "camouflaged mythology" (to use the author's own terms) can be found in the Balzacian universe—due to the sheer number and vitality of the characters, the dramatic nature of the plot—of the novel *The Forbidden Forest* (1971). With the exception of two volumes of short stories, all of these books were published in Romania (where Eliade is a cult figure in intellectual circles), but only after the fall of the Communist regime. Around the same time, two autobiographical works, which had been elaborated in Romanian were also published: *Memoirs* (1907–60) in 1991 and *Journal* (1941–85) in 1993.

On Writing and Writers

A friend was talking to me recently about the following proposition: "The young ought to belt up for ten years." That is, each one ought to retreat into one's little room, in order to work, suffer—and write only after ten years. Their entrance into the world of publishing would then be dazzling. They would impose themselves so definitively that no one would be able to resist them. And the doing away with cultural and literary corpses, which some of us are working on now, would then be almost automatic.

I do not want to debate whether success, after ten years of "silence," would mean anything or bring consolation. I am simply considering the efficacy of this solution—withdrawal. Because the problem is both very complicated and very subtle. For instance, I know a man who has been publishing for ten years almost daily and who, nonetheless, *has not yet started to write;* he is merely preparing to write. And there are many others like him, who refuse to publish what they have written, or refuse to write what they really think. In the end, writing is not as simple as it appears to be; it does not mean that everything that *gets published also gets written.* To be or not to be in the world of publishing, to enter or to leave it—these things are of no consequence.

The only thing that matters in all of this is you. Your being—your thinking, your experiences, your reactions, your therapy—matters. I believe that we have now rid ourselves of the superstition of "style," with which writing has long been confronted. To develop a "style," seclusion is perhaps necessary; not for ten, but for fifty years. Perhaps style already implies perfection, improvement through technique—and this perfection is never reached.

But what of writing? What connection can there be between writing and "style," "perfection," or "improvement"? You write as you are *now.* Not in ten years from now. In ten years you will be other, more defined, more profound, perhaps—but other. I am only interested in the being in you, as you are now, and only writing can reveal it to me. I care very little about imperfections, naiveties, contradictions, obscurities. This is you as you are now; the one who is definitely alive; and if you feel the impulse to write (which is also a way of betraying yourself, of confessing), then write and do not correct yourself a year from now. We have lived long enough with the myth of corrections and perfections. The time has come for us to put aside all prejudices and to face the truth: all our efforts here on earth are transient, no coming back or drive for perfection is worth it after the hour that called for them has passed; everything we do, but absolutely everything, is destined to be destroyed like all earthly things, and, the moment we pass beyond, into true life, everything of ours from down here will be lost in the mist of complete indifference and will not exist for us except as *fact;* and facts have this virtue—they are all of the same value, or all equally futile.

I am reminded of one of my professors from university who asked me once why I wrote and published "so young"; that I should ripen and wait I don't know how many years (about twenty, I think), that I will regret it later, etc. To which I simply replied: Professor, *perhaps* in ten years I will die. And this is the truth. (Not "perhaps," but certainly.) Since we are urged to grow up, we are destined to change, and what I think at twenty (and which has value in itself, when not judged in terms of "style") I will not think at forty, no doubt about it. I will not for the simple reason that the young one in me will have passed, leaving in his place another individual, calmer and more mature. And it would be stupid for that man of forty to regret the enthusiasm and the mistakes of his younger self. What does one have to do with the other?

It seems to me that this entire question of waiting, of perfecting in silence, of being compromised, etc., has its roots in one's name. For that reason—if the proposition to renounce one's name is too inhuman (demiurgic) to ever come true—it would be useful for writers to change their names every three years. This, so that they no longer be encumbered by their past, but have a fresh judgment always, be full of life, alive and not carrying a legendary shell on their back. The perfection of writing had a purpose only when it thought itself to still be "in style." In those days, the writer would work on each page, put his book in order, transcribe his manuscript seven times. He was constantly unsatisfied with what he had accomplished. But this feeling of "dissatisfaction" is completely extrinsic to writing. No one (or perhaps only an idiot) will ever be satisfied with what one writes. Then, the effort and suffering for the improvement of a long-gone thing, are they not futile?

I do not know when it will be understood by all that it does not matter how a book is written. Only the one who writes it matters. And did you note that only "imperfect" books have defied and continue to defy time (Rabelais, Cervantes, Shakespeare, Balzac, Dostoyevsky)? There are books that can be written in twenty ways (*Gulliver*, for instance, or *Don Quixote*). We were left with the book as if by chance. It could have been written entirely differently, and it would have been no less savory, or brilliant, or deep. *Tristram Shandy* is a book that any amateurish novelist, journalist, or professor of English could have written in a "more accurate" fashion, more stylized, more orderly. And Maurois's *Climats* is, simply put, a "perfect" book.

No, gentlemen, this story of waiting, preparing, and perfecting makes no sense. We ought not to be so concerned with the future, just as the past does not concern us. It is almost absurd to believe that in a given number of years I would write any "better" the book that I am writing right now. I would just write it differently, that is all. The problem I am struggling with at the moment I would not solve "more accurately"—I would simply ignore having other problems to worry about. This is how it is and how it should be.

Finally, all these things are, in fact, of little import; they partake of the vanity of the present hour, and they too are transient. It is good if we do them, if we feel the impulse, and if it is necessary to do them. But that is all. You forget them afterward, as you forget so many urgent, hot, crazy, painful, sweet things of the present hour—and which tomorrow will appear to you as mere *facts*.

If we succeed in making each page of ours into a *fact*, then it matters little if we are writing it at fifteen or at seventy-five. These "facts" have nothing in common with perfection, with style. At most they can be called "work" since behind them one intuits a mind and a soul that matured and did not sculpt the same block of marble for an entire life in order to obtain a perfect statue. I pity such provincial "immortals."

Translated by Raluca Manea

Mihail Sebastian

(1907–1945)

Born in a Brăila, a city on the Danube, Sebastian (né Iosef Hecter) studied law in Bucharest and pursued a doctorate in Paris. He was the editor of a number of important cultural publications. During World War II, he was forced to take up a position as a teacher at a school located in the Jewish ghetto of Bucharest. He was a good friend of Eugène Ionesco's and Mircea Eliade's, but he distanced himself from the latter during Eliade's ultranationalist period. He died in a car accident, at a time when his life seemed to become infused with renewed energy. An encyclopedic mind, fascinated by contemporary events, Sebastian published actively in the press and wrote literary, theater, and music reviews as well as articles on political and social themes. In 1939 he wrote an important study on Proust's correspondence. His literary fame stems from his work as a novelist and playwright. He was the author of the novels *Fragments from a Found Notebook* (1932), *Women* (1933), *For Two Thousand Years* (1934), *The Acacia Tree City* (1935), *The Accident* (1940); and the plays *Holiday Games*, *Star without Name*, *The Island*, *Breaking News* (all published posthumously in 1946). In 1996, fifty years after the death of the author, his *Journal (1935–1944)* was finally made available. Documenting an intense inner life, the journal addresses the difficulties of the act of literary creation; psychic, erotic, and moral problems; and the traumas caused by the anti-Semitism of the time.

Sebastian was also the author of an autobiographical essay, *How I Became a Hooligan: Texts, Facts, People* (1935). Banned during the Communist regime and published only in 1990, it exercises a great subversive fascination on Romanian writers. Differences in literary genre aside, the thematics of Sebastian's writing that appear time and again are the search for authenticity, an elegance of style, a melancholy deriving from a lack of assimilation, and the warmth specific to one who aspires constantly toward an (always failed) communication. As a portrait with self-reflexive valences, his work shows "a certain intimate acuity, a certain vehemence of the inner life, a certain inclination toward a vivid way of conceiving of moral problems and their transformation into dramas."

FROM "THE CURSE OF WRITING"

[. . .] "Why do you write?" is the question posed to our writers, a question that has harvested a large number of answers up until now.

Simple though it may appear, this matter is as difficult as all the matters that refer to our common, everyday actions. We always find it difficult to justify our current actions—the more current they are, the harder they are to justify. A simple "why?" directed at the most normal of our gestures always finds us perplexed. Life is not lived with too many justifications. There are habits, there are distractions, there are superstitions that determine what we do or do not do, and when someone forces us to account for these actions, we are simply stunned.

Why do you walk on the right sidewalk and not on the left? Why do you smoke cigarettes and not a pipe? Why do you wear a hard hat? Why do you comb your hair over your head and not to the side?

I would not like to appear frivolous with respect to a serious problem, but my belief is that the question "why do you write?" belongs to the above-mentioned category of questions. It involves—like all others—a series of small, ridiculous, simple, and varied answers.

Why do you do a certain thing? Out of boredom, distraction, habit, laziness, disgust, need, impulse. To forget, to remember, to make a living, and finally—as an ultimate reason!—"so that you can ask."

Each one of these explanations, especially the last, suffices to clarify why a writer writes. It seems, though, that few men of letters can bring their confessions to such impious statements, and thus their answer becomes more serious, more profound, more complex.

In the series of answers harvested by *Facla*, there are some entirely pathetic statements.[1]

"I write because I can't do otherwise." Or: "I write just as I breathe. I would suffocate if I didn't write" Or: "I write because writing is a vital function for me." Or: "I write because I am cursed to write. I was born that way."

Without doubting the sincerity of these confessions, I believe nonetheless that they represent the overstatement of a preconception that has been around for too long and that we ought to revise, at last.

"The curse of artistic vocation" as a formula smacks of Romanticism.

Personally, I consider writing to be a very responsible act—and I would regret it if this comment of mine seemed jesting or skeptic. But I do not see, in our current literature, the writer who is so tragic, so tormented, so demonically enslaved that writing be to him an act of salvation *without which he would perish*! Such specimens constitute unique cases in the history of poetry. Maybe Verlaine, maybe Rimbaud, maybe Dostoyevsky, maybe Proust . . .

It is melodramatic to construe writing as "stigma" which you cannot avoid.

If there weren't any publishing houses, printing presses, journals, reviews, audiences—if there were not, in one word, *a literary industry*—how many of those "stigmatized" by writing would still be writing?

If literature created the press, in the way in which a function creates its organ, it is no less true that the press took revenge in creating literature and stimulating it in turn.

Let's not forget that literature is organized labor. It has frames, functions, a market, offers, requests, contracts, obligations. It is a machinery that must function because it exists. A machinery that has to be fueled. Once he has gotten involved in this industry, a writer writes inevitably.

There is no shame in recognizing this. This is how Molière—who used to create depending on when his theater company needed a repertoire—wrote.

1. *Facla*—social-democratic publication. It was printed in Bucharest, in several installments, between 1910 and 1940. Beginning in 1930, Ion Vinea took charge of the publication and changed its focus to cultural debates.

This is how Balzac wrote. Neither Molière nor Balzac ever considered themselves "cursed."

Perhaps in Bucharest one doesn't write in a different manner after all. We are drawing our colleagues' attention to this modest proposal. [. . .]

Translated by Raluca Manea

Max Blecher

(1909–1938)

As a young man, Max Blecher attended medical school in Paris but was forced to end his studies prematurely, having been diagnosed with bone tuberculosis in 1928. That year, he began a series of peregrinations through the sanatoriums of Europe that would have a marked impact on his writing. He later retreated to a small provincial town in Romania and began contributing to literary magazines (mostly avant-garde publications). He also undertook a fruitful correspondence with local and foreign writers (such as A. Gide, A. Breton, and M. Heidegger). Bedridden for most of his life, he died just before turning twenty-nine.

Blecher established his name as a poet with the volume *The Transparent Body* (1934) and subsequently penned two novels: *Happenings in Immediate Unreality* (1936) and *Scarred Hearts* (1937). The 1999 posthumous collection contains all of the above-mentioned works and *The Lucent Den*, as well as journal entries, articles, and correspondence. Attempting to convey the paradox of "existing and nevertheless not being wholly alive," Blecher wrote a literature that progresses from the investigation of the body, navigates through immediate reality, and finally comes to x-ray different states of consciousness—from lucidity to hallucination and dream. His prose is often compared to that of Kafka and Bruno Schulz.

from *The Lucent Den*

When I evoke one of these memories with my eyes closed, and it is reborn with the intensity of former reality, when at other times décors and happenings that have never happened pass through my head with the same intensity and the same convincing light, when then opening my eyes I gaze round me in the sunlit afternoon and in my gaze gush, like artesian fountains, all the colors and forms of the day, the minute and dissipated green of the grass, the luscious yellow of Chinese silk of the dahlias, and the childish blue of the forget-me-nots that is answered by the intense and smooth blue of the sky, so intense and so smooth that its mystery envelops my brain in the steam of a lucid daze; when memories, dens, and décors peregrinate so, on the here and there of my eyelids, I often wonder with great emotion what the sense of this continuous inner illumination might be and how much of the world it constitutes, so that the answer is always inexorably just as discouraging. . . .

There is in the background of reality a misunderstanding of immense amplitude and of grandiose diversity from which our imagination extracts a minute quantity, as much as it needs, so that by gathering a few lights and a few interpretations it forms the "thread of life," and this thread of life becomes like a fine and continuous lock of light and hair, each man extracting it from the maternal reservoir of reality, full of décors and occurrences, full of life and of dream, much as the unknowing child presses the mother's breast and sucks the gush of milk, warm and nourishing.

In the time that "has not yet run" lie all the occurrences, all the sentiments, all the thoughts, all the dreams which have not taken place and from which generations upon generations of men will draw their necessary bit of reality, dream, and madness. Immense reserve of the world's dementia from which so many dreamers shall be fed! Immense reserve of the world's reverie from which so many poets shall extract their poems and immense reserve of nocturnal dreams from which so many sleeping men will populate their nightmares and their dream terrors!

It is the unknown deposit of reality, full of tenebrism and surprise.

All of these things lie crowded together in an enormous time and will unfold themselves only cell by cell, dream by dream, fiber by fiber, constituting themselves into an immense mosaic in each moment, in each little corner of the world, pebble by pebble, to form that unthinkable painting that is "the universal life in all of its unfolding."

And I think of this unfolding in only one moment of my life.

In the moment in which I write, through small obscure channels, in live snaking rivulets, through the dark cavities dug into the flesh, with a small rhythmic gurgle of pulse, it outpours into the night of the body, circulating among flesh, nerves, and bones—my blood. In the dark it flows as a map with thousands of rivers through thousands and thousands of pipes, and if I imagine that I am minuscule enough to circulate with a raft through one of these arteries, the rumble of the liquid that carries me quickly fills my head with an immense roar in which can be distinguished the ample beats, as of a gong, of my pulse beneath the waves, and the waves brim and carry the sonorous beat further, into the darkness, beneath the skin, while the waves take me quickly into the darkness and in an unimaginable rumble throw me into the cascades of the heart, into the cellars of muscle and fiber where the overflowing of blood fills the immense reservoirs so that in the following instant the dam might be opened and a terrible contraction of the cavern, immense and powerful, terrifying as if the walls of my room would converge and contract in a moment so as to spew forth all the air of the room in a tightening that ruptures the red liquid upon the face and crams it, cell upon cell; it takes place suddenly, the expulsion of the waters and their banishment, with a force that beats in the flaccid and luscious walls of the dark canals with the blow of ample rivers that fall from the heights.

In the darkness, I plunge my arm to the elbow in the river that carries me and its waters are warm, steaming, and terribly mephitic.

I ladle my hand to my mouth and suck the warm liquid and its salty taste reminds me of the taste of tears and of the ocean. It is dark, and I am imprisoned in the rumble and the steam of my own blood.

And I think of all the rivers, cascades, and obscure canals of blood of so many people who are on earth, at this obscure overflowing that takes place beneath their skin in obscurity while they go about or are sleeping, of all the beings that have arteries and veins, of all the animals in which this boiling carries to the extremities of the flesh this steam and this rumble of blood. And if I try to imagine the universal life of blood, only its life, I imagine that the people and animals have lost the flesh and the nerves and the bones off of them so that all that remains is the arbor of arteries and veins, keeping the exact form of the disappeared body, but existing only by their virtue, as some fine network, red of people and animals, as some people and animals made of fibers and roots and lianas, instead of the full flesh, yet still people, yet having a head as a ball, yet full of hollows and woven only from strands through which the blood circulates, and the nose is a tapestry of strands in an aquiline or straight shape, while the lips as a gauze, red and small, move and part, and when the wind blows, the entire body rustles like a dried plant in which the breeze of autumn has blown.

And these sorts of bodies made from networks of fibers and arteries, without flesh, are in the whole world right now, and they circulate, sleep, and feed as the normal beings once did, walking through leaves, grasses, and trees, as a sanguine vegetable world next to the world of sap and chlorophyll of the plants and trees.

It is the world of pure blood, the world of arterial beings and of fibrous bodies, it is the world that I do not imagine, but which exists as I see it beneath the skin of people and of all animals. In the moment in which I write and when I think of it.

It is the world of the reality that lies beneath the skin, beneath the décor and the light that we see with eyes open wide.

In this manner, I imagine the world of blood and I realize that my blood is only an insignificant weave of strands and arteries in the forest of sanguine arterial trees of the whole world, and the rumor and rustle of its circulation is only a minute vibration in the ample cadence and the ample noise that the gathered blood makes in all the arteries through which it circulates through the world.

And the rumor of blood is lost in the rumor of the wind and in the lapping of the ocean's waves and in the flowing rivers and tributaries of the whole world, which also produce noise, in ample unfolding of vast sounds in the entire world. Oh! Immense clamor of our planet in space! And lost in this din, the pulse of my blood! With everything lost, everything meaningless!

And I think of something else that terrifies me.

While I write, while the nib flees across the page in curves and lines and undulations that will mean words and, to my complete stupefaction, will have a meaning for people unbeknownst to me who will "read" them (for, to me, the act of writing up to this point remains profoundly incomprehensible and the subject of a great bewilderment) yet, while I write, in each atom of space something is happening.

In the garden, a bird has flown and has traversed the distance between two branches, and the wind has blown and a leaf has rocked, a baby carriage has passed on the street with a small creak of a wheel, the child has whimpered, a sharp and strident instrument has penetrated a hard body, the carpenter across the street has hit into a block of wood, a cow has drawn out its lowing, a small noise that I cannot identify is coming from the neighbor's shed, in the adjacent garden someone is shaking a fruit tree so as to make the ripened fruit fall from it, in the depths of the slum a violin has resumed its screech and a bark has crossed the moan of the violin, and I stop, and it is impossible for me to follow everything that is taking place around me, here next to me.

And if I think of what is happening just a little off from the circle of these actions that I can listen to or see, the movements and the occurrences that take place multiply extraordinarily, in every street happen things that I can guess at and many others, frighteningly many others. How many? Terrifyingly many, piles of movements and of occurrences and of people who talk and others who smoke and others who drink tea in coffee houses and some who sleep and dream and some who slowly shake the dust from their clothes and the horses who pull the carriages to which they are saddled while in a darkened theater a film is playing and in the scalding steam of an overheated room people are bathing and trains are circulating on their tracks and the wind blows amply over everything disheveling the rustle of the forests, and the rivers carry with them rafts of wood, in a vertiginous descent . . .

And things are taking place in the world, at this very instant, as I write, so many things and occurrences so that all the words that people have pronounced from the day when the very first spoke, and all that they will pronounce from now on, would not be sufficient to describe the occurrences that take place in the world in a single instant.

And so, every instant of my life, every movement I make, every pain I feel, everything that seems to me to happen in my life, every occurrence that I think extraordinarily important for me, is only an atom lost in the vast ocean of the whole world's occurrences.

And my life is only an extra occurrence in the pastiche of occurrences in the world, amorphous in its totality and indistinct.

It is the barrenness of happenings in the world that surrounds any life, and any life remains lonely and isolated in this consummate desert of acts that happen again and again.

When I think of this, of the rumor of blood that as a curtain of whispers hid from my view the rumor of the whole world, and of my life lost in the happenings of the world, everything that I do, everything that I write seems vain, and the visions that illuminate me, lost in this immense diversity, appear to me as oceanic phosphorescences lost in the darkness of the night, somewhere, on the quietness of an aquatic surface when the winds have ceased and the star-studded sky covers with a cupola of silence the vastness of the tropical seas.

And phosphorescences such as these, lost forever in the night, without meaning, are also my lines and my phrases. . . .

Translated by Carla Baricz

Octav Şuluţiu

(1909–1949)

A graduate of the School of Letters and Philosophy of the University of Bucharest, Şuluţiu worked as a teacher in several middle schools and high schools and published articles in several cultural journals. A number of his literary reviews were collected in the volume *On Book Margins* (1938). During his lifetime, he published only two novels: *Ambigenous* (1935) and *Redemption* (1943). The former investigates the psychological trauma of an androgynous being, while the latter focuses, in Dostoyevskian fashion, on the relation between crime and the possibility of redemption. His *Journal* was published posthumously, in 1975.

FROM "AN INNER DAIMON"

[. . .] Why do I write? In order to detox. I must say it from the start: writing is the elimination of certain impure residues from the soul. And, in this sense, it can be said that writing is the exhalation of the soul. Just as in breathing carbon dioxide is eliminated in order to be replaced with oxygen and to replenish the blood, writing takes out from the soul the poison accumulated by the writer's observation and imagination. That is why I see writing as a purification. After I write, I am a different man. I feel transformed. The essence, the state of the soul does not change, obviously, but it becomes purified. It becomes more limpid, more crystalline.

But writing is not a purely literary phenomenon. Anyone can write, and what I said above is to be applied to any kind of writing. He who writes a letter, in any form and of no literary value whatsoever, performs the same act as the writer who composes a novel. Writing is not therefore a uniform phenomenon that consists of a certain category of people but an absolute necessity divided equally among all. This explains everyone's aspiration toward literature, at a certain age and even at a mature age, when earnestness should convince an individual of the futility of any form of expression. What distinguishes, however, the writer from someone who writes—the former, a rare bird; the latter, a multitude—is that the latter does not possess the consciousness of the act he performs, while the former does. The act of writing is not important: it represents the initial, elementary and rudimentary stage of a normal spiritual tendency. Over it comes the intelligence that conquers, refines, and transforms the brute product, which the body could no longer maintain in the state of a transparent crystal. But here begins a different story.

Writing is thus an organic necessity. That is why a great thinker was able to speak of an inner daimon. There is, in truth, a daimon of writing, who pushes both the chosen ones, and the unchosen ones, to sin . . . on paper. Because if we didn't write, we would not always stay the same. The human being wants permanence. And if he kept in him all that penetrates his life, he would find himself in a perpetual state of becoming. In writing, man eliminates that which could change him, in order to remain at a necessary level of stability. Here perhaps one finds a reason for reason; that is, the reason why the human being feels the need to eliminate the contents of the soul. However, why does the human being want to stay self-same, always? [. . .]

Translated by Raluca Manea

Eugène Ionesco / Eugen Ionescu

(1909–1994)

Born in Romania to a Romanian father and a French mother, Eugen Ionescu spent his childhood in both Romania and France. Remaining in his father's custody after his parents' divorce, he graduated from the University of Bucharest, having completed studies both in literature and philosophy. For a time, he made a living as a teacher at high schools in the area and worked for newspapers and magazines. His debut came in 1931, in the form of a volume of poems, *Elegies for Small Beings*, followed in 1934 by *No*, "a false study of literary criticism," part pamphlet, part essay attacking Romanian literature and its consecrated writers. In 1942 he departed for France, though he continued publishing articles in Romania until 1946. That year (in an absurd trial) he was condemned in absentia to six years in jail for slandering his country and its army. Interestingly, 1946 also marked the definitive appearance of his piece (in Romanian) *English without a Professor* (first published in 1965 in a literary magazine), the first variant of the famous *La Cantatrice Chauve* (1950). With similar characters, scenes, and visions (of a world of marionettes incapable of communication), the piece is, in fact, the first manifestation of absurd theater, which Ionescu initiated in his French works published in the 1950s and '60s in Paris. From among these works, of particular importance were *La Leçon, Jacques ou la Soumission, Les Chaises, Tueur Sans Gages, Rhinocéros, Le Roi se Meurt, La Soif et la Faim, Jeux de Massacre*, etc. Also in France, he published short stories (*La Photo du Colonel*, 1962), the novel *Le Solitaire* (1973), his journals *Journal en Miettes*

(1967) and *Une Quête Intermittente* (1987), and the essays *Notes et Contre-Notes* (1962), *Antidotes* (1977), and *Un Homme en Question* (1979).

    Though he never returned to Romania, Ionescu always maintained a tortured tie to his native country; in the 1980s, he even implicated himself in a number of campaigns against the abusive Communist regime in Romania. (*Translated by Carla Baricz*)

FROM "WHEN I WRITE"

When I write I do not worry about whether I am being avant-garde or not, whether or not I am an avant-garde author. I try to say how the world appears to me, what it seems to me to be, as honestly as I can, without a thought for propaganda, with no intention of guiding the conscience of my contemporaries; within the limits of my own subjectivity, I try to be an objective witness. As I am writing for the theater I am only concerned with personifying and incarnating a sense of reality that is both comic and tragic. Putting the characters I imagine onto the stage—and for me they are real, as real as they are imaginary—is something that happens naturally or not at all. If you want or do not want to be avant-garde before you start writing, if you deliberately choose or reject an avant-garde approach, you are, as a creative artist, putting the cart before the horse, you are evading the truth that lies within you and missing the point, you are acting in bad faith. I am what I am, take it or leave it. Genuine self-examination is most successful when it helps you to be yourself. And it is by being completely oneself that one has the best chance of being other people too.

    When I was a boy I used to live near Vaugirard Square. And I remember—how long ago now!—that ill-lit street one autumn or winter evening: my mother was holding me by the hand and I was frightened, as children often are; we were shopping for the evening meal. Dark shapes were flitting along the pavements, people hurrying by: hallucinating, ghostlike shadows. When memory brings back a picture of that street, when I think that almost all those people are now dead, everything does indeed seem to me to be shadow and evanescence. My head spins with anguish. Really, that *is* the world: a desert of fading shadows. How can revolutions change anything at all? The tyrants are dead, but so are the masterminds who succeeded them. The world is something else too; I was still a child when, as soon as I arrived in my second country, I saw a fairly young man, tall and strong, beating and kicking an old man. Both of them are dead now too.

I have no other pictures of the world apart from those that express evanescence and callousness, vanity and anger, emptiness or hideous, useless hate. Everything has merely confirmed what I had seen and understood in my childhood: futile and sordid fits of rage, cries suddenly blanketed by the silence, shadows swallowed up forever by the night. What else have I to say?

Obviously, it's not very original. It has been said thousands of times. But a child had discovered it for himself, before he learned it from so many others, who therefore simply confirmed his childhood vision. It matters little to me whether this vision is or is not surrealist, naturalist, expressionist, decadent, romantic, or socialist. It is enough for me to think of it as perfectly realistic, for reality is rooted in the unreal. Is it not true that we are going to die?

It will be said that this view of the world and of death is petit bourgeois. Are children petits bourgeois so soon? Perhaps. I find this vision of the world in a great number of petits bourgeois throughout the centuries: in Solomon, that petit-bourgeois king; in Buddha, that petit-bourgeois prince; in those petits-bourgeois, Shakespeare and St. John of the Cross; and in a great many more petits-bourgeois, saints, peasants, townsfolk, philosophers, believers, atheists, etc . . . I notice too that this same age-old and enduring vision of life and death is also modern or contemporary: when we read Proust we can catch a great feeling for the uncertainty of existence, which permeates his world of love and memory, of phantoms decked with lace; in Flaubert's *L'Education sentimentale* do we not see an illustration of man destroyed by time, a time in which everything comes to naught, in which everything crumbles against the roar of revolution and a shifting background of societies overthrown and reconstructed and overthrown again? And do we not become aware of almost the same thing in Brecht's *Mother Courage*? This is a play attacking war, of course, but that is not its main theme: time erodes and kills; we are shown this in time of war, but this only makes it more violent and more blatant, the pace of destruction is quickened; fundamentally, it is not about the destruction of man by war but rather the destruction of man by time, by the fact of living.

Is not the theme of many of Chekhov's plays also the theme of evanescence? It is not principally the death agony of society that I see in *The Cherry Orchard* or *The Three Sisters* but rather, through one particular society, the destiny of all men and all societies.

In all these authors one can see diverse situations, various countries, different periods, and conflicting ideologies, but all these particular situations are simply a series of happenings in time, which again and again show me one and the same situation, one eternal event in conditions that change, like the varied expression of one invariable thought.

I do not refute the possibility of a different attitude of mind; I am not opposed to the hopes of Teilhard de Chardin's disciples or those of the Marxists, but I think I can claim that a work of art must express one or the other of our fundamental attitudes, that it is nothing if it does not go beyond the ephemeral truths or obsessions of history, if it is held back by this or that fashion—whether it be symbolist, naturalist, surrealist, or social realist—and fails to attain a universality that is positive and profound.

So the avant-garde is nothing but a topical historical expression of an event of timeless topicality (if I can put it thus), of a supra-historical reality. The importance of Beckett's *Endgame,* for example, consists in the fact that it is closer to the Book of Job than to the plays of the boulevards or to the *chansonniers.* Across the ages and the ephemeral fashions of History, this work has rediscovered a less ephemeral type-history, a primordial situation that all the rest follow.

What is called "avant-garde" is interesting only if it is a return to sources, if it rejoins a living tradition by cutting through a hidebound academic traditionalism that has been rejected.

To belong to one's own time, all that is needed is a certain awareness, a sincerity that is blind and therefore clairvoyant: either one does belong (through one's idiom) or one does not, and it happens almost instinctively. One has the impression too that the more one belongs to one's own age, the more one belongs to every age (once the crust of superficial contemporaneity has been broken). Every genuine creative artist makes an effort to get rid of the relics and clichés of a worn-out idiom in order to rediscover one that is simplified, reduced to essentials and renascent, capable of expressing realities old and new, topical and timeless, alive and permanent, both particular and universal.

The freshest and newest works of art can easily be recognized, they speak to every age. Yes, the leader I follow is King Solomon; and Job, that contemporary of Beckett.

Translated by Donald Watson

E. M. Cioran

(1911–1995)

Son of a priest and beneficiary of a solid religious upbringing (which his antireligious discourse would use to the full), Emil Cioran completed studies in philosophy at the University of Bucharest and then worked as a high school teacher. He was one of the major figures of the generation of young writers growing up between the two world wars and is best known for his essays: *On the Heights of Despair* (1934), *The Book of Delusions* (1936), *The Transfiguration of Romania* (1936), and *Tears and Saints* (1937). A passionate nonconformist thinker, a veritable prophet of uselessness, Cioran meditated on the desperate condition of the human being, the authenticity and "intensity of experience," and the condition of being a prisoner in a culture "too small for my exigencies." In 1938 he departed for Paris on a scholarship provided by the French government and never returned to Romania. He later worked with the extreme right in a kind of nihilistic admiration of Hitler. Along the way, he would decide to no longer speak Romanian (though from time to time he was visited by a deep nostalgia for his homeland and continued to see Romanian friends) and to dedicate himself—in a linguistically refined French—to writing. He is internationally renowned for *Précis de Décomposition* (1949), *Syllogismes de l'Amertume* (1952), *La Tentation d'Exister* (1956), *La Chute dans le Temps* (1964), *Le Mauvais Démiurge* (1969), *De l'Inconvénient d'Être Né* (1972), *Aveux et Anathèmes* (1987), and others. With the exception of the language employed, Cioran's themes and the vision of his works remained unchanged. During his last years, in a tragic irony of sorts, Cioran became ill with Alzheimer's and completely forgot French, reverting back to his mother tongue. (*Translated by Carla Baricz*)

FROM "ADVANTAGES OF EXILE"

It is a mistake to think of the expatriate as someone who abdicates, who withdraws and humbles himself, resigned to his miseries, his outcast state. Upon closer examination, he turns out to be ambitious, aggressive in his disappointments, his very acrimony qualified by his belligerence. The more we are dispossessed, the more intense our appetites and our illusions become. I even discern some relation between misfortune and megalomania. The man who has lost everything preserves as a last resort the hope of glory, or of literary scandal. He consents to abandon everything, except his *name*. But how will he impose his name when he writes in a language of which the cultivated are either ignorant or contemptuous?

Will he venture into another idiom? It will not be easy for him to renounce the words on which his past hinges. A man who repudiates his language for another changes his identity, even his disappointments. Heroic apostate, he breaks with his memories and, to a certain point, with himself. [. . .]

Let us say a man writes a novel that makes him, overnight, a celebrity. In it he recounts his sufferings. His compatriots in exile envy him: they too have suffered, perhaps more. And the man without a country becomes—or aspires to become—a novelist. The consequence: an accumulation of confusions, an inflation of horrors, of *frissons* that *date*. One cannot keep renewing Hell, whose very characteristic is monotony, or the face of Exile either. Nothing in literature exasperates a reader so much as The Terrible; in life, it is too tainted with the obvious to rouse our interest. But our author persists; for the time being he buries his novel in a drawer and awaits his hour. The illusion of a surprise, of a renown that eludes his grasp but on which he reckons, sustains him; he lives on unreality. Such, however, is the power of this illusion that if, for instance, he works in some factory, it is with the notion of being freed from it one day or another by a fame as sudden as it is inconceivable. [. . .]

Equally tragic is the case of the poet. Walled up in his own language, he writes for his friends—for ten, for twenty persons at the most. His longing to be read is no less imperious than that of the improvised novelist. At least he has the advantage over the latter of being able to get his verses published in the little *émigré* reviews that appear at the cost of almost indecent sacrifices and renunciations. Let us say such a man becomes—transforms himself—into an editor of such a review; to keep his publication alive he risks hunger, abstains from women, buries himself in a windowless room, imposes that which confound and appall. Tuberculosis and masturbation, that is his fate.

No matter how scanty the number of *émigrés*, they form groups, not to protect their interests but to get up subscriptions, to bleed each other white in order to publish their regrets, their cries, their echoless appeals. One cannot conceive of a more heartrending form of the gratuitous.

That they are as good poets as they are bad prose-writers is to be accounted for readily enough. Consider the literary production of any "minor" nation that has not been so childish as to make up a past for itself: the abundance of poetry is its most striking characteristic. Prose requires, for its development, a certain rigor, a differentiated social status, and a tradition: it is deliberate, constructed; poetry *wells up:* it is direct or else totally fabricated; the prerogative of cave men or aesthetes, it flourishes only on the near or far side of civilization, never at the center. Whereas prose demands a premeditated genius and a crystallized language, poetry is perfectly compatible with a barbarous genius and a formless language. To create a *literature* is to create a prose. [. . .]

What could be more natural than that so many possess no other mode of expression than poetry? Even those who are not particularly gifted draw, in their uprooted state, upon the automatism of their exclusion, that bonus talent they would never have found in a normal existence.

In whatever form it happens to take, and whatever its cause, exile—at its start—is an academy of intoxication. And it is not given to everyone to be intoxicated. It is a limit-situation and resembles the extremity of the poetic state. Is it not a *favor* to be transported to that state straight off, without the detours of a discipline, by no more than the benevolence of fatality? Think of Rilke, that expatriate *de luxe*, and of the number of solitudes he had to accumulate in order to liquidate his connections, in order to establish a foothold in the invisible. It is not easy to be *nowhere*, when no external condition obliges you to do so. Even the mystic attains his *askesis* only at the cost of monstrous efforts. To extricate oneself from the world—what a labor of abolition! The exile achieves it without turning a hair, by the cooperation—i.e., the hostility—of history. No torments, no vigils in order for him to strip himself of everything; events compel him. In a sense, he is like the invalid who also installs himself in metaphysics or in poetry without personal merit, by the force of circumstances, by the good offices of disease. A trumpery absolute? Perhaps, though it is not proved that the results acquired by effort exceed in value those which derive from a surrender to the inescapable. [. . .]

One danger threatens the exiled poet: that of adapting himself to his fate, of no longer suffering from it, of enjoying himself because of it. No one can keep his griefs in their prime; they use themselves up. The same is true of homesickness, of any nostalgia. Regrets lose their luster, wear themselves out by their own momentum, and after the fashion of the elegy, quickly fall into desuetude. What then is more natural than to establish oneself in exile, the Nowhere City, a *patrie* in reverse? To the degree that he revels in it, the poet erodes the substance of his emotions, the resources of his misery as well as his dreams of glory. The curse from which he drew pride and profit no longer afflicting him, he loses, along with it, both the energy of his exceptional status and the reasons for his solitude. Rejected by Hell, he will try in vain to reinstate himself there, to be reinvigorated by it: his sufferings, too mild now, will make him forever unworthy of it. The cries of which he was only yesterday still proud have become bitterness, and bitterness does not become verse: it will lead him beyond poetry. No more songs, no more excesses. His wounds healed, there is no use pointing to them in order to extract certain accents: at best he will be the epigone of his pains. An honorable downfall awaits him. Lacking diversity, original anxieties, his inspiration dries up. Soon, resigned to anonymity and even intrigued by his mediocrity, he will assume the mask of a bourgeois from *nowhere in particular.* Thus he reaches the end of his lyrical career, the most stable point of his degeneration. [. . .]

"Fixed up," established in the comfort of his fall, what will he do next? He will have the choice between two forms of salvation: faith and humor. If he drags along some vestiges of anxiety, he will gradually liquidate them by means of a thousand prayers; unless he consoles himself with a reassuring metaphysic, pastime of exhausted versifiers. And if, on the contrary, he is inclined to mockery, he will minimize his defeats to the point of rejoicing in them. According to his temperament, he will therefore sacrifice to piety or to sarcasm. In either case, he will have triumphed over his ambitions, as over his misfortunes, in order to achieve a higher goal, in order to become a decent victim, a respectable outcast.

Translated by Richard Howard

Gherasim Luca

(1913–1994)

Gherasim Luca, Salman Locker's pseudonym, pursued—though never completed—university studies in polytechnics (in Bucharest) and philosophy (in Paris). He had a vast publishing history in avant-garde Romanian journals and was a participant in the surrealist movement, as evidenced by his volumes of poetic prose and essays: *Romance* (1933), *Fata Morgana* (1937), *A Wolf Seen Through a Magnifying Glass* (1945), and *The Inventor of Love* (1945). In 1951 he departed for Israel, and in 1952 he finally settled in Paris, writing in French, a language he had used in some of the books published in Romania, including *The Passive Vampire* (1945) and *The Secret of Void and Plenitude* (1947). By cultivating irony, the grotesque, the unconventional, and, above all, images like those practiced by the surrealists, Luca aimed at creating a poetry in which "the tensions rise higher than a flame."

Tragedies That Must Occur

I am free
and can pay close attention to the things that surround me
my fingers quivering like poplars and short like bullets
have taken fast hold of the white, female neck
just as the bards during their frequent excesses of love for nature
used to take hold
of the flowers—the sheep—the field and the stars
the poets of today, the poets with fingers quivering like poplars and short
    like bullets
each have at home a white, female neck that needs to be assassinated
the lucidity with which we will then look upon the things that surround
    us is so necessary
and their violet tongue, such a comical spectacle.

Now that we are free our strolling in the streets holds a significance of
    which we must
be fully aware:
the women are more elegant and attractive today
the gentlemen more cheerful
the shopwindows richer and brighter
and our pockets usually filled with candy and notes now carry pebbles of
    all sizes.

Other people came out to stroll in the large boulevards of the city at the
    same time as us
their fingers are white and fat like lard, they keep their fingers in their
    pockets
and next to them, alongside a photo of their beloved, a handkerchief full
    of snot.
The poets of today, the poets with fingers quivering like poplars and short
    like bullets
the poets with pebbles of all sizes in all their pockets
should know that the only difficulty is breaking the first shopwindow
    they come across

in the large boulevards
because the other shopwindows break on their own
just as it suffices to turn off one star in order for the others to turn off on
      their own
I ask to be forgiven for the star simile
poets,
it is a bygone memory
from the time when I would become ecstatic standing before trees in
      bloom and pass
out at every sunrise.

The poets of today, the poets with fingers quivering like poplars and short
      like bullets
can cast stones at the star simile
it will be perhaps the first shopwindow you will break
as the other shopwindows break on their own.

Translated by Raluca Manea

Gellu Naum

(1915–2001)

Gellu Naum studied philosophy in Bucharest and then at the graduate level at the Sorbonne in Paris. He served as a cavalry officer during the Second World War after having worked as an editor of an antifascist publication during the late 1930s. He was a prolific poet, publishing *The Incendiary Traveler* (1936), *The Freedom of Sleeping on a Fore-head* (1936), *Vasco da Gama* (1940), *The Corridor of Sleep* (1944), *The Tree-Animal* (1971), *My Tired Father* (1972), *The Description of the Tower* (1975), *The Other Side* (1980), *The Blue Shore* (1990), *Ascetic of the Shooting Boat* (2000), and *The Way of the Snake* (2002). He is also esteemed for his prose writings: *The Medium* (1945), *The Forbidden Terrible* (1945), *The Castle of the Blind* (1946), and *Zenobia* (1985).

With the exception of his books for children (his story *The Book with Apolodor* [1959] and its traveling penguin have become classics), and throughout his career, regardless of style or medium, Naum was consistently a surrealist. He wrote an unconventional and antirational ludic literature that, through its ironic and sarcastic character and its astounding and sometimes baffling associations, attempted to free "the other half"—the authentic and mysterious aspect of being that pursues the oneiric vision and the inexhaustible "grammar of the labyrinth."

FROM *WHITE OF THE BONE*

[. . .] Perhaps it would be time to discern with attention from among the numberless shards in full contradiction with one another, which are covered—by dilation to the maximum—by the word *poetry*. The multiple usages, in current terminology, of this word seem to indicate something more than a tacit recognition of the existence of shards.

I know that, as necessary as it might be, a delineation of the zones of poetry cannot prevent prejudices against poetry itself, even if this delineation would only touch an infinitesimal number of the incalculable possibilities of the mysterious poetical resources.

However, this is the secret and the strength of poetry: to shatter systems, to force them to derail, to produce in its curious game spontaneous fusion, to enlarge until the fissures of any ossified direction explode. It is the secret and the strength of this poetry to assure the permanent preparation of a stiff "top-end," with the help of the aroused elements, laid bare from the most profound part of the "bottom-end," to maintain a constant exchange, a fertile transmutation of the top-end and bottom-end. Poetry tends, before any other thing, to break the wretched curses in which the human spirit struggles, to direct this spirit on a propitious path.

This allows poetry to escape easily from any attempt of the definite, to enlarge any limit, any definition that might try to contain it, to not show itself—except as a perpetual mobility—to those who try to establish it, as a heresy to those who try to dogmatize it.

To tear and to refashion ceaselessly the forever-impenetrable veils that cover the living thread of poetry. In this battle which, in the eyes of those warned, seems more and more fierce, the usual instruments of the poet (or that which, through a funerary blindness, he takes as reality) betray him, having been weighed down by all abuses, opposing one another through the grimmest resistance.

It is what makes me entrust the whole of my attention to a certain *passionate bearing* characteristic of the great lovers and heretics, a bearing that, in my eyes, has never betrayed the hopes placed in poetry.

Translated by Carla Baricz

Vintilă Horia

(1915–1992)

Having completed university studies in literature, philosophy, and law, Vintilă Horia worked for the newspapers and founded a literary magazine. During the Second World War, he was a press attaché in the Romanian embassies in Rome and Vienna; in 1944, he was deported by the Nazis to a concentration camp. He survived and, in 1948, immigrated to Argentina, a country from which he would return to Europe in 1953. He subsequently traveled through France and Spain, the latter becoming his home in 1964. Working as a university professor, he was active in the press and wrote essays, literary criticism, poetry, and prose (in French, Spanish, and Italian). His first books were written in Romanian: the novel *There Even the Stars Burn* (1942) and the collections of symbolist poetry *Processions* (1936), *Fortress with Spirits* (1939), and *The Book of the Lone Man* (1941). He continued to publish poetry in Romanian even in exile: *A Saint Has Died* (1952), *Journal from Childhood* (1958), and *Spent Future* (1976). His best-known works are the novels that make up the *Trilogy of Exile*: *God Was Born in Exile* (1960)—which won the Goncourt Prize, not awarded because of a scandal relating the writer with the political right—*The Knight of Resignation* (1961), and *Persecute Boețiu* (1983). Though the first two novels were written in French and the third in Spanish, Horia considered them to be "some direct translations of an interior Romanian, impossible to undo." (*Translated by Carla Baricz*)

FROM *GOD WAS BORN IN EXILE*

FIFTH YEAR

People often say: "He has come back from the war a different man"; or else: "His wife's death has completely changed him"; or again: "I met Caius after that absurd religious crisis he has just gone through. I didn't recognize him; he has become another man." All this is false. Man never changes, nothing in the world can change him. The most far-reaching experience never transforms his essential character, which is something final. One merely grows older. One finds it less easy to judge things and, after a crisis or a deeper revelation of the world, one acts more wisely. Illusions fall away like a bird's feathers. One is wiser, or one goes mad.

Here I am at Tomi. Months have passed since my journey into the land of the Dacians, where I learned more in a few weeks than in all the rest of my life. There, I saw purity and death, I saw suffering and the simplest joie de vivre; there, the secret of life and death was partly revealed to me. I ought to have been utterly changed and become another man, as people say. Yet I find myself once more in the state of expectation that tormented me before I set out, the same expectation, I now realize, that drove me at the age of twenty to visit Greece, with the same intensity and the same hope in my heart and thoughts. Was I not the same at Sulmo, in Rome, and here in Tomi? The difference, because there is one, is that previously I did not know what I was expecting and that, since I have been at Tomi and especially since my journey beyond the Danube, I know. But the certainty is not calculated to reassure me. Thousands of men before me, not only Virgil but Sophocles and Plato, Pythagoras and Thales, have no doubt awaited the same thing. And as they received no answer, each responded in solitude to his torment. But this simply led him round again to the same expectation, it was simply a new way of stretching out one's arms to one who vouchsafed no reply. I have not many years to live and I doubt whether this age will be a privileged one. The expectation is greater than ever. It no longer tortures a few privileged beings but has become a general torment. We live in the age of expectation, and no human solution is now acceptable or possible. Yet how dare we believe that our ears are attuned to catch the word for which mankind has hoped for thousands of years? And if I did catch it, could it change me?

The winter this year has been milder, the sea has not frozen, and the north winds have died away before reaching us. The sky is often veiled, yet there are no snowfalls. Honorius has just told me that winter is practically over and that some Greek galleys are expected here tomorrow. Though it is still only February, the shipowners and seamen were informed last September by an oracle that spring would come very early. And now they have no time to lose.

Translated by A. Lytton Sells

Ion D. Sîrbu

(1919–1989)

A student at the Faculty of Letters and Philosophy in Cluj, Sîrbu was forced to interrupt his studies to fulfill his military service on the Eastern Front in the USSR, where he was taken prisoner and contracted typhoid fever. Hired after the Second World War as an assistant professor at the Institute of Dramatic Arts in Cluj, he was fired in 1949 because of his connection to Lucian Blaga, whom he would consider a mentor until the end of his life. In 1957 he was sentenced to seven years in prison for the sympathy he had expressed (in private) toward the anti-Soviet movement in Hungary. After his release, he worked in a mine and then as literary secretary with the theater in Craiova. He wrote fiction—*Concert* (1956), *Stories from Petrila* (1973), *Why Does Mother Cry?* (1973), *The B Mouse and Other Stories* (1983)—and theater: *Theater* (1976), *The Arc of Good Hope* (1982), *Poor Comedians* (1985). He was one of the few Romanian writers who lived with the conviction that the end of the Communist regime was imminent, a perspective from which he wrote novels destined for posthumous publication: *Goodbye Europe!* (1992–93) and *The Wolf and the Cathedral* (1996). The autobiographical volume *The Journal of a Journalist without a Journal* (1991–1993) was released posthumously, together with a few books that bring together his rich correspondence: *Crossing the Curtain* (1994), *Letters to God Almighty* (1998), and *Winter III with Cancer* (1998). Through their artistic nature and moral force, these books secure for their author a privileged position in Romanian literature.

Not to forget . . .

September 27, 1973

Dear Mr. Carandino,

The pages that I now dare send you carry the inscription "The day of my retirement, September 27, 1973," and represent the continuum of a night during which, finding myself weak and miserable, at an important threshold of life, I wanted to declare at customs, just in case, in one breath, everything I have (everything I hoped to have) in the suitcases with which I would board the final train. . . .

Not to forget . . .

Not to forget that, beside the intelligence related to meditation and the intent observation of the world, there is a wisdom which is obtained through writing, while writing and following the inclinations of the pen,

Not to forget that I must always be careful not to lose in the process the metaphoric synthesis-*idea* between a psychological problem, on a social background, and philosophical implications, always carrying hidden metaphysical or moral finalities,

to look after the poetry of protagonists and situations, to know and be able to eliminate a lot, not to let myself be carried away by a sentence (there is a whirlpool of the temptation of the spirit, an intoxication of writing), to be thrifty and prudent with metaphors "in themselves," to have in any scene and for every character an anchor-reply with which to fixate the part of unity of the whole (how were the Greeks able to fit perfectly the flutes of columns?),

to respect the emphatic curve (emotional, existential, maieutical), while not forgetting that every scene implies an end and that the big end must "discharge" the arena in "charging" the audience,

may ten aphoristic statements at least come out of stone, to last even if the play is forgotten,

to run away from the minimum of resistance, commonplace, warm conventionality (although I know, from my great teachers, that to be simple is the most complicated thing in the world), to encounter the landscape and people like a Romanian living today, unin-terested in today, even free of today, not forgetting that, ever since childhood, my mother taught me to differentiate the sacred from the profane,

not to be an apologist nor a priest nor an executioner of ideas, but a lucid judge, solitary and in solidarity with the drama that ideas experience today, everywhere,

to forget how much I have suffered and to always think of those who are still suffering, because suffering is the raw material of history; when it comes to judging people (and works of art), the quantum of suffering implied involves the specific difference, the ultimate criterion of fate and immortality [. . .]

to combat the state of "religiosity" in beliefs, just as I combat the state of "belief" in religiosity, to stay, as much as I can, faithful and in permanent serfdom to critical lucidity, a slave to teleological values, the stupid-naïve propagandist of liberty (through common sense and modesty), a soldier sworn to the Word,

not to think whether I have "style" or not, whether I am modern, contem-porary, known—but to have and not have patience always, to be careful not to get "unscrewed" from my essence, not mistaking, at key moments, the instinct of preservation of life for the instinct of preservation of *Being* [. . .]

to be convinced that people, words, truths, if you encounter them or use them too much, become empty of content, get dwarfed, tend toward their contrary, moving in a different house, in a different syntax; that Theater is the literary genre that is based par excellence on the capacity (and need) of man to talk to God, simultaneously being part of several horizons; my best works (*The Ark, Simeon, The Threshold*)[1] *appear to have been dictated to me*—any manuscript having a human fate,

nothing is born and nothing dies, everything morphs into a different form; literature, before being an expression of art, is a heavenly contract with the earth; words make up a logosphere, an intelligent and stringent supra-nature of whose leader I am terrified—if I break the contract I am done for and so is my name,

to understand all kinds of stage directors, they came along with the age of great dictatorships (in which everything must and can be staged),

---

1. Titles of plays by the author.

in every man there is *un cochon qui sommeille*, a fascist who wants to fire his gun, and a "demagogue" who can't wait to be summoned to the podium [. . .]

we are cursed, here, at the gates of the Orient, condemned to a wait without relief, to infinite patience and humiliation, our only happiness consisting of the moments when we can gossip about our own unhappiness, gossip being the only cudgel we can still use,

because it's been proven that the force of any idea is directly proportional with the quantum of criticism that it allows [. . .]

when I am most miserable, to think of Actors, they are serfs on my property, *ad scripta verbum*, reduced to the freedom of acting in the chains of my intentions (and, more recently, of the director's intentions), to act respectfully when I reside in their rented soul,

not to forget that the stage is an altar, that Theater is the cathedral that will not sink, to be afraid of my heroes, of those who were born, even more so of those whom I have not yet had the courage to bring into the world, with them I will cross the Styx, they will pay the ferryman in my place,

nulla dies sine linea, nulla linea sine veritas, nulla veritas sine . . . sine . . .

Translated by Raluca Manea

Paul Celan

(1920–1970)

The most important postwar German poet, Paul Celan was born Paul Antschel, in Romania, at Cernăuți (a city later annexed by Soviet Ukraine) in a Jewish, German-speaking family. The death of his parents in the concentration camp at Transnistria and the Holocaust both profoundly marked the poet's memory and verse. His fissured lyricism draws from roots firmly planted in a wound in which language battles to survive the blasphemy of silence through broken and codified pleas.

After the war, Celan lived in Bucharest among writer friends, translated Russian and Soviet literature, wrote verse in Romanian, and made his debut with the celebrated poem "Todesfuge," which first appeared translated in Romanian as "Tangoul Morții," in the May 1947 issue of *Contemporanul*. After a brief stay in Vienna, in 1948 the poet took up residence in Paris, where he would later marry the graphic artist Gisèle Lestrange, father a child, and continue to write until his suicide in April 1970. Celan earned his keep in Paris by teaching German at the École Normale Supérieure. His meeting with Heidegger in Freiburg in 1967 added to the large body of literature that deals with the philosopher's ambiguous Nazi sympathies. As Lacoue-Labarthe and Jacques Derrida observed, it was not Heidegger's association with Hitlerism but "his silence in regards to the extermination" that disturbed.

The unique and irreplaceable tone of Celan's poetry, the anguished auras and somber resonances of his austere and profoundly moving lament, the codified invocation of the sacred within a tenebrous and profane immediate reality that has been brutalized, can be found in volumes such as *Mohn und Gedachtnis* (*Poppy and Remembrance*, 1952), *Von Schwelle zu Schwelle* (*From Threshold to Threshold*, 1955), *Sprachgitter* (*Speech-Grille*, 1959), *Die Niemandsrose* (*The No-One's Rose*, 1963), *Atemwende* (*Breath-Turn*, 1967), and *Fadensonnen* (*Threadsuns*, 1968). Also of note is his correspondence with Ingeborg Bachmann, Nelly Sachs, Ilana Shmueli, Petre Solomon, and Gisèle Lestrange. (*Translated by Carla Baricz*)

Partisan of the Erotical Absolute

Partisan of the erotical absolute, reticent megalomaniac even among the frogmen, harbinger, simultaneously, of the halo Paul Celan, I choose not to summon the petrifying physiognomy of the aerial shipwreck except at intervals of one decade (or more) and will not attempt skating except at the most belated of hours, on a lake patrolled by the gargantuan forest of acephalous members of the Universal Poetic Conspiracy. It's easy to see that around here you can't pervade with the arrows of a visible fire. A vast curtain of amethyst dissimulates, at the outskirts of the forest facing the world, the existence of this anthropomorphic flora, beyond which, I, selenic, will undertake a dance to stun me. I have not yet triumphed and, with eyeballs side-shifted to the temples, I spy myself in profile, awaiting seedtime.

Perhaps One Day

Perhaps one day when the rehabilitation of solstices becomes official, required by the atrocity with which men will wrangle with the trees of the great boulevards of blue, perhaps on that day you four will finish yourselves, simultaneously etching the hour of your death on the leafy skin of your foreheads of Spanish dancers, etching this hour with the arrows yet timid, but no less venomous, of the adolescence of a farewell.

Perhaps I'll be in your proximity, perhaps you'll bring me tidings of the great event, and I'll be there when your eyes, lowered in the distant chambers of the greenhouse, where, for the time yet allotted to you, you exiled your-selves voluntarily, so as to contemplate the eternal motionlessness of the boreal palm trees, when your eyes will voice to the world the unperishing delight of the sleepwalking tigers . . . Perhaps then I will find the audacity to contradict you, that instant when, after so much unfruitful waiting, we'll find a com-mon tongue. It's up to you, if I incite, with fingers out like a fan, the faintly salted windbreath of the requiem for the victims of the first rehearsal for the end. And likewise, it's up to you whether I lower my handkerchief into your mouths, devastated by the fires of a false prophecy, so that then, strolling out into the street, I'll brandish it above the concrescent heads of the multitude, at the hour when it assembles near the single fountain of the city, so as to gaze, one by one, into the ultimate drop of water at its bottom; yes, I'll brandish it incessantly, silent, and with gestures that forbid any other message.

It's up to you. Understand me.

Translated by Julian Semilian & Sanda Agalidi

Alexandru Sever

(b. 1921)

A graduate of the Faculty of Letters and Philosophy of the University of Bucharest, Alexandru Sever (the pseudonym of Solomon Silberman) worked as an editor at a publishing house. In 1990 he immigrated to Israel. He published volumes of short fiction—*Boyards and Peasants* (1955), *The King, the Spy, and the Actor* (1957), *The Memory of Suffering* (1985)—and novels: *Cezar Dragoman* (1957), *The Massacre of the Innocents* (1966), *The Circle* (1968), *The Imposter* (1977), *The Insomniacs* (2000), and *The Chronicle of a Deferred Ending* (2006). The author is also an essayist—*Critical Essays* (1982), *Iraclide* (1988), *The Inventory of Circular Obsessions* (1999)—and a playwright: *The Maid* (1979), *The Old Angel* (1982), *Don Juan the Apocalyptic* (1982), and *The Book of the Dead* (1997). In this selection, Sever used themes and classical motifs (the Oresteia, the Faustian myth, Don Juan), which he interpreted from the perspective of a modern sensibility, characterized by the absurd and nonsensical part of existence, by the atrocious and cynical violence that marks the history of the twentieth century.

Assyriology (The Library of Clay Books)

Imagine a gramophone record in the hands of a man older than us by six thousand years, who lacks the fine and faithful needle capable of unearthing all the treasures of our civilization from those circular dents . . . a depository of millions of records startling our millenary posterity with questions no mind could give an answer to . . . We would understand, perhaps, to a certain extent, the surprise and the emotion of those who laid eyes on clay tablets for the first time: a rectangular tablet on which, with a willow twig, generations of scribes had imprinted signs in the shape of a nail, of a feather, of a triangle. These tablets were mute. Birdcages for sleeping words! A brilliant genie was asleep in a clay bed, and no one knew the formula that would release him from the heavy curse of lost time. No dictionary, no reference, no scholar was able to make him talk.

And yet, here begins the resurrection of a language. The force of Logos has something of the force of life. In the resurrected words there is the promise of eternity. The discoveries made between the Tigris and Euphrates, which preceded the deciphering of the tablets, were recounting something about the ancient Assyro-Babylonian civilization, but the voice of the monuments was weak and uncertain; their whisper could not have the definitive force of the word. It was about an ancient language, a language in which an ancient civilization had thought for thousands of years. Ten years of excavations were necessary; there was a need for the collaboration of scholars of various nationalities—Danish, German, French, English, Russian; there was also a need for specialized archaeologists who had just enough of either travelers' curiosity or the interested support of some researchers improvised from dubious diplomats and adventurers; an assiduous study that did not shun the fecund light of chance; what was needed the most was the concerted effort of history, archaeology, mathematics, comparative philology, and even the ingenious help of chemistry and physics in order to find a purpose for each sign, a meaning for each word and each sentence, a tablet consecutive to another, for each shard the shard that completed it in order to be able to reconstitute the most astonishing monument ever unearthed from clay: an entire language, with its lexicon, its syntax, its phonetics, with its fineries and bizarre originality, with the history of its evolution. The written history of a world.

But how dead can a language that contains the very principle of life really be? It was a language whose memory—that which makes up the posthumous shadow of an existence—had been lost. The deadest of the dead languages; a language that no one spoke anymore, that no one needed for everyday life, that had not perpetuated its being into any sort of literature, that could not remain in the community of human knowledge except through the effort of dozens of scholars and through the poor mediation of some difficult books. And when this astonishing language, whose words had not resounded under the skies for thousands of years, finally revealed its secret, from the clay tablets there emerged in all its complexity and splendor the whole civilization situated between the Tigris and Euphrates rivers. Assyriology was an established science, at last. This final triumph will have resounded in the world with the clarions of Universal Resurrection. Death, ashamed, rendered if not the being of a world, at least its memory! A body reanimated once clinical death had been declared would not move me more than such a scientific triumph. Everything that time and catastrophes—the fires, the floods, the winds, the sands, the wars, the earthquakes, the invasions—had buried, covered, altered in man's memory, was now revealed. A cell in the brain of humanity afflicted by a millenary paralysis was regaining its attributes, and with each pulse it was pushing in the vast memory of the world a content that had been sequestered for so long: an unique episode in man's long youth. The Assyro-Babylonian civilization could be reconstituted not only in its defining lines, but detailed at times to the point where the Babylonians themselves were ignorant of the significance of each detail. The social structure, the economic, political, and cultural relations, the history of kingdoms and of domestic relations, science, literature, the entire people of kings and slaves, magicians, and astrologers—it was all about to be revealed.

I am seduced by the idea that the death of certain peoples and languages, like the death of an individual, will have only been the moment of a becoming, of a necessary metamorphosis, meant to ensure the continuity of the world. What I mean to say is this: one can't conceive of the death of a civilization like a sudden, definitive exit from the cycle of life with no consequences. Perhaps this astonishing and unique past had secretly circulated in the veins of humanity, summed up, indecipherably, in so many beliefs, so many literatures, so many monuments, so many sciences and customs. But by discovering the formula that solved the millenary sleep, by bringing back in the thesaurus of human knowledge, in the great cycle of life, the meaning of a language and the image of a world, by refreshing the memory of humanity, the scholars completed the image humanity has of itself and gave it the opportunity of a better self-understanding.

Therefore, once the world is seen as a connected whole, it is difficult to conceive of a definitive caesura—a dead space—between two points in history; there is, of course, an underlying solidarity, the underground passages between past and future, between one moment in history and another; a solidarity whose detailed map we'll never know perhaps, but which is no less real or efficacious.

It is especially from epics, myths, and Assyro-Babylonian legends that certain familiar profiles come to unsettle us—certain gestures from the dictionary of our significations, certain hopes that were never foreign to us. Gilgamesh—with the head of a Ulysses and the body of a Hercules—an embodiment of cunning and force is the hero of an epic that evokes, in certain episodes and by the common technique of wandering, the *Odyssey*. With Gilgamesh next to Enkidu, half-man, half-beast, a kind of Caliban more apt for civilization, we have perhaps the oldest couple of friends; Achilles and Patroclus, Orestes and Pylades are perhaps only the most noble embodiments of a literary impulse that dates way back. Ishtar is, in one instance, a Circe, ready to corrupt Gilgamesh. But in another legend her image is completed with unique attributes: she is the goddess of beauty and fecundity, a mix of Venus and Ceres; and when, like Orpheus, she descends to the underworld to regain her lover, all beings, deprived of the sweet protection of her spirit, stagnate, ready to die.

I am fascinated by the possibility man has to build connections and establish contact with all the epochs and all the ages, not solely out of an ambition to reconstruct the spiritual being of humanity—paleontology is better at that in this domain—but in order to fortify each generation with the knowledge of the whole of history, just as the individual himself draws his powers from the secretly incorporated memory of his entire past.

To organize the memory of the world!—here is an idea of our century. The clay tablets from the great library of Asurbanipal are not all deciphered yet. Perhaps similar depositories will be discovered. They reveal themselves in silence, as though the communication through time and space can only take place through a strictly cerebral effort. It is a communication through time: the emitting voice is long gone, the receiving ear is still vibrating; there is still news on the way that must reach us. At the other end of time, the Assyriologists continue to decipher the messages of another world . . . And, all shaken up, I wonder if in this gigantic effort to communicate with posterity, with other ages and peoples, one does not see triumph the same ancient desire of the human species to overcome its solitude.

Translated by Raluca Manea

Marin Preda

(1922–1980)

Born into a family of peasants, Preda attended a school for teachers, after which he worked as a clerk in a statistics institute and then as an editor and copyeditor. After 1970, he was named the head of the most important literary publishing house in Romania. He was the author of short stories—*Meeting from the Depths* (1948), *Ana Roșculeț* (1949), *The Proceeding* (1952), *Darkened Windows* (1956), *The Daring* (1959), and *Chills* (1963)—of the play *Martin Borman* (1968); the collections of articles *The Impossible Return* (1971) and *Creation and Morality* (1989); and the memoirs *Life as a Pradă* (1977; the term *pradă* is the Romanian word for "prey") and *Intimate Journal* (2004). He also published the novels *Moromeții* (1955, 1967), *The Squanderers* (1962), *The Intruder* (1968), *The Great Lonely One* (1972), *Delirium* (1975), and *The Most Beloved of Earthlings* (1980).

For his artistic focus and his dedication to the profession of writing, for the coherence and impetus of his creative universe and of his characters (through the valorization of major themes in the history of Romanian literature), as well as for his disquieting work in a period of optimist certitudes, Marin Preda is considered the most important postwar Romanian prose writer. His best-known work, the novel *Moromeții,* chronicles the lives of a family of peasants, featuring as protagonist a wise and mysterious patriarch who cannot prevent the breakup of his home and hearth. Placing itself squarely in Tolstoy's long line of descent, the novel alludes through its moral theme and vision to the prose of Siberian writers such as V. Rasputin and C. Aitmatov, while also embracing the meridional evanescence of Kazantzakis's *Zorba the Greek.*

from "The Writer and the Word"

Perhaps a meditation upon the writer's condition has never been more pertinent than now, in our times. Of course, the reader wants to see ideas in movement, to have them related as briefly as is permissible and, if possible, in a visual montage in which the image is pleasing, the thoughts of the writer alluring, and the allusions to the condition of our life eliminated; man knows without being told that he is stalked by disease, that often he is a toy of history—regardless of whether he lives in a larger or smaller country—and that, in the end, he must forcibly abandon this life.

But why would a meditation on the condition of the writer be more pertinent than one on man in general? Because the writer uses the word, which is at hand for everyone's use, while the scalpel is only handy for the doctor and the measuring rod only for the specialist. A worker can exclaim with pride when his professional livelihood is threatened: No one can take the hammer from my hand! However, can a writer exclaim with the same pride that he is master of the word? Not an absolute master, for no one is master over an absolute anything, but only as much as is necessary for his profession to maintain its prestige and his trust in the word to be unwavering. Nevertheless, the writer of our epoch, together with his reader, have unabashedly assisted in the manner in which, with the help of the word, colossal myths have been created, primitive and barbaric, myths that have produced unprecedented tragedies in the world, with enough victims and enough executors so that only a humanity cured and ready for new adventures (as, bizarrely enough, humanity looks today) can still quiet us. Torrents of lies have been poured into the world for scores of years, on the radio, through the press, and in books, proving, through their effects that took place, the terrible power of the word. It's a miracle that the writers of this century did not all appear as the sorrowful disinherited, since so many of them have become true martyrs, dying in concentration camps or before the firing squad. Their art, however, has not remained untouched. The prestige of the word has tottered, and the current generations have fought for its reestablishment in their eyes and in the eyes of the reader.

Following this situation, in a paradoxical manner, some think that a way out of this situation might be the negation of the consecrated meaning that the word holds for us. For them, the word would no longer be the instrument of great epic or poetic constructions in which the hero or the soul of the poet, riding unexpectedly, would disappear in the great fire of the event. The hero must be an antihero, a cardboard cutout, or a plastic figurine, a figure in any case deliberately dead—the author declaring proudly that he knows but one manner of creating live men, and that being in bed . . . In the happiest of circumstances we are given a play on words that barely, if at all, explains a play on reality, but without a solid relation to the life of man as he lives it in real life. Is it a form of protest against the diminution of the word's power? An attempt of renewing it through devalorization? This would be the better justification of this view, and of course, the future will quickly tell us if they are right or not.

Others, on the contrary, maintain a naïve trust in the word and calmly construct moralistic stories and novels, firmly convinced that they have their readers and that the purpose of art and the writer's condition have remained untouched by the traumas of the century. Their comfortable position is an illusion that unravels at the first encounter with reality, however; they do not answer any question, nor do they ask any, and do not even have the instinct to bury their morality in events. They do not see that the instrument that they use so serenely and so credulously, so as to move the reader through the description of the chick's drama (which is left by its kind because it cannot fly), is at the same time the instrument of the great cynics, who encourage the reader with friendly pats on the shoulder not to lift his eyes toward the world of his time; a tear torn from the reader, he is told, does much more than a tragedy (which scares more than convinces).

What is the purpose of the word and the condition of the writer in these extremes? There is no doubt that whatever the writer's condition might be, and whatever the situation of the word, the writer must not abandon man, even if man, fed up with his own actions, would not wish the mirror to be placed in front of him and his face to be revealed. It is not always pleasant to see yourself as you are. Nevertheless, you cannot climb any moral peaks or any peaks of conscience if you do not know how you look. In the 1950s–60s this sort of thought, which we have inherited from the ancients, was considered a grave heresy; man needed not to be shown as he was but as he should be, in this manner putting art under the guidance of an abstract code of Byzantine morality, which, as expected, could only condemn creation to bareness and syrup. And all this precisely in a period of great social convulsions and spectacular overthrows.

The strengthening of art's prestige is only possible through the creation of durable works, in which words, much like carved rocks, should stand close together until the edifice rise—lasting and imposing. There is no other path for the creative destiny of the word.

Art creates abstention in her enemy. The work of art gives birth to a superstitious fear, as before a goddess that, as her enemy well knows, once created cannot be destroyed. We must know how to profit from this magical effort of art, to attempt to obtain it. Then the force of the word will increase and the condition of the writer will be better. Who else should believe deeper and more fervently in the eternity of art if not the writer himself?

Translated by Carla Baricz

Ion Caraion

(1923–1986)

Before studying at the University of Bucharest where he took classes in literary history (graduating in 1948), Ion Caraion worked as a reporter. During the Second World War, he was the editor of a leftist publication with antifascist tendencies, which eventually allowed him, in 1944, to become editor of a number of Communist newspapers and magazines. In 1946 he accused the Communist regime of suppressing creative freedom and lost his job. Four years later, having been accused of further subversive behavior, he was condemned to five years of hard labor. In 1958 he was arrested for a second time for having composed anticommunist poems, which he was accused of distributing outside the country. He was sentenced to hard labor for life, a sentence he carried out in the Romanian lead mines. Along with a number of other political prisoners, Caraion was freed during the ideological thaw of 1964. He was subsequently recruited as an informant by the Secret Service; he collaborated actively, gathering information about fellow writers. In 1981 he exiled himself to Switzerland, after the Secret Service threatened him and made public some of his informative notes. Obsessed with publishing, he founded two cultural magazines abroad, one of which (*Correspondances*) published work in six languages.

Having an ulcerous temperament and a convulsive biography (perhaps the most contorted of those modeled by the totalitarian regime), Caraion was the author of an expressionist poetry in which the reoccurring themes of nightmare, anguish, abjection, and apocalypse predominated. Some of his more important volumes include *Panopticon* (1943), *Black Songs* (1946), *No One's Morning* (1967), *The Mole and the Near* (1970), *The Cemetery of Stars* (1971), *Perpendicular Tears* (1978), and *Love Is the Pseudonym of Death* (1980). *Arrested Poems* (1999) was published posthumously and contains poems that were confiscated at the time of Caraion's arrest and were used as evidence against him in the trial of 1958. The poet also penned a number of books of essays—*The Duel with Lilies* (1972), *Enigmatic Noblesse* (1974), *The Syllable Hatter* (1976), and *The Insect of Comrade Hitler* (1982)—and of confessions (*Journal I–III*, 1980–98). He was also an acclaimed translator, especially of poetry.

FROM *THE SYLLABLE HATTER*

Poets are individuals who live all of their lives building with discretion, in anonymity, the lives of others. The others—sometimes—know it; sometimes they do not.

Every time a poet has angered a society without horizons or with a historical reservation, he has strengthened both society and history in futuristic projection.

The dialectic illustrates it.

There are many difficult things in the world.

I have seen arms digging, carving, breaking stone. And I have dug, carved, broken stone with them.

I have seen men making houses, paving roads, draining swamps, raising the terraces of railroads or of dams. And I have numbered myself among the shadows of each of the masses of the aforesaid occupations.

I have seen wagons pushed through the undersides of mountains, galleries strengthened with healthy logs, perforators biting the mined hollows, vaults collapsing, naked bodies from which the acidic water mingling with sweat ran in an intermittent salting of boils and eczema.

It was not difficult; it was exceedingly difficult. Most of the time it was indescribable.

But to make humanity dream without asking it for anything in return (for this is the position of the authentic poet in the universe!) is much more difficult than any of the other difficulties. For all the other difficulties would be impossible without dreams.

A blind, animalistic work, an ellipse of windows, and the memory of solar aims would turn men into termites and robots.

And human intelligence was not born for the harpoons of this shipwreck.

For the poet belongs to all of humanity, even without its approval, and to all times, even without time's approval.

A cosmic escalator with lights and umbrellas, with the questions and silences of this world, moves through his brain and his heart distributing ozone, fantasy, the solutions of each molecule of the energy of waiting another minute; another halting, another sign: the revelatory one.

Poetry is like a bizarre cipher.

To await the sign that can reconnect every meaning, every hope, every aspiration to the colossal turbine of dreams where the waters boil bewitchingly and imbibe the human planet with the superb illusion that life has a meaning, that the discourse of existence is—besides that of a tragic toy and besides only blackmail, exploitation, anarchy—also beauty, and morality, and equilibrium, and music, and the prodigious blooming of all principles and privileges of thought and liberty.

The work of the poet—so often defamed, ordered to the corner, to the stump, or to the electric chair; so fragile that only rarely it tempts any lily liver to deride it and beckon it to the circus, between buffoons, where cheap fun is prepared and sunflower seeds are eaten; the work of the poet, his song, the urge through which he (clumsy!) introduces into the world trust, dream, mystery, illusion; through which he makes possible the impossibility—also of bearing life; the work of the poet is the dosage—simultaneously—of the fascinating inexpressible, of impalpability, of the essential without which life would be more impotent than if it were lacking in air. For we cannot name life that which has not yet arisen from the biologic.

Translated by Carla Baricz

Constantin Țoiu

(b. 1923)

A graduate of the Faculty of Letters and Philosophy at the University of Bucharest,
Țoiu worked as editor at several publishing houses and literary journals. A part of his
vast journalistic production (especially the portion concerned with literary themes) is
collected in the volumes *The Fate of Words* (1971), *Pretexts* (1973), *Other Pretexts* (1977),
Caftans and Beatings (1994), and *Morbus Diaboli* (1998). He has published a memoir
(*Memoirs from Time to Time*, 2003) and a great number of translations. He is considered
one of the most important Romanian fiction writers of the period following the Second
World War. He is the author of a volume of short stories (*The Sunday of the Mountains*, 1967) and of several novels: *Death in the Forest* (1965), *The Ivy Gallery* (1976), *The
Companion* (1989), *Obligado* (1984), *The Fall into the World* (1987), and *Barbarius* (1999).
As a fiction writer interested in the refinement of style and narrative construction, Țoiu
often works with themes characteristic of one's experience of living in Romania during
the Communist regime. He is particularly interested in the ways in which the individual
is crushed or, on the contrary, saved through modest strategies. Among his frequent
themes one finds the trauma of memory (in a society that mystifies the past), guilt, the
relation between the individual and power, the preservation of inner freedom, and the
authenticity of the human being.

FROM "THE TEAM PASSING THROUGH THE WORLD"

1991

I come into M.'s office one morning in November 1975: into M.'s who has now started to resemble—pale and corpulent as she is—Nașa Primavera, the typographer, Aurica's wife, Chiril's godmother. I have not come in with the intention to see A.M. I'm still not too sure if the existence of my book depends on him. On him, who in turn has started to resemble Bunthe, giving shots to dogs in Dobrogea, although, I repeat, the text is already *written*! [. . .]

M. was kind, calm, a perfect secretary. We would use the informal "you" with each other, with no intimacy besides the feeling dictated by the routine of the job. I no longer know why I had stopped by her office; in any case, I remember it was not related to the manuscript that was waiting to go to print. Today I am surprised by this naïveté. It was lucky that M., after having solved the problem I had stopped by for—I think it had to do with the typing, she had recommended a typist who could be trusted, I think that was it—asked me if I didn't need to see A.M. because he was in his office and had no other appointments. Yes, indeed, it would have been good to see him—he was the most punctual and good-willing director and an informed literary critic. When I came into his office and saw his thick glasses shine in the morning light, directed toward me with a smile that I would understand much later on as a "complicitous smile," a heavy character dozing inside me woke up and signaled: well, Sir, this is your man! The man in whose power rested editorial publications that had several problems. He asked me to have a seat in the most collegial of ways, and, while talking, I saw him bend over behind the massive desk, staying there for a while, as though he had pulled out a drawer down there and was looking for something in it, and then he got up again—and I noticed that his face had turned somewhat red. This was around 10:00 A.M. We talked about other things, then we came around to talking about the manuscript of *The Gallery*. It was difficult, it had many problems, but the most difficult one was that the main character committed suicide, and such a thing had not been published since August 23.[1] He could not commit suicide,

---

1. On August 23, 1944, following a coup, Romania turned against Germany and joined the Allies. Although the Royal House (Romania was at the time a constitutional monarchy) and other political parties contributed to this change, the Communist faction took credit

another ending had to be found—and he bent over again, behind his desk and stood there for eight, nine seconds. When he raised his head, his physiognomy, that of a kind man from Ardeal, had gotten redder and you could see on it a type of perplexed candor . . . A vague smell of high-quality wine, somewhat sweet—I could swear: Ottonel—passed under my nostrils . . . I did not know it then, I found out later, that A.M. was suffering from a malady for which it was necessary to ingurgitate a certain quantity of wine every day. Thus, it was not a vice; it was a necessity. But then, not knowing the cause of it, I was very surprised. A director, at the Combinat, consuming alcohol at 10:00 A.M.![2] Not to mention the imprudent nature of such habits. He would have been fired instantly. Someone had to point it out to him, get him out of trouble, otherwise who knew what kind of brute could come and take his place? This is what I thought, kindly inclined as I sometimes am, up to a point!

A.M. talked to me afterward for a while about the difficulty of publishing a novel in which the main character committed suicide—while bending over every now and then, with a jerk of his right shoulder . . . Later on, recomposing the scene, I found an analogy—his gesture resembled that of a driver handling the stick shift, putting it in first, second, third, then fourth gear—while the bottle itself, placed down there, by his foot, was like the known mechanism that regulates, stage by stage, the driving regimen of an automobile.

It was 11:00 A.M. now. M.'s head peered in; someone else was waiting. A.M. with a kind of gentle euphoria made a sign that they could wait further. And we went back to Chiril's suicide. A.M.'s eyes were tearing. I said I was a good person up to a point. And, well, when I get to this point where something in my existence comes into play and no compromise is possible, I change and can become stiff, stubborn with a determination that surprises me too. I also do not think that I am so removed from a certain *natural* theatricality. Now, this was different. I had in front of me a sentimental man, softened up by his gearshifts during several quick rounds, the teary nature of his eyes— typical of natures sensitive to other people's troubles—bearing witness to it. I had to attack! To discover the weakest side of this man, wounded not only by

---

and declared it the day of inauguration of the new regime, which would take full control of the country three years later. Up until 1990, August 23 was Romania's National Day.

2. Combinat—communist industrial platform.

his malady but also because of the time he had done unjustly (this I knew, he had been previously locked up because of some banned books). We had agreed on certain small corrections. I know that good negotiators compromise on insignificant matters so they can win on the important points. Fine, I would do this as well, I will humanize Roadevin, I will have him say this and that, I will make the page, the line stronger—I was jotting everything down in the fever of negotiations; I will also cut out that sentence. Great—he would say—but how about the suicide? How can *you* think that something like that can come out today, do you not see that it can't be . . . *don't you know that?!* . . . And what if no other hero committed suicide until my novel, this will be the first one, we will start with this one—I would say with determination, raising my voice a little, feeling that the man in front of me needed a determined guy, uncompromising on this matter in order to back out, defeated. But he would not admit defeat—he would say, this can't be, *don't you understand?*, find something else, make him live, find a trick, you novelists have imagination. That's it, I answered aggressively, I don't have imagination, what kind of imagination?!—and I did not go on, which meant that reality surpassed imagination. It can't be, he would repeat, it can't come out like this, change it . . . make him live, no matter how, but make him live! . . . I got up in a grave manner, and instead of yelling, I murmured (*qualisartifex pereo!*): I cannot, dear A.M., I cannot—*the grass has grown on his grave!*

A.M. looked at me for a while. Then he looked down, extended his hand over the desk separating us, managing to get up halfway: a hand whose handshake was formal in appearance, but which was in fact a sign of defeat . . . And *The Gallery* was going to come out very soon. Only because, by chance, I stood before a man, and I uttered, involuntarily, the key sentence, the magic formula, and that man appreciated the word, the *logos* that opens up everything. Although, I have to admit, later on, repeating to myself: I CANNOT, *the grass has grown on his grave*, these words appeared theatrical to me; although, when the fight is unequal, one cannot really choose one's guns.

The truth is that this character, on whose grave the grass has grown, was real and I had known him, and when I uttered those words I was not referring to a fiction. A young man of great value, who had hanged himself, while in detention, with a pair of long underwear that he had fashioned into a noose. He helped me, perhaps, from Beyond, to finish and to impose *The Gallery*.

The second character, who also could have helped me from his void, was the paralytic adolescent, from my childhood in Urziceni,[3] Ialomița, who would sit all day on the gallery of the ivy-shadowed house that exists even today. When I pass through Urziceni to light a candle at my parents' graves, I also pass by the little street where the house with a gallery is located, and I stop and look at it, both grateful and surprised. The novel began here. In the most distant summer of my childhood. I was about nine, ten years old; Paul (the paralytic) was fifteen and because he sat still, he had become our feared and respected leader. Perhaps because of his illness, perhaps because of his bestial grin with which he commanded us from the deck (the commanding post) of his motionless ship, the Gallery . . . I revealed long ago the origin of the novel. Now I return, redefining the confession; being of a certain age, it becomes more and more important to show your gratitude to those who really deserve it. A paralytic, a man who does not move . . . to remain so vividly in your memory . . . His most powerful look, of all the looks he gave, that which would subjugate us the most, was when, bellowing like a bull and undoing his pants—we could only see his chest!—he would suddenly cry out *attention!* and a long and blurry stream of urine would go up over the wooden edge of the Gallery, making a big arch in the air—quite a performance—while we, his subjects, ran away in terror. [. . .]

Only today, after the fall of the dictatorship, am I aware of the importance of the book. There will never be another dictatorship of this kind; nor a *Gallery* written under so much tension, the two being tied forever in some strange way.

Translated by Raluca Manea

3. Urziceni—a small town in the southern part of Romania. C. Țoiu's birthplace.

Nina Cassian

(b. 1924)

A poet of many talents, Nina Cassian studied painting, acting, and symphonic and instrumental music, among other things. She began—though never completed—studies in philology in Bucharest. After her debut in the literary world with avant-garde poetry (*At Entrance 1/1*), she engaged in propagandist writing—*Our Soul* (1949), *Youth* (1953), *The Flower of the Homeland* (1954)—but soon found her own voice and went on to create original and innovative verse: *Open-Air Spectacle* (1961), *Let Us Give One Another Gifts* (1963), *The Blood* (1966), *Parallel Destinies* (1967), *Requiem* (1971), *Loto-Poems* (1972), *Of Mercy* (1981), and *Backward Countdown* (1983). Cassian is also the author of a volume of prose entitled *So Awesome and Adio: Fictive Confidences* (1971), and of an interesting autobiographical series, *Memory as Inheritance* (3 vols., 2002–05). She has published a number of volumes of verse for children, which were very well received by their intended audience, and completed an impressive number of translations into Romanian (especially of poetry). In 1985, due to the degradation of living conditions during the dictatorship, she relocated to the United States, where she continued to publish verse.

Nina Cassian writes a nonconformist, ludic, protesting, experimental poetry that invents and subverts languages and displays a flair for the dramatic that unites the cerebral and emotional registers. (*Translated by Carla Baricz*)

THE IMMIGRATION DEPARTMENT

Me with my pen
hoping the ink won't run out
before I register a new defeat.
Look I'm waiting—as I've waited year after year—
for them to deny me
the right to poetry, to an orange,
perhaps even the status to be human.
My identity—more and more uncertain.
In vain I keep writing my name on books,
on scores, in the right-hand corner of an idea,
my name—a convention;
my being—an abstraction;
distinguishing marks—none.
(Oh yes: a rash of pride on my left cheek . . .)
in the end
the denials which besiege me
define my very being
just like the knife thrower   .
who gets his victim's perfect outline
from the knives he throws at the board.

So
I've no chance
although I'm wearing
the protective glasses of my loved one
(things have outlived him:
his purple jacket brilliantly patterned,
the absurd hat bought on Barbe's Boulevard,
the gloves lost then found,
and of course the photographs,
three of them carried on me always:

the one where he strangles me, smiling,
and me with a happy smile
letting myself be strangled.
The one in which he wears the glasses I'm wearing now
looking at me with slight admonishment
sometimes with benevolent irony.

Finally the one where he only looks
at something that looks at him
inviting him politely to leave the world . . .)

The immigration office is not the ideal place
to keen your dead,
but I can't control it
and the public eye me
as they would a miserable creature . . .
which in fact I am
if you take into account my loss
of parents, of pair, of pastures,
of shared pillow, of shared passion . . .

The clerk won't be convinced
of my metaphors;
I almost long to be refused
my respectful application to poetry
to conform with my destiny
familiarized with its commandment
(hope unbalances me).
With the glasses of my loved one
on my famous nose,
I'm waiting, waiting,
for centuries, always waiting
to be called
by the clerk.

Translated by Andrea Deletant & Brenda Walker

Petru Dumitriu

(1924–2002)

Following unfinished studies in philosophy (in Munich) and law (in Bucharest), Dumitriu practiced journalism. In the 1950s he led a literary journal and then an important publishing house, being considered a "red prince," a favorite of the Communist regime. In order to attain this status, the writer abandoned the refined style of his debut volume (*Eurydice*, 1947) and adopted the formula of social realism required by the Communist Party, which he practiced in works of propagandistic fiction such as *June Nights* (1950), *Road without Dust* (1951), *The Bird of the Storm* (1954), and others. He also published enthusiastic notes on his travel to the USSR (*For People's Dignity and Happiness*, 1954) and articles and essays collected in the volumes *On Life and Books* (1954) and *Us and the Neobarbarians* (1957). Dumitriu would later qualify this part of his literature as a "pact with the devil," necessary for survival during an epoch of terror (his father was detained in a labor camp built by the regime that his son was praising). Displaying unusual talent, he published the novel *Family Chronicle* in 1957, a work that surpasses ideological clichés with a remarkable force. It is a massive Balzacian construction that follows the life of an aristocratic family for five generations. In 1958 the writer initiated another fresco (*Biographical Collections, Autobiographies and Contemporary Memoirs*), which remained unfinished. In 1960 he sought political asylum in the West, an act punished by the regime, which arrested his family and held in custody his underage daughter. Once settled in Germany, Dumitriu held modest jobs and underwent a continuous crisis of adaptation. He wrote (with long interruptions) and published in French, both novels and essays that engage predominantly religious themes. After 1990, Dumitriu reentered the literary circuit in Romania; his books were republished, he became active in literary journals, and several volumes of interviews around his tumultuous biography came out.

COGNITIO INCOGNITI

I write these lines in view of knowing the unknown that I am, a complex and contradictory man, so contrasted even in his multiple character yet having a stable, central axis oriented toward God and his fellow beings. Self-conscious during puberty, hiding during the ten years when I called the bear "uncle" till I was safe across the bridge, this axis has been manifest since 1960—*Incognito* (1962) being the first and main reference point—then, from around 1979 (*Au Dieu inconnu*), until this day.

Around this backbone, qualities, pulsions, various faults organized and inter-collided, generally characterized by the gift of love, the gift of friendship, the gift of moral consciousness even while sinning: capable of making mistakes and committing sins, I am not capable of being blinded, not as far as myself nor others are concerned. And more: it is easier for me to be more lenient toward others than toward myself. But when confronted with one who is unjust to me or humiliates me, I turn to stone. I do not wish him evil, I do not wish for him to suffer; I wish neither to see him nor hear from him any longer.

From a heavenly childhood—protected, loved and loving, surrounded by French books and magazines, a childhood in which the gift of writing was already shining forth at thirteen (in French: at fourteen "Les trois combats avec l'hydre," a story with a prophetic title for my life), at fifteen, sixteen *Master Manole* (a play in verse), at seventeen "Niobe," the first prose piece in *Eurydice*. The most important event was, for me, beginning to pray, having an inner life—a religious life—between the Holy Scripture and Eliade's *Yoga*, published by the Royal Foundations.

At seventeen, in the fall of 1941, Paris. France, my natural goal, motherland of my spirit, inaccessible under German occupation; but with my knowledge of French, German, English, Latin, and Italian, I received a scholarship from the Humboldt Foundation, which, since the nineteenth century, has helped worthy students from Eastern Europe study in German universities.

How so? Hitler? The war? The genocide of the Jews?

Answer: I prepared at the University of Munich a doctoral thesis about a work of the brilliant mystic Jakob Böhme (1575–1620?, if only I could remember), who inspired Hegel, Schelling, and Balzac. In passing, it should be noted that through Hegel, Böhme is the inventor and inspirer of Marxist dialectics. The thesis remained unwritten and I did not graduate, because in August 1944 I was at home, on break, and I did not complete my studies. There, in Germany, I learned what dictatorship is, what totalitarianism is, what war is, what unhappiness and human folly are. And I read, I read insatiably, from the two million volumes of the State Library in Munich; and I learned yet another language, Spanish.

One of my professors, Kurt Huber, was decapitated by the Nazis because he was against the war; two students, his disciples—whom I knew from his course and with whom I used to fence in the hall of arms—were decapitated in turn, as was the sister of one of them, for spreading manifestoes against the war.

Having returned home, the house where I was born, the heaven of my childhood and adolescence, was destroyed by German cannons, while we (my mother, my sister, and I) were hiding in the cellar, the shell splinters gushing through the cellar door, red in the dark, as the house was being hit by explosions falling onto our heads.

Then came the liberation via the Russian-Asian despotism and its political-military barbarism and its packs of pillagers and rapists. Such a pack left me without a coat in December 1946 and with three scars on the top of my head: blows with the pistol barrel, for lack of cartridges. Had there been a bullet, only one, I would have died then, at twenty-two.

We were betrayed at Yalta by President Roosevelt, left to the Russians' beck and call for almost half a century. I was starving and I wanted to write. In 1947 I published *Eurydice*. Then the Communist Party got a hold of publishing houses and the press. Not able to do anything other than write, with no door open toward the West, I became an editor at *Flacăra*,[1] I wrote short stories adjusted to the ideology of the Communist Party, among which *Family Jewels* was going to remain in the history of Romanian literature because as far as the revolts in 1907 were concerned, my heart was on the side of the rebellious peasants, crushed by cannons.

Other short stories will not last, although here and there shone forth a gift for dramatic dialogue, for empathy with human suffering—all of it being nonetheless falsified by the Marxist-Leninist political tendency—a system of illusions, lies, and barbaric cruelty to which all humanity from the border with Austria to the Pacific Ocean was subjected, with the approval of the Western allies and without any one Sovietologist, not one, being able to predict its collapse in the fall and winter of 1989.

The victorious tyranny, accepted and tolerated by the West, was ruling in Romania. I complied, gnashing my teeth. A great pharaonic building site opened. I wrote the beginning of a novel on this theme. On my second visit to the Canal I saw a novelty: the penitentiary colonies of the Ministry of the Interior.[2] The first chapters had come out in *Viața Românească*.[3] I could not go back on it. When I was writing *The Wolf Hunt*—good beginning chapter, the rest a lie and unworthy—my father, innocent, was locked up in the prison in the center of Timișoara. At that point, my life and that of my family— parents, sister, companion—all depended on me, or else everything would have gone down had I lost my life heroically. I lived there for eight more years—back there, long ago. *The Bird of the Storm:* the first chapter, powerful, a storm out at the Black Sea, the rest, shameful, guilty. And still, Leontiev Scremutu called me on it, to tell me how to give a twist to the story.[4]

1. *Flacăra*—a sociocultural magazine founded in Bucharest around 1948.

2. the Canal—the Black Sea canal was built in the 1950s with the forced labor of political detainees. In 1951 P. Dumitriu published a novel, *Road without Dust*, in which the canal was depicted as a great achievement of the people. "The beginning of the novel" to which the author alludes are the parts of *Road without Dust* already published in *Romanian Life*.

3. *Viața Românească (The Romanian Life)*—a literary journal founded in 1906 in Iași. After 1930, it was published in Bucharest.

4. Leontiev Scremutu—the satirical nickname of Leonte Răutu (1910–93). Member of the Central Committee and the Romanian Communist Party, Răutu occupied several important posts, among them head of the Department of Propaganda and Culture; he was

His unforgettable words to me: "My death is not the same as the death of a well-to-do peasant!" As if death would differentiate! What arrogance! The Marxists, beginning with Marx: an arrogant tribe, contested and wiped out by history.

1954: thirty years, in the prime of life. *A Family Chronicle.* A strong construction, twisted and disfigured by the blind pressure that came from above and crushed us all. Twenty-four short stories, some unforgettable. State Prize? Not at all. Not even because I had given it the twist that they wanted. The book wasn't bad enough for the State Prize.

Afterward, *Contemporary Biographies*, in parts, in *Steaua*,[5] in *Viața Românească*. Underneath, from the shadows, disgrace. Suspicion, envy, ill will.

I knew where this was going. I knew the program. Ever since Esenin, Mayakovsky, Mandelstam, Fadeev, Pasternak. Suicide. Or the hidden, but not too hidden, persecution. (And now I know even better: murder, as with Marin Preda.)[6]

I decided not to wait. I wrested myself away. My parents, my younger sister, my sister-in-law, my ex-wife, my close friends: in prison. The child: in an orphanage.

None of them reproached me for the escape from the big prison. They understood. They knew I wasn't the jailer, the torturer, the executioner. But Burghiu-Vrej, Chivuță Scoica, and whatever the names of the sinister clowns were, the former dead of cancer, the latter a pseudo-suicide, murdered by the Secret Service agent who was guarding him, that entire, horrible system from which I had wrested myself.[7]

Only to end up in the midst of the intellectual Left in the West.

Immediately, in 1962, I wrote *Incognito*. What? This deserter? This traitor? Anticommunist, anti-Soviet, antihumanist, anti, anti, anti?

---

also in charge of the media and press section. He exercised tyrannical power and imposed an anticultural agenda while holding these positions.

5. *Steaua (The Star)*—literary journal published in Cluj beginning in 1954.

6. After Marin Preda's death on May 16, 1980, in a writer's house owned by the Writers' Union, it was speculated (though with decreasing interest) that Preda's death might have been the result of an assassination.

7. Chivuță Scoica was the satirical nickname given to Chivu Stoica (1908–75), an important member of the Romanian Communist Party.

The most talented fiction writer from after the war, Marek Hłasko, committed suicide in exile, at Wiesbaden. The second most talented, Jerzy Kosinski, committed suicide in New York. The greatest German poet after the war, Paul Celan—a Jew from Bukovina and Bucharest, whose friend I had the honor to be—committed suicide in Paris. The Russian who wrote *I Chose Freedom* committed suicide in the United States. The nice Romanian dancer, whom you remember, perhaps, and who rejected the sexual advances of Comrade Ocnăraş, committed suicide in Paris.[8] And Marin Preda was murdered at Mogoşoaia, in secret, under the seal of lies and silence.

This is how I would have perished, had I stayed in the country. Through suicide or through murder camouflaged as suicide.

On the other hand, in the West I have been so unhappy that, for years, looking at trains go by at great, striking speeds—like thunder and lightning— through the train station in Bad Godesberg (relative to Ben, Bad Godesberg is what Băneasa is to Bucharest; I live there), I have been thinking until yesterday: "You have one more step to make. From the edge of the platform to the place between the rails. The collision, the instant, darkness, nothingness. Clothes ripped apart, meshed in with broken bones and torn flesh, in a puddle of blood. Over. You're gone. You are nowhere."

And this, for thirty-three years. The temptation.

I say I have expiated. I say that he who wants any more from me is a persecutor. I say this is enough. He who does not believe me, may he live in the West for thirty years and remember then what I say here and that he did not believe me and that he was completely wrong.

Here I am, at seventy. The third period of my life, perhaps a short one, is about to begin. The first was the happy childhood, the adolescence, the youth, the writer of poetic myths. Then, the state and party liar, gnashing his teeth as a sign of weak revolt, capable of writing lasting pages and seeing these pages sullied by the tyranny of the party. Thirty-six years, then the dislodgment, as if wresting oneself from the jaws of the dragon, leaving it with a bloody arm in its teeth.

The second period, thirty-three years in the barren, hostile, heartless West.

---

8. Comrade Ocnăraş was the satirical nickname given to Emil Bodnăraş (1904–76), an important member of the Romanian Communist Party.

Out of ten years, unemployed for one. Out of five, clerk for one. Out of ten, one communist, even now! Out of ten, all ten: dumbfounded, lost, disoriented.

And in their midst you write in a foreign language, for strangers, a stranger among strangers. You are lost. You survive by miracle. Not as if by a miracle, but by miracle.

Readers of *Incognito*, now friends, turn out to be the embodiment of human kindness. One in a thousand or in ten thousand. But that one gives me his hand and does not let me drown. And he passes away, but look, another one, and I elude drowning again. And I write novels, religious and mystical essays. And look how in my loneliness and my lost state—a woman comes and tells me: "I read *Incognito*. I love you."

Now begins the third stage, the last, from the liberation of Romania onward, and for me, from seventy to the more or less distant death. Now I write again in Romanian. And in French, as before. I am no longer exiled, I am at home, among friends. Tired, but happy. I must hurry because I do not have a lot of time left but a lot left to write.

Translated by Raluca Manea

Leonid Dimov

(1926–1987)

Dimov attended classes in several departments and schools of the University of Bucharest (letters and philosophy, biology, law) without ever earning a diploma. In 1957 he was arrested for two months for having insulted Stalin's statue. He worked as associate editor and editor for several cultural publications. He was prolific as a translator and authored several volumes of poetry: *Lyrics* (1966), *Seven Poems* (1968), *On the Bank of the Styx* (1968), *Book of Dreams* (1969), *Eleusis* (1970), *Heavenly Signs* (1970), *Openings* (1972), *ABC* (1973), *Litanies for Horea* (1975), *Youth without Aging* (1978), and *The Show* (1979). Posthumously, in 2003, an insightful volume of correspondence, *Love Letters (1943–1954)*, was published.

One of the most original Romanian poets and founder (with Dumitru Țepeneag) of a movement called Aesthetic Oneiricism, Dimov wrote a poetry of great refinement, with a predilection for fixed forms. Through the latter and by means of a lyrical idiom, the writer built a baroque universe, populated with sumptuous, theatrical, clownish spaces, given to illusion and games (often macabre and grotesque). His privileged theme was the dream, made manifest in diverse hypotheses (from reverie to hallucination and nightmare), yet treated not surrealistically, but in a lucid and aestheticizing manner.

The Noble Fool of Totality

A predominantly sensitive being, destined to explore the pre-noumenal chaos, the poet plays the part of a boomerang of the spirit. Hurled into the shadows of the unknown, he comes back into the world, but not as he departed—on the sinuous line of his thought will soon glimmer the grains torn from the invincible thing-in-itself.

The poet lives like any other being endowed with thought. Moreover, the world holds a double importance to him: of maintaining him in relation and of sustaining his primordial fragments of obsession or vision. Between the poet and the world there is a double bind twice as strong as the one between the world and the nonpoet (with the exception, for instance, of Jakob Böhme, the poet-shoemaker). Everyone can experience states of daydreaming, poetic states—so everyone can be, for a moment or more, a poet. Only the true poet, however, is urged by mysterious powers to forge a noble alloy between poetry and world. He thus becomes an emperor's fool. The noble fool of Totality. For the poet, to renounce the world is to give up on life, Totality—in which death, as we well know, represents a single moment—to renounce poetry.

The ban on the renunciation of life is not just under the jurisdiction of the church. It is postulated by the very principle of poetry. Silence, as the final goal of poetry, is a gross paradox, although it enjoys a certain notoriety in modern aesthetics. Less severe than the church, poetry does not ban the renunciation of any kind of life, does not postulate existence at all costs, on the edge of a cliff, when everyone and everything has disappeared. In this sense, of the poet's absolute demand of the world, we can say that he is constantly in *articulo mortis*. Always ready to sacrifice himself for poetry, he only surpasses, with mortal peril, the region in which the ethical intermingles with the aesthetic. And when he is taken by force from this region, when injustice alters poetry, he perishes virtually at the moment when injustice becomes essential, meaning that it can no longer be amended. We find ourselves faced with fragility, with finitude. But a fragility in strength, a finitude in infinity. [. . .]

There is, however, a way of conceiving of these things that is less Cartesian, proper to the poet. In his imagination, he can bypass unfavorable phases until he is able to move freely, in a world, it seems, of his own. Who were the great Utopians? Precisely the kind of poets urged to live in a world that did not satisfy them. What is at stake here is to anticipate (with all the implied transfigurations) a future, better world.

If such a poetic production also holds an epistemological function, if the world imagined by the poet presupposes an explanatory structure in relation to the world in which he lives—this is a question whose answer goes beyond his prerogatives. The positive role of the invasion of the future by poetry (I am not thinking here about the technological future whose anticipation is relegated to science-fiction productions, but about the aesthetic future, meaning the axioms of a world that is beneficial to aesthetic beauty) is nonetheless twofold: in the first place, it rescues the poet, offering him the palliative of a fulfilling phantasm; in the second place—and this is the important one—it gives the reader the power to enfold the "things" degraded by the quotidian through a connective stratum, meant to emanate connections both on the vertical and the horizontal axes, beyond and below zero. Poetry thus regains its demiurgic function, and—who knows—the relation between poet and Totality (fool-emperor) may become mutual.

Translated by Raluca Manea

Octavian Paler

(1926–2007)

Having completed university studies in philosophy and law, Octavian Paler worked as a radio and television journalist (reaching the post of director) until 1970, when he became chief editor of a well-known Bucharest newspaper, *Romania Liberă*. He held this position until 1983, when he was fired for political reasons. After 1990, following the fall of the Communist dictatorship, he reentered the publishing world, becoming an important opinion-maker. Though he made his debut in poetry (*The Shadow of Words*, 1970) and though his writing has a lyrical dimension, Paler's main contribution was in the form of prose. He was the author of the novels *Life on a Train Platform* (1981) and *A Lucky Man* (1984) and of the autobiographical novels *Paths through Memory* (1972–1974), *Caminante* (1980), *Life as a Bullfight* (1987), *Don Quixote from the East* (1994), and *The Desert Forever* (2003). He also wrote essays, including *Subjective Mythologies* (1975), *Imaginary Letters* (1979), *Cordial Polemics* (1983), *A Museum in the Labyrinth* (1987), and *Solitary Adventures* (1996). Both his parabolic novels and his confessional literature cultivate in a desperate and at times pathetic register what Paler considered to be the central moral problem of his time: guilt, forgiveness, and human strength in the face of violent and crude mystification. (*Translated by Carla Baricz*)

THE SECOND LOVE

You wrote somewhere in a verse: "What good is a poet,
in a time of drought?" And just this question gives me the courage
to address myself to a great writer and to say that genuine courage,
the genuine courage of poetry does not necessarily lie in praising the rains
when everybody can see them, but genuine courage is to see
the burnt sky and to hope. Because the rain must first be
hope and song, and only later genuine rain that waters the deserts.
A poet announces to the city, to the earth that there is rain,
he announces to people that it is their duty to keep hope
alive. A poet under a burnt sky, in front of a burnt plain,

who is not able to sing and to believe in rain,
and to remind us that rain exists,
and makes the sick earth blossom,
therefore, a poet who is not a prophet of hope,
a poet with burnt lips who does not feel the need to sing
the rains of the world

does not understand that poetry is first of all a form of hope.
What good is a poet in a time of drought?
To praise the rain just when we need it, when we miss it,
and when we long for it,
when the sun burns and hands smell of doubt,
when the trees of sand vanish at the slightest breath of wind,
when memories taste of error and hope is a dangerous word
and one who praises rain risks being despised and beaten
even stoned, persecuted by both gods and people
for his foolishness and the courage with which he goes on praising
the rains, and the torrents, while the people raising up their arms
remain crucified in the air as on Golgotha. What
will announce the rains if not poetry? Who will have the
courage to see rain clouds in the empty sky,
who takes the risk of predicting rain if poetry does not,
that poetry which was with the Greeks at Troy's walls
and climbed down with Dante into Inferno?

Translated by Crisula Ştefănescu & Emily Chalmers

Radu Petrescu

(1927–1982)

After graduating from the Faculty of Letters at the University of Bucharest in 1951, Radu Petrescu worked as a teacher of Romanian at a number of public schools throughout the country. He returned to Bucharest in 1954 and took up modest posts, as a functionary and documenter at local research institutes. A discreet, unassuming man with few friendships in the literary world, the writer saw literary creation in the absolute sense, driving himself energetically and mercilessly. He kept a journal from adolescence on, recording the books he read, his feelings, and his perennial concern: how one might go about writing. Some of these journal entries were published as *Through the Other End of the Spyglass* (1978), *Berenica's Hair* (1981), and, posthumously, as *The Catalog of My Daily Movements* (1999) and *Prisoner of the Provisional* (2002). Petrescu also published the novels *Matei Iliescu* (1970), *A Single Age* (1975), *What Is Seen* (1979), and *Prose* (1971). He was also the author of essay *The Meteorology of Reading* (1982) and of a number of articles about the fine arts, collected posthumously in *The Place of Revelation* (2000). Considered an important postwar prose writer, Petrescu attempted "mythological transpositions," which he camouflaged in quotidian universes. His best-known work, *Matei Iliescu*, is a romance in which the psychology of passion is minutely and painstakingly transformed into a metaphysics of love that is of "aerial essence."

FROM "ILL FROM UNWRITTEN BOOKS"

28 JUNE [1949]

We must not think that to write means to have at hand a table of sensations and ideas, a nib, and plenty of time to move it across the page. The responsibilities of this act are infinite, and he who performs it is indebted—to the highest degree—to the virtue of prudence. After all, what he does is a work that implicates him completely, a splendid body (*splendidus* = lucent) which tempts the unskilled to profanation. This, however, is only one of the dangers. There are others, less sinister in appearance, but in reality more dangerous because more subtle. A book, a phrase, a true page must not be flung upon the market but guided. Behold a principle of whose importance I am too late aware and, having ignored it, of whose consequences I will suffer God knows how long, perhaps all my life. I mark this down quickly. The accumulation of my papers constitutes a debt to myself. Happily enough, I am not a criminal. I will not use the powers that I have received for a grimace. This is the third danger (I have not formed hierarchies, though among the ones listed here, it would come first). But do I not deceive myself?

10 NOVEMBER [1949]

Writing must be a lot like *this* gaze—to arrive at the possibility of making life through the simple adjoining of two or three words and then to no longer be interested in what I write, for anything will have life. To make, from two or three words of ink, a tree, a woman, a cloud, a dog. Can there be a simpler voluptuousness? And then to write the universal catalog. Any opus is, after all, a catalog of what the artist has seen, of *all* that he has seen. We no not even have to claim further ambition knowing that, like Pliny, even if we write about humble things (a cloud, a dog), we find ourselves before a tragedy, before the Eternal.

7 OCTOBER [1958]

After years and years of searching at chaotic crossroads, searching that leads to nothing, suddenly the arduously desired fruit is made visible. You have found *your* voice, *your* volumes and colors. Yes, well, this sacred moment is only the beginning. Until now you have done nothing but incite its coming, readied yourself for it, put yourself in the state that will make you capable of seeing. Now, however, you must consolidate and build yourself. Regardless, the danger is that any gesture can be a straying, which will irrevocably remove you from the discovered essence. *You can forget this essence.* The sirens surround you, but you must tie yourself to the mast very tightly. The more you suffer, the better. In regards to myself, I have strayed but little and returned quickly. Rigorous tower. All the conditions for the continuation of the work with an accretion of violence. First of all, solitude, now complete, and the knowledge of the misery of those who contest it. I see clearly, as always, but very deeply, very wide.

SATURDAY, 17 [JANUARY 1959]

How a novel is written. A *volume* colored so and so is dreamed of. Then, around two or three figures that beckon, a certain intrigue congeals, chosen nevertheless so as to give the author the maximum capability of development and yet not overstep beyond the believable. From this intrigue a moment is chosen and is developed on a few pages in a few images—and from here on everything comes on its own if you can persist on paper, unbefouled, absorbed, concentrated upon it even when you do not write. Let us define the novel as a prolonged captivity between Ideas.

27 JANUARY [1959]

Margareta C. and Mrs. Sch. from the ICAR are frightened for my head, ask me if I am not ill for—as they pretend—I have lost much weight and have a yellowed cast.[1] Ill? Yes, I am ill of life, of the immense work that I cannot manage to accomplish, I am ill of all the unread books, of all the unwritten books.

Translated by Carla Baricz

---

1. The ICAR stands for the *Institutul de Cercetări Agricole Romania (Romanian Institute of Agricultural Research).*

Mircea Horia Simionescu

(b. 1928)

Graduate of the Faculty of Philology at the University of Bucharest, Mircea Horia Simionescu was a newspaper editor, clerk for the Central Committee of the Communist Party, and director of the Romanian Opera House. He is the author of an ample novel cycle, *The Tempered Ingenious One*, which contains the volumes *Onomastic Dictionary* (1980), *General Bibliography* (1970), *A Half Plus One* (1976), *The Breviary* (1980), *Toxicology or Beyond Good*, and *On This Side of Evil* (1983). He has also published the novels *Never-ending Dangers* (1978), *Teachings for the Dolphin* (1979), *The Frock Coat* (1984), *The Auction* (1985), and *The Siege of the Commonplace* (1988). Simionescu is also a short-story writer known for *After 1900, Around Noon* (1974), *The Banquet* (1982), *The Angel with a Kitchen Apron* (1992), and *Gallant Stories* (1994). He writes a prose composed of fragments and divagations in the course of which the epic of the whole is pulverized or relativized. Creating a complex network of associations, he combines fantasy with the ludic, parody with the literary, and the real with the fictional, often citing nonexistent works.

FROM "WANDA, OR THE INTERPRETATION SYNDROME"

Solicited by the doctor to enlarge upon and, if possible, to interpret my symptoms, I took up the pen and reporting notebook and, sitting down on a bench near the pavilion where once, in a little barred room, the Poet lay ill, I wrote the notes that follow, promising myself to transform them into a story later:

• Writing, I pray hopelessly to the heavens for something to come and wrench me from the whirlpool that I bring about by pressing forward: for my mother to come from the provinces, for a storm to begin, for a compressor to explode in the street, for the phone to ring, for the brick wall near the kitchen to collapse, for someone to yell, for someone to call me, for someone who burst into the house or had been sitting for a long time in the wardrobe to hit me, for my lover who left me and tormented me with her memory to come back twenty years later.

But nothing happens, the clock ticks quietly, the pen slips, scratching on the luster of the page. The cheated waiting fills my soul with bitterness, and, at long last, no longer able to wait for something to happen, I begin to think that the modest deeds which delineate themselves on the page are the only important events in my life.

Writing, I pray hopelessly to the heavens to keep anything from happening that might undo this sheaf of dried flowers after I have tied it, fearing that even a slight breath could scatter what came together along with my possible life.

• Much like love—the more impassioned, definitive, voluptuous, the more the lovers are threatened (look at the ill factory-workers, or at those suffering from incurable diseases, or those awaiting their sentence or their departure for the war!)—it's the same with literary creation: the paper becomes miraculously fertile and the writing very virile in states of great fatigue, of acute existential disquiet.

On the contrary, the states of equilibrium, of reconstruction, of prudent care and toning are sterile, comfortable until the tightening of all desires.

It is natural that a true artist, who wishes more than anything to have a proper disposition for writing, will attempt to reedit the marvelous moments of exhaustion, of self-loss, which tachycardia, cerebral congestion, insomnia, melancholy, coffee, and the sentiment of desperation sometimes bring.

The writing table can be called the place where one signs the contract with death. As is the case with other contracts, this Faust also sells his soul with the hidden thought that he will be capable of tricking his partner in some manner.

· The terrible, insupportable, infernal suffering of feeling that the passing of time works against the fixing of your ideas: while thought slides and tumbles maddeningly forward, the remainder of one's being remains behind and the hooks, the nets, the set traps no longer manage to reach and catch anything but the solitary thread of stirred-up dust. While you run, you keep looking backward, knowing that you are there and knowing that you have not escaped and you cannot escape from here.

In order to truly penetrate into the kernel of an occurrence, of a scene, of a shadow, you need an immense quantity of time that opens into the receding past and would like to close somewhere in the most uncertain of futures, though never really closing; you, however, have at your disposal only a very short fragment of this time, its magnifying glass does not encompass in its field more than the present and a thin strip of circular penumbra.

If you try to catch the idea when it has just begun its tumbling, the idea is frail and the prey does not tempt. If it has drawn away and flees madly, filling out like a snowball, it is either too far for you to reach it or so beautiful that you prefer to let it fly as it will until, like an asteroid, it will scatter into nothingness, dissipating.

You prefer the waste of a shameful, barbarous hunt. [. . .]

· Sleep prepares itself throughout the duration of the day, when you choose the pollen of images for the famished honeycomb. Forms, colors, slivers of action, articulated motions charge the retina and create in the depths a three-dimensional space. Sleep delays when the desert stretches beneath the eyelids, only the words passing from one sky into another, like the birds at night, murmuring but formless, traveling in a precise direction with an unknown destination.

Painters sleep well, are never anxious that they will not close their eyes all night because their images are spatial. Writers, however, torment themselves terribly: the words are dry, reality reduced beginning at the level of sensation, electrical current without the lamp. Undone by what evokes and represents, the words lay waste to space, and conscience feels again their superficial movement as a physiological impotence. A certain Madam Precup sleeps like a log, the words through which she has gained information regarding the world have become visual images, she sees scenes and casts aside the carrying words. . . .

· The idea fluttering about my temples nails me to the cross of the chair, with the paper before me: as always, all the spectacle of life interests me. As in a film, short happenings peregrinate before my eyes, the countenances of people, corners of the world, known landscapes or others little forgotten, silhouettes of beautiful women, much desired, episodes from books, phrases delineating the histories buried in the depths of being, and little by little I am flooded by the thirst to plunge into the living torrent of all these scenes, to join the countenances and the silhouettes and to live with and through them the ineffable charm of life. But the paper stands before me as a fastened gate, I cannot pass beyond. All that is left to me, so as to taste the inaccessible, is to make up some pretty words, to form from them a construction more or less similar to the glimpsed world, to make do with the sketches and copies made in resignation—not after I have truly seen, but after it seems to me that I have, when I had thirsted to see.

The great happiness of living is consumed with each word added on paper, and I rise after a few written pages with the violent wish of never seeing or hearing anything ever again.

Writing is a daily exercise for the definitive leave-taking. [. . .]

· I am not interested in my beloved who awaits me, in the sky that wants itself looked at, in the steadfast fragrant forest, in the concert of a great pianist, in the trip to Greece, in the shoes that delighted my eyes from a display window, in the book borrowed by a friend, in the conversation with an acquaintance recently returned from Africa . . . And this acute anorexia only because in the depths of my being has stirred the wish to sit down at the table as soon as possible and to write something lived a long time ago.

I clearly know that, most often, the novelty of my discourse arranged on the page does not suffice to compensate even a quarter of the novelty of out-side events that had solicited me.

But if? . . . It happened once that the occurrences put down by me on the page were more masterly than those helter-skelter ones preferred at the time. A single experience of this kind immobilizes me for days on end before the writing table, before the page.

How wonderful it would be if some sign—an eyelid flutter, a stomach rumble, a skin itch, a certain nausea—would indicate with certainty that you do not keep at your writing without some sort of usefulness. . . .

You advance quickly or perhaps with difficulty, always however living the painful sentiment that you relinquish something contoured and named for something vague and improbable.

• Nevertheless, if the door has closed the need for me to push and to slam it, if it seemed to me to be five to ten, but it is only ten to five, if, reaching out my hand after a cigarette I find it immediately and the match does not break in its lighting, if, if, if . . . I can have some hope, and in the evening, an unimaginably voluptuous contentment. . . .

Translated by Carla Baricz

Radu Cosașu

(b. 1930)

Fascinated by the Communist regime's ideals of social justice and determined to place his "life on the altar of the revolution," Radu Cosașu (pseudonym Oscar Rohrlich) broke ties with his family at the age of sixteen and ceased taking piano lessons, an instrument for which he had unusual talent. Also for purely proletarian reasons, he would later interrupt university studies in philology and pursue the coursework of a school of literature organized by the Communist Party. Cosașu worked as an editor in the quotidian press, then as a barber, and after a period of intellectual unemployment (he was removed from the press for his ideological "impurity") lasting over a decade, he became an editor in the cultural press. He is the author of several volumes of articles that manifest a propagandist's enthusiasm but reach a substantial humanistic and artistic quality: *We Serve the Romanian Socialist Republic* (1952), *The Opinions of an Earthling* (1957), *Energies* (1960), *Light!* (1961), *Man Escapes after Thirty-three Years* (1966), *Personal Monkeys* (1968), *An August on a Block of Ice* (1974), *Life in the Movies* (1971), *Around the World in One Hundred News* (1974), and *A Life with Stan and Bran* (1981). He also published memoirs: *Survivings* (6 vols., 1973–89), *Sonatine* (1987), *The Aunts from Tel Aviv* (1993), and *Self-Denunciations and Statements* (2001).

The history of a being who renounces intransigent convictions, as well as the black and white reality generated by them, in order to open himself "to shades" and to the disquieting plurality of the world. *Survivings* is Cosașu's most important book. It is

considered an autobiographical work of exceptional quality, a narrative that surpasses
the boundaries of self-ironizing pity (for which Cosașu was compared to Hašek and
Kundera), to reach an understanding of "the supreme curse, that of simultaneously
living both comically and tragically, and the salvation inherent in doing so."

FROM "MY ART WAS BORN FROM FEAR"

My art was born from fear.
I was a frightened debutant and I created so
as to conquer this fear. I had no other motive.
I felt from the very first that as long as
I narrate and play in the movies, no one attempts
or wants to bludgeon me. My art was
not premeditated, cerebral, it began spontaneously
from my shaking limbs, on a particular evening,
at the corner of the alley Popa Nan, when four boys from
Țepeș-Vodă wanted to steal my new football.
Then, as I struggled
not to belt them one, caught as in a rugby heap
(rugby seemed to me eternal, more
heroic than the everyday football), I yelled
a Tarzan yell, they freed me
and immediately I began to walk—not run—
like Stan and Bran at the tail of the soldiers' platoon
from the *Foreign Legion*.
I walked ten meters forward,
toward Prau's tailor-shop, and came back in
the same manner. They formed a column behind me
and I traveled the distance home in that
happy step—from which, psychoanalytically, also came the title
of one of my films, twenty years later, in '58,
written while in a bad fix: *Five Men on the Road*.
At the gate, I told them, without a script,

from where I had taken the scene. They had grown quiet. I gave them
the ball until the following day but they didn't want to take it:
"Tomorrow, if you don't tell us another movie, we'll
cobble you." From this burden was born
all of my cinema. The next day, I told them about
Robin Hood with Errol Flynn. They had brought with them
three little girls from Delea Veche. It was
extraordinary. They listened to *Zaendul*[1]
with their eyes to the ground. My basis wasn't gesturing.
The word was all. Rarely did I raise my arms
to show them how Robin Hood jumped from liana
to liana. Epic predominated. From the balconies
of the houses, parents and grandparents watched me.
My own lived on the ground floor, they couldn't
watch me and anyway they dreamed me a pianist. [. . .]

Translated by Carla Baricz

1. "Zaendul" is a Romanian tongue-in-cheek rewriting of "The End," which appears at the
end of British and American films.

Mircea Ivănescu

(b. 1931)

A graduate of the Faculty of Philology at the University of Bucharest, Mircea Ivănescu worked as an editor at a publishing house and at several literary journals. He translated abundantly from Fitzgerald, Faulkner, Capote, Joyce, and Kafka. He was also the translator and author of an anthology of American poetry. He wrote collections of poetry with titles that are intentionally nondescript: *Lyrics* (1968), *Poems* (1970), *Poetry* (1970), *Other Lyrics* (1972), *Other Poems* (1988), *Poems, New and Old* (1989), and *Lyrics Poems Poetry: Other Same Old New* (2003, an anthology by Matei Călinescu). Ivănescu employs the long poem form and depicts, in a voice that combines melancholy ("a wintry melancholy") and self-irony, rich interiors, and ordinary moments in everyday life or the conversations of certain characters. These scenes are, in fact, pretexts for the investigation of nuanced states of being and feeling.

FROM "THE TEXT WRITES ITSELF"

INTERVIEW WITH TITU POPESCU, 1983

We must not forget that the text, as far as I am concerned, writes itself. Starting from the nostalgia of the arrest, of fixating the moment, or—which could amount to the same thing—from a title somebody else suggested, I realize that the text writes itself; and without being dishonest even for a second,

I realize that I speak by placing the words—the same words, disposed in the same way, in the same lines so as to avoid calling them verses ("You still write in long lines," as Pica said to me a while ago)—placing, I say, words, I express certain things that I would not have expected to come from me. Let's understand each other, though. This does not mean that I renege with them, or that I say them in order to create literature. I simply did not know them before. I am aware they are true, as far as I am concerned, I believe in them, with all my being, but I know that they did not correspond, at any moment, to the intention with which, let's say, I had begun a certain text. This means that the moment I wished to fixate or which I evoke through recollection when I write a poem—entitled, for instance, "The Prayer of the Golden Passions" (since I wrote it, this poem)—was hiding within itself these words that now constitute the lines strung under this title. The sin, as I was saying, is that these things hidden within are always the same, so we are back to the issue of scarce resources. But this is a different story. Or, perhaps, the same . . .

How does the poet impart truth? The simplest answer would be to repeat what I tried to say in that initial answer. The fear of untruth, of the literary, of the fact that one or another of the moments that I experience conforms so much to literature, to what I know from books—so the fear that they are lies—sometimes makes me believe that, in writing them, I could give them an appearance which—by not coming from the outside, from what conforms too much to the formula of being—could have a truth of its own. Let me give you an example: a number of years ago, in places that, by deliberate chance, I have revisited over the last few days, in the region of Sinaia, Bușteni, etc. [. . .], one night, very late, I happened to be coming home, to the house where I had taken a room during that vacation. The thing—the trip—took place on Furnica Hill, on the way back from the Par restaurant in Sinaia, toward a street that one could go up either by Bratianu's villa or by climbing some steps. The person I was accompanying—and who, as they say in literature, of course, was at the time the most important person in my life—said to me after we went up a first set of steps (numerous, abrupt, difficult, since there was snow on them): "And from here on we have so much more." It is that moment which I keep trying to express and write, and each time I am under the impression that, if I were to write it endlessly, it would be true. . . .

Translated by Raluca Manea

Nichita Stănescu

(1933–1983)

Graduate of the Faculty of Philology at the University of Bucharest, Stănescu worked as a proofreader and editor for a number of literary reviews. Though fascinated by the library and the act of reading (a fascination that becomes visible in the allusions and quotations present in his texts), the poet was best known as the legendary and principal figure of the bohemian literati. As his own saying goes: "The poet, like the soldier / has no personal life. / His personal life is dust / and ashes." He was the author of many books of exceptional poetry: *The Sense of Love* (1960), *A Vision of the Sentiments* (1964), *The Right to Time* (1965), *Eleven Elegies* (1966), *Vertical Red* (1967), *The Egg and the Sphere* (1967), *Laus Ptolemaei* (1968), *Unwords* (1969), *An Earth Named Romania* (1969), *In the Sweet Classical Style* (1970), *The Greatness of Cold* (1972), *Epica Magna* (1978), *Imperfect Works* (1979), *Crying Bones* (1982), and *Nodes and Signs* (1982). He is also the author of two volumes of essays: *The Book of Rereading* (1972) and *Breaths* (1982).

Possessing a great talent for metaphor and an unusual linguistic ability, Stănescu combined the most divergent of poetic registers (from the slang of the slums to a hermetic and parabolic language) and was a visionary poet who projected psychological states in universal, cosmic, overwhelming landscapes. Through the intermediary of a few metaphorical figures (many of mythological provenance), he expressed "the brutal state of being"—the self-devouring, the hunting, the fear, the disquieting anticipation of death, the human being reduced to "a stain of blood that speaks." He is considered the most important poet of his generation. *(Translated by Carla Baricz)*

FROM "MY SOUL, PSYCHE"

I was traveling with my soul, Psyche, when suddenly, I asked myself: But animals, what do they think about the world? What thinking! They do not think, they have only wishes and appetites. Only verbs pass through their mind, not even verbs. Aspirations toward verb, nervous states, halos, objects in the process of destruction or birth, all, absolutely all, tending toward verb.

As strange as it might seem, the verb has no memory. It is difficult to possess memory when you yourself are in the midst of action. The cessation of actions, their fulfillment or their death, it alone has memory.

To think in nouns is to have a fabulous memory. Who could have a memory more fantastical than the word "tree," which remembers all other trees in the world? And not only the trees of the world, but also all the verbs that they have incited, acting by one means or another, existing.

My soul, Psyche, asked of me: You who run, what do you think of those who run, you who stand still, what do you think of those who stand still?

Only when I stand still do I have opinions about those who run, but when I run, I simply run; I do not even think of those who stand still.

Thus, it is made evident that what I can speak of are verbs rather than nouns.

When verbs overgrow my spirit, when I find myself in their midst and I myself become a verb, I become interested in their tensions, I feel their tensions, I run in their directions, I read upon them as upon the face of a clock with an infinite number of hands, showing an infinite number of hours and minutes.

When my state of mind rests in the ample armchairs of nouns, even then I think of verbs, for verbs are the memory of nouns. A strange memory, I would say, sometimes even a memory of the future; though verbs themselves have no memory, for they themselves are memory.

My soul, Psyche, said to me: It would befit you, who enjoy poetry and proclaim yourself a romantic, crazy after verbs, of a madness similar to that of old Hokusai, crazy after painting, it would befit you to be given the penitence of memory. I would punish your body so as to force it to remember the history of all bodies before itself . . . Fine, I answered, but this is exactly what is happening with my body—it seeks to forget what it remembers so as to have the ability to create (before itself and not after) memories that have not yet taken place.

It doesn't love nouns because its greatest pleasure is to create rather than to judge that which is created. To crave after the sense of creation alone means to refuse yourself, to some degree, the judgment of value; this not because you might not want to enjoy it, but only from a pressing lack of time always absorbed in the movement of verbs.

My soul, Psyche, with whom I was traveling, said to me: The canter of the horse on the field is agreeable, but even more agreeable is the field itself, for on it one may canter! You, Psyche, always hurry me into speech, when I am only just beginning to prepare for the invention of words. You hurry me, when I am only just beginning to prepare for the invention of a word suited for hurry. Psyche! Make yourself into a hawser with an anchor at its end, so that we may stop a single verb and see it with our own two eyes. Come, let us try to check its flight so that its letters may clank together, as the steel brush plates of train carriages at the entrance of the station.

To come with large magnifying glasses, with microscopes, to shade our eyes with our hands, to bring the lunette, to play the music, to bring talking birds, to unroll flying carpets, to align fruits, and to stand together chained by astonishment and gaze at the strange verb travelers! . . .

To stop a verb is perhaps harder than stopping a beam of light. Light itself is movement. But the movement of abstract lights has a different sort of beams, perhaps is the verb form.

Not the abstract world, Psyche, but its movement, this I would like to see, if we can.

My soul, Psyche, is uneasy: What are you doing, it asked me, are you trying to define poetry? You are venturing into such a delicate domain! No, I shouted, I do not want to define poetry, though, sometimes, it stops one verb or another and with its astonished eyes watches beings, also astonished, descending from verb. That which is in movement cannot be anticipated. That which cannot be anticipated is very difficult to define. It can only be surrounded by large unmoving spaces, it can only be delineated.

Psyche! You, my soul, remember that, in antiquity, fire was obtained by rubbing two pieces of wood. I want to see what that is—a verb—even if I will be forced to take two nouns and rub them together until they catch fire. Often, searching for one thing, I find another. Wanting to find out what a verb is, I am afraid that I will instead find out what heat is.

From the antique elements of matter—earth, fire, air, water—only fire had the characteristics of the verb. The earth, water, air, and fire of poetry also have the same characteristics. You, Psyche, you dwell in fire, on you depends the heat or the coldness of poetry, on you and your verbs. You ask me questions, but I cannot ask you anything, for your structure is interrogative, you yourself are a question.

Better make yourself a hawser with an anchor at its crest, Psyche, and come, let's pull a verb to the shore, like a Noah's ark, and let all diverse beings that make up the nuances of heat descend into the intelligible. We communicate through hot or through cold.

Blessed are the hot or cold, for he who is lukewarm, as the legendary text states, *God spits from his tongue.*[1]

Translated by Carla Baricz

THE POET, LIKE THE SOLDIER

The poet, like the soldier,
has no private life.
His private life is dust
and ashes.

With the tongs of his circumvolutions he raises
the feelings of the ant
and brings them nearer, ever nearer to his eye
until they are part of his eye.

He puts his ear to the belly of a starving dog
and smells its half-open mouth
until his nose and the mouth of the dog
are one and the same.

1. The legendary text to which the writer refers is the Book of Revelation in the Bible.

In the terrible heat
he fans himself with the wings of birds
he frightens to make them fly.

Do not believe the poet when he cries.
None of his tears are his.
He has wrung the tears from things.
He cries with the tears of things.

The poet is like time.
Sometimes faster, sometime slower,
sometimes lying, sometimes true.

Refrain from telling a thing to the poet.
Especially refrain from telling something true.
And better yet, refrain from telling something you have felt.

He will tell you straightaway he said it
and he will say it in such a way
that you will also say that certainly
he said it.

But most of all I beseech you,
do not touch the poet with your hands!
No, never touch the poet with your hands!

. . . Only at that moment when your hands
are thin as rays,
and only in this manner could
your hands pass into him.

Otherwise they will not go into him,
and your fingers will remain on him,
and again he will be the one to boast
he has more fingers than you have.
And you will be forced to say that, yes,
in fact he has more fingers . . .

But it is better if you will simply trust me—
it is best if you never
touch the poet with your hands.

. . . And it is not worth laying hands on him . . .
The poet, like the soldier,
has no private life.

Translated by Thomas C. Carlson & Vasile Poenaru

Nora Iuga

(b. 1933)

A graduate of the Faculty of Philology at the University of Bucharest, Iuga worked as a German teacher and editor. She also became well known as a translator from the German. A writer in her own right, she published several volumes of poetry: *The Fault Is Not Mine* (1968), *The Captivity of the Circle* (1970), *Unsent Letters* (1978), *Thoughts on Suffering* (1980), *The Heart Like a Boxer's Fist* (1982), *Sky's Square* (1986), *The Night Typist* (1996), *Insidious Whims* (1998), and *The Mannequins' Hospital* (1998). She also wrote fiction: *Leopold Bloom's Soap* (1993), *The Sexagenarian and the Youth* (2000), *Fasanenstrasse 23: A Summer in Berlin* (2001), and *Let's Steal Watermelons* (2009).

The writer's imagination is marked by an abundance of associations and great mobility, moving swiftly from the everyday to the oneiric, from the dramatic to the ludic and the grotesque, from straightforward confession to baroque staging.

PRISONER OR MASTER OF LANGUAGE?

The writer—prisoner or master of language—here comes a question both inviting and complex; if you attempt to penetrate its essence, you realize that you cannot answer it. At first, the two hypotheses—"prisoner" and "master"—which exclude one another, seem to delineate two distinct spheres, but things are not as clear-cut as they appear to be. The most immediate answer would be the equivalent of a truism: *In his native tongue, the writer is a master, in a foreign tongue, he is a prisoner.* One could refer here to the drama of the writer exiled from his community and his language, made to express himself by means of an uncomfortable, not easily accessible foreign instrument—this would be the case of minority writers or exiled writers who, in order to penetrate the circuit of their adopted literature, must change, along with their language, their sensitivity, and, in many cases, even more dramatically, their identity. To a writer, language is not only an instrument, it determines his inner structure, it situates him in a particular space, it is his own way of thinking and feeling, it is his home, his tradition—language is memory. When you have to express yourself in a foreign language, you experience discomfort, as though your intelligence and your sensitivity were reduced by half. Passing to a new language has the aggressiveness of giving birth, it is the Fall from Eden, from the maternal womb. I tried to write in German, and my intellectual and affective register felt unsatisfying to me, like an act without a closing scene.

Thus, I was starting with the premise that the writer is a master in his language and a prisoner in an adopted language. I met a writer of German origins, from Banat, who told me that what convinced her to move to Germany was the language, which was insufficient here. I understood her. She was not referring to Romanian in particular but to the German spoken in Romania, which, as any minority language, is an ankylosed, aged, inexpressive language. The texts of minority writers, when published in the country where their language is spoken, undergo, with a few exceptions, a process of ablution, of revitalization. This is also what happens with translations done by those who do not live in the natural environment of their language.

But I am wandering away from what I had meant to say. I wonder whether the writer is ever the master of his own language. I try to answer with examples drawn from my own experience. I cannot write whenever I want, but only when I am granted permission; more precisely, when I am ordered to write. For a long time I entertained the thought that, just like any artistic toil, writing is in turn conditioned by a state of being. A special state characterized by a certain eroticism, which reaches orgasm not through senses but through words. At that moment the poet does not speak, he is spoken. The poem writes itself. "Who is he who tells my story by heart?" This state, the idea even, becomes a substitute for language; language dominates everything.

The poet is possessed by words, he is the captive of his own language. Can the poet really be considered a master when rhyme calls for his words beyond his will, when dictation spills on paper a conglomerate from which a surreal world is configured, a world to which he succumbs voluptuously? Can the medium be a master of his trance? Is God a master or a captive of the Universe He created? But is the writer a medium so passive that he does not have any options? Is he just a receptacle open to receiving a foreign message, which he accepts as given? The writer intervenes, selects, he is not always content with that which is dictated to him, he is a type of farmer who weeds the field, separates the wheat from the chaff, deforests new land, tries to force nature to work in his favor. The writer has always been dissatisfied with the scarcity of the words available to him. "Where is the word that speaks the truth?" The history of literature with all its movements, trends, experiments, revolutions is nothing but the writers' constant struggle with the limits of language. Free verse, in its time, automatic writing, the association of seemingly incompatible words, the unusual opening up of new spaces of exploration; oral speech, the democratization of poetry through the acceptance of any form of expression, the rehabilitation of the ugly and the abject, the repudiation of complexes of any kind, the multiplication and diversification of registers—they all make for a more inclusive poetic language, for a larger and more comprehensive communication. But perhaps under this struggle with the limits of language there remains hidden a struggle with the limits of a degree of civilization. Up to a certain point, language is civilization, there are evolved and primitive languages, privileged and disadvantaged languages. The handicap of literatures written in quasi-unknown languages is the very handicap of these countries in the general European ensemble. These two dimensions essential to our national existence mutually condition each other, one triggers the other. The writer has always worked on language like someone who wants to surpass his condition, he is a superior craftsman who has been entrusted with a monstrous and sublime mechanism that can lift him out of anonymity or refuse him a future. Is this an argument in light of which he may conceive of himself as a master?

We are the masters of language only to the extent to which we regard language as an instrument like any other, to the extent to which we diminish it. It has the attributes of an instrument only when it is used consciously and

logically to communicate your own ideas or those of others. The virtuosity
with which you handle this instrument entitles you to consider yourself its
master. I am very familiar with this feeling. I consider myself the master of my
language only when I translate. This seems to be a paradox. But it is precisely
the dependence on another linguistic pattern that, by delineating the degree
to which I can move, offers me a freedom scaled to the possibilities that I master. At that moment the words do not possess me, they obey me. I no longer
have the impression of a miracle, I no longer hear that secret voice speaking in
me at such a speed sometimes that I am unable to record it.

You see then how difficult it is for me to answer the question of whether the
writer is the master or the prisoner of his own language. I believe he is both
at the same time, which increases his greatness by humiliating him, putting
him in his rightful place among the ambitions and ambivalences of the world.

Translated by Raluca Manea

Nicolae Breban

(b. 1934)

Born into the family of a Greek-Catholic priest (a religion banned by the Communist regime in 1948), Breban was expelled from high school as a senior, due to his "unhealthy" origins. For similar reasons, he was excluded from the Faculty of Philosophy at the University of Bucharest; after a few years, he began studying philology, which he would later also abandon. He worked as a laborer and driver. After becoming a prestigious writer, he was elevated to the position of editor in chief of an influential literary weekly journal, a position from which he resigned after Ceaușescu initiated a politics of re-ideologizing literature. He lived as a freelancer, moving, in the 1980s, between Paris and Bucharest. From 1990 onward, he was the director of the literary journal *Contemporanul*.

Although he published poetry (*Parisian Elegies*, 1992) and essays (*Taking Risks in Culture*, 1997; *The Romanian Spirit Facing Dictatorship*, 2000; *Rigorous Literary Memoirs*, 2001; *The Betrayal of Criticism*, 2009), Breban is, first and foremost, a novelist. He is known for *Francisca* (1965), *When the Masters Are Away* (1966), *Sick Animals* (1968), *The Plaster Angel* (1973), *The Annunciation* (1977), *Don Juan* (1981), *The Road to the Wall* (1984), *Still Hunt and Seduction* (1991), the trilogy *Amphitryon* (1994), and the tetralogy *The Day and the Night* (1998–2007). Much like the writers who fascinate him (Dostoyevsky, Mann), Breban writes novels in which he combines psychological investigation (of abysmal, confused, and convulsive psyches in particular) with essayistic and ideological prose. He is particularly interested in the power dynamic found in male-female or master-disciple relations.

Why Do I Write? What Do I Believe In?

[. . .] I write because "ambition drives me," but also because I cannot do otherwise. I could not *stand* myself otherwise, without writing, my life (and life in general) would seem to me insufferable, unworthy of being lived. What is more, my faults, my mistakes—which I repeat with mysterious tenacity (really, how nondidactic experience is!)—the evil, the antipathy that I create around me (with my vanity, no question about it!) the *shadow* that I cast on the ground, etc., I could not accept these things without the bridge, the saving plank of writing conceived as profession. You see, with a certain naïveté, with a certain perseverance, everything can be redeemed—at least in our eyes!—by a single quality. If it is quality we are talking about, if our writing has, therefore, value. And yet!

· In fact, perhaps there is something human in this instinctive prejudice: the whole is redeemed by the part. Obviously, with the condition that at least this part be absolutely necessary (to others), meaning, of value. Let's strive to perfect this unique quality of ours, and in this sense, our life could be grounded, could become meaningful. Honesty in one's profession. Goethe would talk about a *passion* for work, including in it the moral dimension, of course.

I write because since I was young, very young, I have had a terrible liking (a sick one) for reading, for the book, this rather uncanny object that came along late in the evolution of humanity, the papyrus of our times, the rolls (sheets) of paper, bound together, protected by a hardcover cut in a rectangular shape, of a convenient size, practical, almost as big as a pocket (could it be that the first tailors of male coats were thinking about the format of the modern book when they came up with a pocket of the same shape and size?! . . .), an object rather lacking in consistency, since it is empty, hollow, in a material way, it cannot even be used as a banal cardboard box: lifted up by the spine, the book flutters its antennae and moustaches like an unarmed insect uprooted from its soil; or, like a wise plant, it unfolds its petals and resigned leaves. I read an enormous amount indeed, I ruined and tired out my eyes as a young boy—to my parents' alarm—and then, like a passionate reader, charmed by the book,

I entertained the thought, the hope that I would write one myself—one of these *uncanny* objects, a kind of parallelepipedon drawn by a surrealist artist. I wrote throughout high school, like some of my classmates, and some of them surpassed me by far. I would write in a tormented way—false, bookish, insipid—I would start all sorts of stories without finishing any, and I would appear to myself as endowed with a deplorable will. Although I also wrote poetry, my dream was always the novel. As a ten-year-old and thirteen-year-old student, I would linger for minutes and hours on end, like an idiot, fascinated by a faded photo of one of the classics of Romanian literature at the time—wearing a necktie or cravat—as they appeared in Romanian textbooks: Cezar Petrescu, Sandu-Aldea, Brătescu-Voineşti, Liviu Rebreanu, Barbu Delavrancea. I would study, fascinated, the lapels of the pictured outfits, the tie knot, the character's sideburns, the drawing of the hand, or—for entire minutes—the ear. Then, with a sigh, I would myself start writing again. It would be bad, lengthy, flat, futile, disappointing, my dear ones would shrug their shoulders; I seemed intelligent and yet I wrote incoherently, like an idiot; I seemed knowledgeable and yet I would express myself at random, like a cabbage. A long, infinite, a thousand times defeated childhood, puberty, adolescence, post-adolescence. My first good sentence—transparent, meaningful, and vigorous, today's sentence—appeared when I was twenty-eight, as I was writing the last version of *Francisca*. I came to this sentence so late—at last capable of expressing myself, of building the great edifices of paper that I had dreamt about—that I grew old and committed suicide many times, failed as many times; when my first book finally came out I was already defeated, a *sage*. This active, vigorous, vengeful resignation gave me power for the rest of them, for the Work, the envisaged Work, the ten thousand pages. (With *The Road to the Wall* I will reach about five thousand; could it be a sign that I am only halfway in my effort?!)

I write to give form, to mold, to "polish" myself. What I am today, as I really am, is, without a doubt, the fruit of the written *word* that came back to the one who emitted it, in order to alter him—as in a galvanic bath—to cut into him, to mold him, to give him another face. A written sentence has two meanings: one facing outward, *intended*, acting upon its recipient, the unknown and eternal reader; another facing inward, backward, *unintended*, directed toward the one who creates it. Who knows, maybe this is the real reward of creation: the polishing of one's self, the long, patient, voluntary-involuntary edification of one's self that takes a lifetime, a work. [. . .]

I write so that I do not feel alone. My books put me in touch with the world, with humans, with my fellow beings, with those who speak my language, with those interested in my range of problems. My books put me in touch with the young generation, with those who will come after me, with those who will be capable and will confront the problems that are of interest to us today; it is they, our not so distant posterity, who will certify to what extent we are to remain in existence, that is, modern. My books, to the extent to which they represent me, situate me in the sphere of values, turn me into a *link* pulsing like a (rather complex) amoeba that inhales and exhales incessantly the surrounding liquid.

I write, of course, with the fundamental mindset of one who plants a young tree, a row of trees; I write out of need, out of the instinct of survival of the one who engenders and rears children in order to become, as Unamuno would say, immortal in their flesh. Obviously, children are a more concrete, more certain immortality compared to books; books are a riskier, more improbable immortality. With one quality, maybe, with one advantage, if one can speak of advantages here: books, the book preserves individuality, the unity of the being—made of flesh and thought—that created it. Artists, creators, those who sign their works, suffer probably more than others from the vanity of the being they want to preserve, to put forth in their work at any cost—like a mirror reflecting neither world nor century, but their own silhouette, to the last nerve, to the last, barely distinguishable nuance of thought.

I also write . . . so that I do not get bored. Life is long, and we would degrade rapidly if we did not work. I was talking before about work or passion, and the only work that I care about passionately is the writing of my books, the *construction* of novels. I prefer it to alcohol, to fishing or hunting, to traveling, even to chatting, sometimes even to friendship or love. If I were not able to write, if I were prohibited to write (in my case, it's the most efficient form of torture!), I would be bored by that intensity one calls despair. (When I say writing, I am always referring to the publication of my pages, my books; there is no efficient, professional, valuable form of writing outside the book or the press; there is no true writer that lives apart from his readers: he needs them constantly in order to give and to receive, to shape and to let himself be shaped and they need him for the same reasons. [. . .] There are no values outside the social sphere, there is no creation outside individuality or self-awareness as such.)

I write out of ambition, it is true, but these ambitions are so big that they become sacrifices, almost involuntary ones. Such is the individual: he can't work for himself alone; a strong survival instinct creates the world and serves it.

Translated by Raluca Manea

Matei Călinescu

(1934–2009)

Graduate of the Faculty of Philology of the University of Bucharest, Matei Călinescu worked as a proofreader and editor, simultaneously teaching literature at the university from which he had graduated. He was a current events critic (he played an important role in the cultural thaw of the 1960s) as well as a literary historian. He was also the author of volumes of poetry—*Sign* (1968), *Verses* (1970), *Water Shadows* (1972)—and gained literary fame with the novel *The Life and Opinions of Zacharias Lichter* (1969), which features a memorable protagonist, a marginalized man who combines buffoonery with prophetic wisdom. In 1973, Călinescu left Romania on a Fulbright Scholarship and settled in the United States, where in 1979 he became a full professor at Indiana University. He published a number of books of literary theory and literary criticism. He returned to Romanian literature after 1990 (his works having been banned by the Communist regime prior to 1989), both through translations of his English works and through new books, written directly in Romanian. He published a number of collections of essays: *About Ioan P. Culianu and Mircea Eliade* (2002), *Mateiu I. Caragiale: Re-readings* (2002), and *Eugène Ionesco: Identity and Existential Themes* (2006). He also wrote a number of autobiographical works: *Memories in Dialogue* (1994, in collaboration with Ion Vianu), *Portrait of M* (2003), and *A Sort of Journal* (2005). In these writings, the scrupulous reconstitution of the past (never resorting to mere documentation) is combined with the expression of a sensitive and cultivated thinking tinged with melancholy. *Portrait of M* is a book of mourning, written after the death of the writer's autistic son.

FROM *WRITING AND READING OR VICE VERSA*

It was only at the onset of adolescence, at the beginning of the 1950s, that I began to want to write: the incitement derived from a wish for self-expression appropriate to that age. At that time, I inaugurated a kind of journal—the type I had not kept as a pupil in primary school, when children are encouraged to have a journal to which to address themselves in need, as to a dear friend—"dear journal, today I met with . . ." It was a journal without dates, comprised mostly of vague aphorisms and coded references, which, after a time, would become unintelligible even to me. There was something else as well: in the collective psychosis of suspicion, generated by the repressive Stalinist regime, to keep an intimate journal was—as my elder friend Paul Georgescu would teasingly joke—"a form of denunciation." How many had not been arrested because their names had figured in the journal of some "enemy of the people," confiscated by the secret police? The abstractions and codes of those notebooks were, beyond doubt, also a reflex of fear. Though the truth is that I did not know how to write because, though I had been reading for a long time, I did not know how to read properly. I did not realize that the writings that fascinated me also tacitly "fictionalized" me, as a reader. In turn, I could not fictionalize my reader except as an alter-ego, which made communication in and of itself useless. I let myself be hypnotized by what I read, without considering that hypnotic reading is the most redoubtable hidden enemy of writing. The political atmosphere indirectly encouraged reading as a form of evasion from a lugubrious, threatening, and opaque quotidian.

At long last, I began to read better, obligated also by the fact that in the meantime I had been asked for—by the magazine for which I worked as a young proofreader—reviews of the books that did not interest the other collaborators; obligated furthermore by having been named an assistant professor in the Department of Comparative Literature at the University of Bucharest, in 1963, at a moment that announced a more general ideological "thaw." As a reader, I came, by roundabout ways, to intuit the unwritten laws of writing and to understand that, in order to capture even only a shadow of truth, a literary text must not necessarily respect such laws but neither ignore them. I finally understood that the art of writing and the art of reading are twins. To read well is to read as a writer, and to write well is to write as a good reader— as a reader that is capable, if I may say so, of reading . . . the reading that succeeds in reaching—how? through what mysterious interior technique?—that state of grace I would call *inspired attention.*

Good readers tend to become nothing more and nothing less than virtual authors of the text they are perusing. They feel free, in their imagination, to rewrite this text in a different manner when they see within it idle possibilities, open but unexplored precincts. Perhaps not without a sense of guilt (also virtual) of having "violated," through a burrowing reading, the text in question, these readers-writers become true members of the so-called "republic of letters." I would illustrate these affirmations by means of a quote from one of Henry James's letters, which imprinted itself on my mind as soon as I read it, many years ago, while I was working on my book *Re-reading* (1993) in the United States. *The Master* had been sent—for the purpose of collegial examination—an early, fragmented version of the novel *Eleanor,* which was in the course of preparation by his friend, Mrs. Humphrey Ward (1851–1920), a successful writer in her time. Henry James writes to her, on July 26, 1899, that while reading her manuscript he had ceded "to my irresistible need of wondering how, given a subject, one could best work one's self into the presence of it. And, lo and behold, the subject isn't [. . .] 'given' at all—I have doubtless simply, with violence and mutilation, *stolen* it. It is of the nature of that violence that I'm a wretched person to *read* a novel—I begin so quickly and concomitantly, *for myself,* to write it rather—even before I know clearly what it's about. The novel I can *only* read, I can't read at all!" In other words, James could not read a novel that was only readable (meaning banal, predictable, mediocre), a novel that did not feed his hunger to "steal" and mentally rewrite it. A text that is only "readable" becomes, for the serious reader, unreadable! Evidently, you do not have to be Henry James in order to read (as part of your "trade," if not as a novelist . . . then at least as a literary critic) in a similar manner.

To the eternal question: "Why do you write?" I would answer simply: because I have fallen in love with reading and because, with the passing of time, I have learned to read. Besides literary criticism—in its university variant, begun in Romanian and continued in English, in the United States, where I have been living since 1973—my reader-writer interests (or vice versa) have inclined, especially in the last two decades, after the collapse of communism in my home country, toward memoir. And my remembrances articulate themselves—have always articulated themselves—in Romanian. The experience of exile has made me realize that Ithaca is for me a language—a small, rocky, obscure island in the vast linguistic geography of the world. Even though I read books primarily in English or often in French, I have rediscovered the lost language, the Romanian language—a secret language for those in the midst of whom I now live—quite different from the English in which I have written my critical academic studies of the last decades, and in which I have always felt I could never become a writer (even though every time I would read Joseph Conrad and even more so Vladimir Nabokov, I felt compelled to try).

The way home toward the Romanian language, after so many years of exile, is not without its paradoxical elements. Many Romanian writers of modernist orientation, to whom I have always felt close, have suffered because of the limits imposed by the use of a language of small circulation and, implicitly, because of the rapport to a culture as recent as it is marginal when compared to the great European occidental cultures. At the time when he was still a Romanian writer, the young Eugen Ionescu declared in the controversial *No* (1934): "I am immeasurably discomfited that I am condemned to remain a poor relative of European intellectualism; the fact that we are only three hundred bodies who beat ourselves over the head with ideas, ink, and paper, and moreover do so poorly, and that, not having readers, we read each other, of this constitutes one of my chagrins, one of my permanent *malaises*." However, isn't the cultural situation of today's Romania, after half a century of communist barrenness, even worse than it was in 1934? Strangely enough, I would have to say that the Romanian literary life of 2007, at least its atmosphere, does not radically differ from that of 1934; quite on the contrary, in certain respects (I am thinking of fundamental ideological conflicts), the similarities are striking, producing an uneasy feeling of déjà vu. But perhaps even more strangely, the linguistic Ithaca from which I have written several books, and from which I write even these lines, has no tie, or perhaps only a superficial tie, to what is understood by the notion of "literary life." The act of writing in Romanian, from far away, from very far away, from another world if not from the other world (is it still necessary to say that the world in which I live was for a very long time, for Romanians living in Romania, the other

world?), at the same time seems to me both extraordinary and perfectly normal. In the meantime, I have tried to return to Romania for good, but after a
few months I realized that I am more of a stranger there than I am here. My
Ithaca remains an island in a linguistic and symbolic geography, to which I
return often and which I always leave.

Ulysses, say some legends, after the unforgettable *nostos* of the *Odyssey*,
might not have remained in Ithaca.

Translated by Carla Baricz

Florin Mugur

(1934–1991)

Graduate of the Faculty of Philology at the University of Bucharest, Florin Mugur worked as a primary-school teacher and then as an editor for a publishing house, playing a crucial role in promoting promising writers during a time of censorship and intimidation. He was an astute literary critic (some of his works from this period appear in his *Sketches about Happiness,* 1987), and his books of literary interviews became standard models for interviewers. He wrote two volumes of short stories—*Evenings from the North Sector* (1964) and *Almost November* (1972)—and a novel, *Antim's Last Summer* (1979), though his literary reputation rests mainly on his volumes of poetry: *The Song of Philipp Müller* (1953), *The House with Silver Windows* (1959), *Myths* (1967), *Intermediary Destinies* (1968), *The Book of Kings* (1970), *The Book of the Prince* (1973), *The Book of Names* (1975), *The Pale Rock* (1977), *The Dance with the Book* (1981), *Delayed Entertainment* (1985), and *The Nature of Things* (1988).

Using a number of reoccurring figures, Mugur wrote in a voice that oscillates between elegy and irony (often bitter), describing melancholy, anxiety, (dis)illusion, and "the slow farce of my life." His moving volume of *Letters from the End of Days* was edited posthumously and contains missives sent to fellow writers and friends in exile, whose absence is felt dramatically and mournfully.

Stanzas

You carry in your arms the book, prince,
as you would a girl. The hard body
full with a tender earth
glistens. The blond water
streaming long from her hair.

What could you save from the profuse
inundation of desire?
The immense mouth of the verbs
moans, stammers, is full
of light and snails.

And from whence the book, prince?
Beneath the sole quake
shelves of yellow clay, shelves
of empty rocks that sing
idle shelves of books.

Quick waters—also in Bibles, kings
sleep with their hands to their mouths
their knees sleep on the slippery
rocks. And fall leaves
from one age into another age.

We are the sleepwalking princes—
We walk blindly on roofs
high, very high, on roofs.
Ancient regal libraries
tremble beneath the pure step.

The Dance with the Book

How to be short and ludicrous
and with a beard like a bride's veil
and with blue eyes

and how to be old
and with your clothes wet with tears
and how to nevertheless trip happily?

On my bed
the old prince dances drunkenly
with the book in his arms.

The shirt on his shoulders streams wet
his cheerful buttons peep
he trips full of sparks and barbs.

And what is written in the book of the old man? My own
tired destiny. Dances slowly. Toward evening
small, pellucid eggs pour sweet from his hair.

What bleating, what stuttering of petals!
Slips soft on a teardrop. Look, he holds
onto the book, which trembles lazily in his arms.

And I am no longer afraid and I am no longer afraid.
How tender it is! My sorrowful and worn out head
Dares to laugh.

THAT WHICH REMAINS

That which remains agonizing after all the leave-takings
The pride of being whole, at last
When you are almost nothing.

The poet—the nodes of an old oak
In which break the silver knives
of haste

the poet—nothing more can be glimpsed
of you
beside the traces left by the others

one of them
(but you must draw quite close, otherwise you will see nothing)
has the shape of an eagle's wing.

a trace
perhaps a wound
the work of a prolonged pain.

And only the irony
with its nostrils mild and thin like Bible paper
blowing in your palm

and only the noble, only the majestic aortic arch
curving in the darkness of the body
like a superb bishop's staff.

Translated by Carla Baricz

Paul Goma

(b. 1935)

Born in Basarabia, a Romanian province that in 1940 was forcefully annexed by the USSR, Paul Goma has always lived the life of a nomad. In 1944 his parents moved to Romania as refugees, only to find that the authorities of the country had come under Soviet influence and would persecute them and their son, who would be repeatedly expelled from public school. In 1954, as a young man, Goma enrolled at the Institute of Literature and Literary Criticism in Bucharest. Two years later, in 1956, he was arrested and condemned to two years in prison and five years of house arrest for having written a seminar paper that expressed his sympathy toward the Hungarian revolutionary movement against the Communist government. After being set free, Goma worked odd jobs (as photographer, trumpeter, day laborer) and published a collection of short stories, *The Room Next Door* (1968). His novel *Ostinato*, rejected by Romanian publishing houses, was published in 1971 in French and German and led the foreign press to speak of Goma as a Romanian Solzhenitsyn. In 1977 Goma signed Charter 77, a human-rights petition circulated by Czech intellectuals. Harangued by the secret police and arrested once again, Goma went into exile with his family in December of that year and took up residence in Paris. He was only published in his home country after the fall of the dictatorship, at which point his novels began appearing: *The Sufferings after Pitești* (1990), *Ostinato* (1991), *Bonifacia* (1991), *Our Daily Door* (1992), *In the Circle* (1995), *The Reverse Guard* (1997), *Altina* (1998), and *Heart Attack* (2008). Goma also went on to publish memoirs: *My Childhood at the Gate of Unrest* (1990), *The Colors of the Rainbow '77* (1990),

Gherla (1990), *The Art of Taking Refuge* (1991), *The Dog's Soldier* (1991), *Astra* (1992), *Letters*

Half Open: Alone Against Them (1995), *Journal I–IV* (1997–99), *Other Journals* (1998),

and *Intimate Novel* (1999). He has also published two collections of articles: *Romanian*

Amnesia (1992) and *The Red Week* (2003).

Regardless of genre, Goma's writings follow the imperative of memory, which is

never without a political dimension (for, as the author himself states, "we Romanians

are like that: not only do we have little history to go on, but even the little that we have

we do not know") as well as the imperative that literature can be a means of fighting a

dictatorship and any other abuses, the word being "sharper than any sword." (*Trans-*

lated by Carla Baricz)

FROM "THE COLORS OF THE RAINBOW"

BUCHAREST, JANUARY 1977

To Pavel Kohout and his Comrades,[1]

I declare myself to be in solidarity with your action. Your situation is mine; the situation of Czechoslovakia is—with nonessential differences—also the situation of Romania. We live, we survive, in the same Concentration Camp, in the same Biafra (capital: Moscow).[2] You, the Czechs and Slovaks, had your '68; the Poles their '56, their '71, and their . . . always; the East Germans had their Berlin and their Biermann. We, the Romanians, do not have comparable points of reference. Though suffering is not always directly proportional to the intensity of the shouts of those who revolt. You (like the Poles, the East Germans, the Hungarians, and the Bulgarians), you are under Russian occupation; we, the Romanians, we find ourselves under Romanian occupation—at the end of the day more painful, more efficient than a foreign occu-

1. Pavel Kohout was a Czech writer, exponent of the 1968 "Prague Spring," and founding member of Charter 77.

2. A reference to the Biafra genocide of 1968, when Nigerian-occupied Biafra became a charnel house of extermination.

pation. We live, all of us, under the same heel (and the heels no longer require qualifying remarks). The same lack of basic rights, the same mockery of the human being, the same imprudence of the lie—everywhere. Everywhere: poverty, economic chaos, demagogy, uncertainty, terror.

Cudgel-Constraining Gag-Corruption—behold (in the Romanian language) the three Cs with which the two Cs have pushed our fellow citizens onto the stairway of history, tens and hundreds of years ago.

Yet behold, it is proven (and it will continue to be proven) that it is possible to fight against the systematic degradations to which man is subjected, here, in this "socialist"-Stalinism.

Word-Writing, Implement-Wary Conscience (the coincidence of another three Cs in Romanian) has upset the digestion of those who, in our name and "for our own good" have stepped all over us, have forced us to build pyramids, have jailed us, have gagged us (a gag they have never removed, removed only so as to permit us to shout praises of gratitude), have killed us. Their digestion was upset, and I am convinced that it was not only their digestion: interrupted forever. And not because of our goal; our goal is just—so many other just causes were defeated—but because our weapon is the Word, the Word that is sharper than the sword. A Russian sword in your case, a Romanian sword (indigenous, Dacian-Romanian—in the end, the sword of our brothers) in our case, in Romania, a sword above our heads, Romanian heads—the sword will be forced back into its sheath.

Perhaps for the small, insignificant reason that the ideology that on one hand pretends to serve man but on the other hand cuts off his head has no tie either with ideas or with man.

I am on your side, the side of the Czechs, the Slovaks, the Hungarians, the Poles, the Germans.

Many, very many Romanian intellectuals are with you, fondly with you, even if they do not add their signature to mine.

Paul Goma

Translated by Carla Baricz

George Bălăiță

(b. 1935)

Graduate of the Faculty of Philology at the University of Bucharest, George Bălăiță worked a number of jobs (draftsman, substitute teacher) before becoming editor of a literary review. He began by publishing short stories—*The Trip* (1964), *Speaking about Ionescu* (1966), *Happenings from the Night of the Milk Sun* (1968)—before moving on to the novels that would make him a consecrated writer: *The World in Two Days* (1975) and *The Disobedient Apprentice* (1977). He also published volumes of essays: *The Nights of a Provincial Man* (1983), *Gulliver in Nobody's Country* (1994), and *Dog on the Leash* (2004).

Bălăiță is a refined prose writer, both linguistically and thematically; his works open the domestic and quotidian space to esoteric and mythic universes.

from "The Raft on the Crest of the Wave"

I do not like to speak about myself; however, in this impossible profession, I have no choice. If I sometimes let myself go, I do so being tempted by the actor in me. I would have strutted the stage with great pleasure had I not been emotive and had the One Above bequeathed me with more hypocrisy and envy. It was not to be! For a long time I was terribly afraid of my loneliness. This fear never left me, but with the passing of time I have learned to cooperate more or less with this capricious companion. I write easily and serenely. This is not to be understood quite as *easily* and *serenely*. I have just reread some of my writings (and not those that were published, mostly "essays"; Camil Petrescu says, around 1923 or '32, something like this: from the Tisza to the Nister, everything's only an essay. . . .[1] This short phrase, with a hidden predicate, like an elite sniper tracking his prey, says more about the autochthonous authors than a doctoral thesis, a bibliography, quotes, academies. And when you think that there are idiots who, today, ignore or make fun of C. P. Camelie, who they say has no opus. Forgetting that *Procrustes' Bed* is a novel of breadth and scope, original and problematic; the French version produced commotion and amazement, oh, had we only translated it in time. "The best Danton," said not too long ago the illustrious men of theater from other sunlit nations.[2] Where was it played? Mostly nowhere. What is there to be done? I don't know. Only if the 1848 call of Heliade Rădulescu still means something: *write boys, only write.*[3] Everyone complains here that we aren't known in the world, that we don't have good translations, translators, institutions, and so on. A tone of *revolt and of mourning*! I haven't, however, heard someone doubt whether perhaps something important is missing; whether our missionary nature is hollow. There are not too many things to say, the temptation of universalism is absent, the horizon ends in the neighbor's garden. In truth, we might not be such enemies to the rest of the world—the anti-Romanian plotters and the rest of the mafias—come, let's do a vivisection. When someone does do it—rarely, very rarely—he finds himself on the blacklist of the nation. Forget it, even that [good] one spits forth his oaths and disdains, goes the way of swearing and coercing I don't know how, and however right he might be, it isn't fitting. Why? Because he does it from vanity and hatred, rather than from love and understanding. What is to be done? I don't know); so I have just reread pages written in the last *polish*, not to say the first post-December five-year

---

1. "From the Tisza to the Nister"—famous line from Mihai Eminescu's patriotic poem "Lament"; the Tisza and the Nister marked at the time of the poem's composition (1877) the frontiers of Romania.

2. Danton—protagonist in Camil Petrescu's play and leading figure of the French Revolution.

3. Ion Heliade Rădulescu (1802–72)—Romanian writer who played an important role in the creation of the modern Romanian idiom.

period.[4] Where is the silence, where the serenity? The hand that writes is a claw, and the mind is haunted by ghosts. As in other, older texts in which the mockery, the coldness, the indifference, the cynicism at the other end mime a state of grace. You can only write *well* when you are undisturbed. You must succeed in this no matter how hard it might be for you to do so, no matter how you live. You don't necessarily have to be deathly ill to write *The Death of Ivan Ilyich*. On the contrary. If Hans Castorp had not been cured in the sanatorium where he had come for a few days and remained for lengthy years, Thomas Mann would never have written *The Magic Mountain*. As for the mammoth parenthesis from before, I made it so because I like to float, to "make the raft on the crest of the wave." Perhaps some teacher mad about literature will give it on a pop quiz sometime: *Analyze from the point of view of. . . .*

Translated by Carla Baricz

4. December 22, 1989, marked the fall of the Communist dictatorship of Nicolae Ceaușescu in Romania. The period that followed was termed "post-Decembrist."

Marin Sorescu

(1936–1996)

Born in a family of peasants, in a village to which he would be attached for the rest of his life, Marin Sorescu graduated from the Faculty of Philology at the University in Iaşi. He did editorial work for a number of cultural publications. In 1995 he was elected Romania's minister of culture. He wrote a number of articles on cultural themes, which were collected in the volumes *The Theory of Spheres of Influence* (1969), *Insomnias* (1971), *The State of Destiny* (1976), and *Easy with the Piano on the Stairs* (1985). *Treaty on Inspiration* (1985) contains interviews with foreign writers. However, Sorescu is best remembered as a poet, having composed a large, diverse, and refined body of work: *Alone Among Poets* (1964), *Poems* (1965), *The Death of the Clock* (1965), *The Youth of Don Quixote* (1968), *Tourists* (1970), *A Wing and a Foot (or How I Almost Flew)* (1968), *Souls Good for Everything* (1972), *At Lilieci* (6 vols., 1973–96), *Descîntoteca* (1976), *Living Water, Dead Water* (1987), *The Equator and Poles* (1989), *Poems Chosen by Censorship* (1991), *The Crossing* (1996), and *The Plank* (1997). Sorescu was also a playwright, publishing *Ioana* (1968), *The Chapel* (1970), *The Thirst of the Mountain of Salt* (1974), *Matca* (1976), *Theater* (1980), and *The Cousin of Shakespeare and Other Plays* (1992). He also wrote the novels *Three Front Teeth* (1977) and *The Vision of Vision* (1982).

With an unusual imagination and a capacity for intricate creative associations, Sorescu resorted to a comic approach (parody, quid pro quo, sarcasm, etc.) in order to treat grave themes: death, captivity, despotism in history, illness, the anguish of temporality, the drama of communication, and others. His writing creates a sense of the uncanny through the modification of the register used to convey the everyday. What is quotidian becomes fantastic, the oneiric is transposed onto the domestic, life is subjected to a rigid mechanics, while the dead (in conformity with Romanian folklore) partake in the vivacious habits of the living. (*Translated by Carla Baricz*)

How to Be a Fakir

No one says you have to write, no one says you have to read. My own writing is simply an energy discharge, a shortcut from mind to heart. I electrify myself continuously, in a state of fakir-like bliss. The nails penetrate my flesh, they hurt me. I'm just an apprentice-fakir, so the double edge of joy and pain becomes visible in me. But it's joy that I hope to transmit.

I've written poetry for a long time, and I still don't know where it comes from. For me it's the highest thing there is, an almost scientific approach to knowledge, an apparatus of unpredictable laws. Intuition is behind it. It's more potent than any mathematical calculation. It sets the most profound and powerful human forces loose. Don't underestimate it.

A Romanian poet from the last century called one of his poetry collections *When I Have Nothing Else to Do*. I've nothing else to do myself most of the time, so I've dedicated myself to the task of cracking the mystery—The Mystery Cracker. Everybody knows the modern mystery *is* locked away in a safe, of course, at the extremity of the world, inside an iceberg. Forever.

So my irony must be sweet-tempered. Almost a smile. First, no one should worry about liberating the mystery; it won't vanish into thin air. Second, poetry should have a crystalline shape—no wrapping paper, no baroque ornament. And though poetry sometimes appears to lose its form, it never abandons ritual—myth is its natural environment, no matter what kind. It could be ancient myth, it could be what we're witnessing today: the slow taking shape of modern myth.

A unique gesture by the poet becomes whole and finds its echo in the unique gesture of a reader. Tongue-tied Homer wouldn't have brought a single hexameter to fruition without an audience of geniuses around him, listening, mouths wide open. We need to find those prodigies of the fertile, illiterate times again, the ones who could *read with their ears*.

How are we going to enjoy *The Iliad* or *The Odyssey* today without some of that old-time emulation and complicity between reader and poet? And shouldn't the intimacy of writing pleasurably entwine with the intimacy of reading, whether the process involves reading aloud or not?

The gods will have to give us a hand here. A new period for the human race is gradually becoming distinct (the modern age), and we've no time to waste. Let's record it swiftly, using black magic spells—in up-to-date versions—and some of those forgotten songs you still can't forget. Material from the past will take on new shapes, verified by suggestion, sculpted by memory. And the poet, bowed under the weight of a tradition he commands, will continue to rearrange the world. Endlessly.

HOUSE UNDER SURVEILLANCE

They've come to take my manuscripts away
with a crane as tall as a tree.
I open the doors of the pages, set free
my poems. They soar into the sky.

Lead pellets fired through telescopes
wound the rhythms of those beating wings.
My stanzas fall. With twisted grins
the hunters fire again. The words are killed.

Greasy palm upon his gun butt,
the guard is watching you, my heart.
You could be silenced with a single shot

and this house they've set on fire
is the dream to which you cling.
Become a poem only if you must.

Translated by John Hartley Williams & Hilde Ottschofski

Dumitru Țepeneag

(b. 1937)

Graduate of the Pedagogic Institute, Dumitru Țepeneag worked, for short periods of time, as a professor of Romanian and as an editor of newspapers and magazines. He promoted, along with Leonid Dimov, an experimental literary movement named Aesthetic Oneiricism, which he theorized and illustrated in the volumes of short stories *Exercises* (1966), *Cold* (1967), and *Waiting* (1972). Finding himself in France at the onset of the 1970s, he criticized the abusive communist system in Romania; in reply, Ceaușescu abrogated his Romanian citizenship, forcing Țepeneag to remain in Paris, where he lived as an exile and gave up literature for a time. Țepeneag eventually began writing in French and published two novels: *Le Mot Sablier* (1985) and *Roman de Gare* (1986). A few days after the fall of the dictatorship, Țepeneag returned to Romania in the company of humanitarian relief groups and very quickly reentered the literary world. He subsequently published a number of articles, which were collected partially in the volumes *The Return of the Son to the Breast of the Stray Mother* (1993) and *The War of Literature Is Not Yet Over* (2000). He is perhaps best known for his trilogy: *Hotel Europa* (1996), *Pont des Arts* (1999), and *Maramureș* (2001). A highly skilled and subtle writer, Țepeneag depicts post-1990 Romania as a "living wound, permanent," a world populated with nomadic characters that peregrinate around Europe and United States. His dynamic, picaresque narration (from which criminal intrigues are never missing) finds its double in the tragic theme of exile from a cursed country.

PRAISE OF THE ANONYMOUS

Reading—the unpunished vice, someone once said. This encouraged vice—even this institutionalized vice, I would add—for which a professional, social category has been created: the writers, meaning men who have the talent necessary for the creation of the object of reading: the book. To have talent, I think, means to have the courage of pride and desperation, though also a little exhibitionism. The pride of thinking yourself a creator, Author; the desperation, because you know that no creation can be absolute, remaining, in fact, an apology, an exhibitionism, because you display the pride and desperation that accompany it.

The only major social justification of a writer is the establishment of a dialogue with the reader. It does not matter of what nature is this dialogue. He who writes knows how to give the impression that he has something to communicate, and he who reads lets it be understood that he needs this message. *Hypocrite lecteur!* . . .

However, if this is so, reading is no longer a vice, but a necessity, a means against loneliness, a dialogue from a distance. Even if this dialogue is not possible in an absolute manner, even if between author and reader the opus—cunning, fraudulent, pretentious (as an autonomic universe)—is imposed.

The reader has before him only a homunculus, an artificial being. And thus begins the vice or, if you like, the sainthood. If things have progressed this far (I won't go on about the other vices of modern society), there isn't anything else left to do, in any case. Moreover, this is the only solution. Since the reader, living within this illusion created by means of reading, is free, consoled by fiction, happy. Through reading, he penetrates into a superposed realm where the sentiment of death, which beleaguers him here, in the quotidian world, disappears. Reading is an annulment of death, of fear. Through reading one becomes Don Quixote immortal. Don Quixote was an ardent reader, a vicious one, actually a saint. Those around him thought him mad, and so he put on that rusted armor, he put on the helmet to defy them. And from reader he became character: he lost his anonymity and liberty, but he proved his immortality.

Therein lies the superiority of the reader: in his permanent virtuality. Cervantes was mortal, like any other creator, since as the Author, he was condemned to remain on the outside, on the cover of the book like God at the gates of Creation, punished for his mad pride. Any creator is a suicide—a simple name, fleshless and bloodless. A man who has emptied himself has become a Job, having desired to establish this dialogue that would socially justify him. His world and his character are now his, the reader's: his are the ideas, these ghosts more powerful than everyday reality. The Author disappears—he is left only with the name—while the character resists time, but is deprived of liberty, a slave to a God who has died. Only the reader is free and at the same time immortal, only he, the anonymous, poor, happy reader, who can venture anytime in the book's world of the beyond, precisely because he has no world of his own. He is not an individual, he is a category, an immutable term. He does not suffer from the individuation to which the writer has condemned himself through pride.

For the writer, reading might nevertheless be a means of escaping from the trap of his own creation, from the loneliness in which he finds himself. I read not as much out of curiosity as from a certain discipline of humility, so as to attempt in this manner to arrive—in spite of the opus, so often deceptive and always parricidal—at my being left on the outside, on the cover. It is an attempt of solidarity with my being, just as hypocritical and desperate as myself, just as indentured, just as mortal; a meeting beyond the heavy and imperfect bodies of books, in a pure space, where only their souls abide.

But oh! I know that it is useless, for I remain bound to my obsessions, and I am not a true reader, an instantiation of purity, one of the happy poor who can slip from one world into another smiling.

Translated by Carla Baricz

Cezar Baltag

(1939–1997)

After graduating from the Faculty of Philology at the University of Bucharest, Baltag worked as an editor at a number of important Romanian literary journals. He was the author of several volumes of poetry: *The Golden Commune* (1960), *Planetary Dream* (1964), *Reflections* (1965), *Rest in Scream* (1969), *Blind Chess* (1971), *The Madonna in the Mulberry Tree* (1973), *Unicorn in a Mirror* (1975), *Eurydice and the Shadow* (1988), *The Calling of the Name* (1995), and *The Eyes of Silence* (1996). Some of his essays and literary publications in the press were collected in the volumes *Essays* (1992) and *The Paradox of Signs* (1996). He was also a translator; among other works, he translated a number of Mircea Eliade's books on the history of religion.

Holding the belief that "the experience of poetry is somewhat similar to the religious experience," Baltag addressed themes such as fate, death, and the soul. He did so in a lyrical and refined poetry that ranges from lucid and ludic meditation to the tragic nature of the last volumes. The poet valorizes motifs from Greek literature (Orpheus, Platonic myth) as well as Romanian mythology (youth without old age and old age without death).

from "Existence Starts to Gain Density"

[. . .] *Since we are talking about discontent, how do you live when you can't write?*

Let me tell you what can save me from such a crisis. The terrible feeling that nothing is of consequence any longer, the feeling that I have done nothing in this world. At the same moment comes a terrible fever of chaotic readings, readings outside the scope of poetry, from various bizarre disciplines. I read books on medicine, the philosophy of science, magic. The only thing that can save you is a feeling of profound humility in relation to what you are as an author and implicitly as an individual—because you can only conceive of your life in light of what you write.

How do these periods end? With a moment of inspiration?

I am not familiar with states of bursting inspiration. The feeling is that of experiencing something larger than life. I have the impression that existence starts to gain density. The same impression you have, for instance, when you find yourself in a supersonic aircraft and suddenly the air acquires consistency, turns solid. You start to swim in existence. You no longer have a feeling of void, of falling, of uselessness, but, on the contrary, you become reintegrated in the natural order of the world. I see inspiration as a state of cold paroxysm, of extreme lucidity. Things acquire a more real and profound appearance, while ideas gain in perspective: it resembles the passage into a world with a dimension in death.

When you begin to write a poem, do you know what the end product will look like, do you know exactly what you would like to say?

I do. Naturally, surprises arise almost always in the process of elaborating the poem. If these surprises partake of the original impulse that hurled me into writing, I accept them. When, however, these poetic surprises do not coincide with the direction of my spiritual state, even though the metaphors being engendered are excellent, they do not satisfy me. They appear to me as foreign to that undefeatable premonition that compels me to write this poem and not another, sprung from the mere zigzagging of accidental inspiration. I will never be a surrealist poet, I admit it with a sense of guilt. [. . .]

Translated by Raluca Manea

Emil Brumaru

(b. 1939)

A graduate of the Medical School in Iaşi, Brumaru worked as a doctor in a countryside dispensary for almost a decade. Later he worked as an editor. He was the author of several collections of poetry: *Lyrics* (1970), *Arthur, the Detective* (1970), *Julien the Hospitable* (1974), *Naïve Lyrics* (1976), *Farewell, Robinson Crusoe* (1978), *The Cabinet in Love* (1980), *The Ruin of a Samovar* (1983), *Out of a Carrot Hollow* (1998), *The Butterflies in the Short-cake* (2003), and *We Get Engaged with a Grass Ring* (2008). In *The Coffee Beggar* (2004), he collected some of the letters he sent to Lucian Raicu (1934–2006), an important literary critic who went into exile in France in 1986. Using a lyrical style, Brumaru writes predominantly about the domestic universe and anthropomorphized nature (lilies, pumpkins, butterflies, stags, etc.), valorizing such themes as sexuality, eroticism, and play.

FROM LETTER TO LUCIAN RAICU

Dear Mr. Lucian Raicu,

I open the *Reasece* and read: "The crisis of words must not, in any way, legitimize the inertia of our spirit in relation to them, *the incapacity or the laziness to awaken them from the sleep of banality.*"[1] And further on: ". . . the tension of the uprooting of words from the anonymity of everyday speech . . ." And more: "we talk and write too much . . ." And again, happy, happy, happy because of the precision of the spindly flame that dances as if on top of treasures: "Poetry, anyway, ought to express *the state of emergency, the state of necessity* of language." Then, as a finely cut stone: "A lack of civility is always preferable to banality." I remember it even now. This is about the "cleansing" of the words. About the failed attempt, in the 1970s, to "write" an eventual, final poem in which to use *all* the words, set next to one another, without grammatical articulations, a kind of testament. I had found the title: *Prayer*. But just that. It seems extremely simple to take words and place them like this: *closet lily angel butterfly* etc . . . Except that through this monotonous, interminable enumeration I would have liked to "awaken" the words, to give them a new "polish," for it all to appear like an ubiquitous dew, terribly round and fresh on the burdocks of the old verbal prejudices. A grievous prayer of the words to the Word! I had intended to use "my" words, only "my own." I could not, I did not even begin, the "incapacity" of doing so preventing me, of course, from the start. I would—lying in my chaise longue, in the afternoon, eyes in the light of the brick wall a few meters away from me—dream of my last poem as of *a woman!* [. . .]

And I remember it again. Each time I began a poem, *the mechanism* would be magically activated through a word, a *word* that until then, although I repeated it, while talking, thousands of times, or read it, had nothing unusual about it. And suddenly—I have not been able to understand why to this day—this word would "reveal" itself to me, I would "see" it, I would "hear" it *for the first time*, different, unusually crisp, bizarre, as if estranged from my human language. It was as if it had been whispered by a "virginal" mouth, by an angel

---

1. *Reasece* is an abbreviation of Lucian Raicu's book title, *Reflecţii asupra spiritului creator* (*Reflections on the Creative Spirit*, 1979).

that came precisely for that purpose close to my ear and soul. And from this blinding word, not previously encountered (although I had encountered it a million times before), aurorally trumpeted under the lid of a genuine horizon, suddenly receiving its true garment, the original one probably, unsoiled in its folds by any signification other than the one of its pure existence, transparent and opaque at the same time, from this invented word, made up of pristine syllables that illuminated my understanding as though in paradise, in front of which I had shaken with the emotion of beginnings, of something mysterious, divine, feeling profoundly happy that I could bestow life on it, that I could, for a fleeting moment, seize it in its unknown shape, from this word, as in a dream, the poem began. [. . .]

Except that *the word* was not enough! I had to be there as well! And perhaps, in fact, the consciousness (which seldom penetrates my understanding) of the gaze, I exist, I live, would summon up *the word*, would replenish it. "Seemingly knowing" subtleties! [. . .]

Yours faithfully,
Emil Brumaru

Translated by Raluca Manea

Virgil Duda

(b. 1939)

Born Rubin Leibovici, Virgil Duda graduated with a law degree from the University of Bucharest and worked as a legal adviser. After 1970, he was an editor and producer in Romanian state-run cinematography. He settled in Israel in 1988, where he accepted a library post and later became editor of a Romanian magazine. He is the author of a volume of short stories (*Stories from the Provinces*, 1967) and of a number of novels: *The Cathedral* (1969), *The Apathetic Investigator* (1971), *Mislead* (1973), *The Second Passage* (1975), *Cora* (1977), *The Masks* (1979), *The War of Memories* (1981), *The Harassment* (1984), *The Saved Mirror* (1986), *Alvis and Destiny* (1993), *To Live in Sin* (1996), *Life with Delayed Effect* (1999), *Six Women* (2002), and *The Last Loves* (2008).

Duda writes a psychologically driven prose in which, through remonstration and investigation, his characters attempt to rediscover the truth (always relativized) regarding obscure or traumatic periods in their past.

FROM "THE STORY OF A TITLE"

I began to write, in the fall of 1957, under the fascinating influence of reading the novel *Buddenbrooks* by Thomas Mann, and under the weight of some
pressing personal dramas, a saga inspired by the "decline" of the family into
which I was born. I was a second-year law student in Bucharest, sufficiently
unripe, ambitious, or crazy enough to believe that I could do "something
like that." If I remember correctly, it was a novel preponderantly historical,
for the majority of the events took place between the two great wars. I was
under the "influence" of some retellings that I owed to a few fabulous aunts. I
don't think anything much resulted, but I was impressed by the few hundred
pages emerging from my toil, which had stretched over a period of some four
years. A known writer had read the text, had recommended it to the press,
and had accompanied me to the discussion of the "manuscript" about which
one of the young editors said that such stories—with merchants destroyed,
let us say, by capitalism—did not fit into the thematic agenda of a socialist
literary press, the sole press (it seems unthinkable!), much like the sole party,
at that time in soviet Romania. He was perfectly right, which is why I cannot
bear him any ill will. It was recommended that I begin with the short story
genre. And since the leopard cannot change his spots, I worked another two
years at a novella about the suicide—evidently from personal motives—of a
young woman. I began "a real case," of which I had heard not in the *Gazette
des Tribunaux*, as Stendhal had for *The Red and the Black*, but directly from
the chambers where I functioned as a lawyer. One magazine after another
dismissed me, invoking artistic weaknesses.

Then came the "thaw" of 1964 from which a kindhearted editor profited,
helping me make my debut first with a volume Chekhovically entitled *Tales
from the Provinces* and then with a novel called *The Cathedral*.

The "material" of my youthful work, understandably, did not give me any
peace. The pages were left "in the drawer" for a time, and then took the road
of no return into the fire ("Manuscripts don't burn," Bulgakov assures us in
The Master and Margarita), however the memories persisted and did not leave
me even in sleep. Until one day and night. Twenty years had passed, as in
Dumas. I crushed them to cinders and spun a few narrative threads, which
constituted the first two parts of a new novel, each having a narrative time

frame of twenty-four hours: *The War of Memories*. The book enjoyed a warm welcome from those whose opinion I treasured, but also from others. The truth is that I had cleverly insinuated choice "bits" of my youthful work in almost all the books that had since appeared, even in *The Cathedral*, though more importantly in the vaguely autobiographical *Apathetic Investigator*; yet only in 1977 had "the hour of vengeance" sounded, for as with first loves, failure, by definition, the first madness, is not easily forgotten.

What was meant by *The War of Memories*, what does this collocation aspire to mean? I remember that at a book discussion which took place in the prose section of the Association of Writers in Bucharest, a discussion in which two critics and two prose writers (all of highest regard) participated, the significance of the title was also debated, among other things. But the author—a wise decision—was not asked to give his opinion! [. . .]

Translated by Carla Baricz

Ana Blandiana

(b. 1942)

Born Otilia Valeria Coman, Ana Blandiana graduated with a degree in philology from the University Babeș-Bolyai in Cluj. She then worked as a magazine editor and librarian. After 1990, she became one of the principal founders of the Civic Alliance (the most important organization of civic commitment in post-Communist Romania) as well as the founder and president of the Civic Academy. With the help of the European Council, this association has put together the Memorial for the Victims of Communism and of the Resistance.

Blandiana has had a rich and lasting career in both journalism and criticism. Her articles and essays have been collected in the volumes *The Quality of Witness* (1970), *I Write, You Write, He/She Writes* (1975), *The Most Beautiful of All Possible Worlds* (1978), *Corridors of Mirrors* (1983), *Self-Portrait with Palimpsest* (1985), *Guessing in the Multitudes* (2000), *Who Am I?* (2001), *To Be or to Gaze* (2005), *A Syllabification of the World* (2006), and *The Fear of Literature* (2006). She has also published volumes of short stories—*The Four Seasons* (1977), *Projects from the Past* (1982), *Imitation of Nightmare* (1995), *The Melted Town and Other Fantastic Stories* (2004)—and the novel *The Drawer with Applause* (1992). Though these books have been well received, Ana Blandiana gained and continues to gain critical acclaim mainly for her poetry. She has published a number of collections: *The First-Person Plural* (1964), *The Vulnerable Heel* (1966), *The Third Mystery* (1969), *Fifty Poems* (1970), *October, November, December* (1972), *The Sleep in Sleep* (1977), *Happenings in My Garden* (1987), *The Eye of the Cricket* (1981), *The Hour of Sand* (1984), *The Preying Star* (1986), *Other Happenings in My Garden* (1987), *Happenings on My Street* (1988), *The Architecture of Values* (1990), *One Hundred Poems* (1991), *The Morning after Death* (1996), *Angel Picking* (1997), *Arpagic's White Book* (1998), *The Scale with One Pan* (1998), *The Sun of Thereafter* (2000), and *The Reflex of the Senses* (2004).

In her writing, Ana Blandiana combines a lyricism of the emotions with the themes of a cosmic expressionism peppered with social and moral observations. This technique can also be identified in her prose, in which the unusual is used as a springboard into the surreal.

from "Fear of Literature"

117. Until not too long ago, I had the clear conscience that I was writing because someone from my depths dictated, word by word, what I only needed to hasten to mark or, on the contrary, to labor for—so as to create the necessary conditions for this inner voice—for it not to cease speaking. And, though it would have been an exaggeration to maintain that that voice was really myself, a profound sentiment of kin, a true tie, of blood, pulsed between me and my pages. Now it seems to me that this someone moved to my outside and, boorish and uncommunicative, no longer tires itself to tell me what we are talking about, but as foreign and almost hostile, simply takes my hand and moves it up and down the paper. The signs, the resulting lines are thus almost unknown to me and the only thing left is to reread them, to choose from among them, to memorize them so as to make them familiar, so as to bring them closer. But this I can do with anyone's verses; they do not necessarily have to be my own. And, in fact, not for one moment do I have the sensation that these verses are mine.

118. Sometimes, I feel like saying regarding that which I am living, like others do: "It's too bad I don't know how to write, it would be a veritable novel." Though whether I would know or not know how to write it

remains to be seen. What prevents me from finding out is not a proper incapability but a certain disdain turned prejudice for the epic, for what Eminescu called "a history on water." I do not see myself describing facts, manners whose only sense would be the realist one. I do not see myself writing: "He sat down at the table, poured water in the glass and said . . ." And, moreover, facts are almost nonexistent. What exists is their ceaseless interpretation and reconstitution. A reconstruction that, if it is to follow the laws of logic, I feel would deviate from truth.

120. When I narrate certain things said, seen, I am moved more than I was at the time when I encountered them. I am moved more by my rendition of reality than by immediate reality. Is it perhaps because of a postponed emotion that strikes me later or because of an emotion that strikes me only in the moment in which it has become artistic (through storytelling)?

121. For me, poetry is a logical advancement from word to word, from stone to stone, on solid ground, to the point at which meaning opens suddenly, unexpectedly, over the void and stands still holding its breath. This moment is everything, this realization of the void beneath, this sudden emotion in the face of the assumed boundary, this halt, more revealing than the unconscious continuation of the path over the precipice. To the miraculous, I have always preferred the questions without answer from which the former eventually springs.

122. The writer is not the creator but the witness of the world through which he passes. If it had been created by writers, the world would have looked completely different.

129. Writing is not as much a means of surviving as it is one of dying, a means of dying ceaselessly, second by second, until you can no longer cease to die. Immortality is nothing more than a death that never ceases.

134. The poet is a precipice in which the pain of the world sonorously falls and in falling disintegrates and burns, so that before reaching the bottom all that is left is a snowed echo of ashes turned heavenward—almost a music.

141. Much like in a language that I do not know very well, while holding a conversation I find myself saying something other than what I mean, only because I do not remember the words that I need, but, on the other hand, I can recall others with a slightly different meaning—in similar fashion, while writing, I can never precisely follow a plan (I don't even try to make one anymore) because my intentions, desirous to materialize into phrases, are replaced by other words than those I wanted, birthing other senses unfaithful to me, faithful only to an often strange beauty.

144. I write prose with a certain wonder, in the shadow, perpetually strange, of the question—"What am I doing here?" Of course, to this was added by long and logical lines only the need of stating truths, of participating in a way in the history that I traverse. However, strangely enough, an antibody exists in my writing, which itself eliminates the too tightly wrought historical bond. From all the sufferings that surround, on my page is glimpsed only suffering in itself, a conquering suffering, but one lacking in determinations. Desperate and humbled, I do everything I can in order to fix, to cover—illicitly and even with the risk of breaking the quiet mirror of art—as many concrete elements as possible, but something deeper and more passionless, something more indifferent to the moment and even to time itself, tells me that everything in me happens as it does for my own salvation.

150. Poetry is what gives, almost as a sixth sense, the sentiment of the Other's presence in the surrounding world. The Other gazes at me from rocks, from plants, from animals, from clouds. An Other that only in moments of great fatigue is named Nobody.

Translated by Carla Baricz

Gabriela Adameşteanu

(b. 1942)

A graduate of the Faculty of Romanian Language and Literature at the University of Bucharest (1965), Adameşteanu worked as an editor for a publishing house. From 1990 to 2005 she led *22*, the most important weekly civic journal in Romania, from 2005 onward being involved solely with its cultural supplement. After the fall of communism, she published widely. A series of her articles appeared in *The Two Romanias* (2000), and some of her interviews were collected in *The Obsession with Politics* (1995). She is the author of four novels—*The Equal Way of Every Day* (1975), *Wasted Morning* (1984), *The Encounter* (2003), *Provisionality* (2010)—and two volumes of short fiction: *Give Yourself a Day Off* (1979) and *Summer-Spring* (1989).

Her novel *Lost Morning* is thought to be a masterpiece (according to literary critic Monica Lovinescu, "a *War without Peace* of the Romanians"). Adameşteanu, esteemed as one of the most important Romanian writers after World War II, achieves in her work a brilliant synthesis between the prose of everyday life and that of interior spaces, using major themes such as memory, history, fate, and family dispersal in an exquisitely rendered and, at the same time, accessible, fluent, and dynamic form of writing.

FROM "LITERATURE AS RELIGION AND FEAR"

When literature revealed itself to me, rather suddenly, at the age of twenty-eight, I had not previously made any "serious attempt" at it, although my parents, who were teachers, had diagnosed me early on as "a child with literary inclinations and no sense of observation." But I had not tried to put to test my natural gift. Since then, perhaps, I have had sketched out in my mind the idea that "a life = a life," although I was obsessed with building something lasting, without knowing whether or not I was capable doing so. I noticed that we often have two projects, corresponding to two diametrically opposed images of life, which appear to coexist peacefully in our mind. In fact, it all comes down to a tension to be solved by opportunities in life or in a moment of choice.

I avoided literary gatherings. I have no patience to listen to speeches or readings of texts, and my first visit to such a meeting in the provinces, as a teenager, planted in me the fear of failure before I ever began writing (the failure of literature, the failure of success, the failure of life). I could never again dissociate the idea of a literary meeting from that initial image, terrifying in its mediocrity. In the end I wrote because life seemed to me insipid, suffocating, and there was in me a repressed energy (I can see this clearly now, I did not know it then). I was afraid of being a writer (perhaps I fear it even today), which is why I wanted to be a literary critic: I was, in any case, addicted to reading like to a drug. I reached some balance when I myself began to write, but every time I am interested in a book, I intend to write about it (although that does not generally happen).

The fear of the profession of a writer, which can push you beyond all frontiers, in a space filled with danger, has for a long time given me the feeling that I ended up becoming a writer because I did not keep myself in hand and gave in to an inner moment of weakness. In fact, because of this moment, my life became richer and opened up to me, I rebuilt myself on the inside, I resisted when faced with a difficult life and world. [. . .]

I believe I have espoused with passion the artistic deontology of a religious type proper to the moment (its theorization may be found in the wonderful books, little perused today, unjustly so, by Lucian Raicu)[1] because, like the

---

1. Raicu (though also Emil Brumaru) dealt with the subject alluded to by Adameșteanu in *The Practice of Writing and the Experience of Reading* (1978); *Reflections on the Creative Spirit* (1979); *Scenes, Reflections, Fragments* (1999).

majority of my fellow beings, living in communist seclusion, I had nothing in which to invest my lofty impulses (I avoid with shame the term "the
absolute," otherwise frequently used at that time, in relation to the Romantic
ideology that had then been partly resuscitated). Gabriel Liiceanu reproduces
in *The Forbidden Door* a statement that I probably made in his presence, and
whose pragmatic brutality causes him fear: "A writer has to put everything
on display, all his feelings are for sale."[2] There is in this formulation a daring,
aggressive note, perhaps I uttered it in a "polemic moment," but I cannot but
recognize myself in it, since it is built, despite the fact that it speaks of trade,
on the idea of art as religion. It is the schizophrenic or monastic condition of
the artist who "sacrifices" (here it is an accepted word, because it is "nobler,"
albeit cliché) every lived moment, making it prey to another's gaze. And then,
when he does not have enough power to do it (we say that he does not have
"enough talent") or when he tries to deceive the inhuman gaze from within
him, he fails: his book will add to the ocean of recyclable paper.

Looking back, I recognize in myself, in the one from back then, the traits of
a secluded world, in which circulated foreign books that were at least fifty years
old, in which instructors taught dated and scholarly languages, in which artists
imagined the "free world" as a paradise ungoverned by the power of money, etc.

Seclusion turns you into an essence, makes of you a half-saint, half-caricature
(saint according to the image you have of yourself, caricature according to the
image others have of you).

Translated by Raluca Manea

---

2. *The Forbidden Door* (2002), autobiographical work by Gabriel Liiceanu, an important
Romanian thinker and writer. He translated from Plato and Heidegger.

Virgil Mazilescu

(1942–1984)

Graduate of the Faculty of Letters at the University of Bucharest, Virgil Mazilescu taught at a village school, worked as a librarian, and was later editor of *Literary Romania*, the most important publication of the Writers' Union. He published little, but his volumes of poetry were critically well received. His work consists of *Verses* (1968), *Fragments from the Region of Once* (1970), *It Will Be Evening, It Will Be Late* (1979), and *Guillaume the Poet and Administrator* (1983). Considered a masterful technician of a fragmentary and enigmatic discourse, Mazilescu created an imaginary universe of convulsions, anguish, and self-devouring, so that "forever, whoever I may be, I will be other."

PREFACE

and after I invented poetry in a clandestine chamber in the depths of the barren earth—the courage and the (human) strength vanished like vapor

and something more, beyond the fact that I was born and that I live and shall likely die trembling (which is what after all I wanted to say even two, three years ago) for now oh I cannot say it

and so I take up again the old tongue: beginning even this very moment I

distort it I caress it I beat it savagely, yet the uncanny syntagmas in which (it
is said) that my soul slumbers as in a lost den do not entice me any longer the
tapered fingers that will dig ditches in the forest and will return there again
and again and will begin little by little to putrefy? the tapered fingers do not
disturb me any longer

HONEY ON THE TONGUE

in order to better remember he must learn to forget.
to bend over backward to learn. day and night—never ceasing.
lord (he has been telling himself for some time) what a ludicrous
        occupation
I seem to have. what a difficult job. in the end: what a ruin lord.

and does he come from afar? well, yes he comes from afar
he comes sobbing loudly and chokes
from so much sweet honey and does not have
an angel to guard him. and does not have
an angel to guard him at night.

his tears resemble large very large
land slides: with small infinitely small—almost invisible—

colored seeds of the century.

Translated by Carla Baricz

Gabriela Melinescu

(b. 1942)

A graduate of the School of Faculty in Bucharest, Melinescu worked as a journalist. She published the volumes of poetry *Winter Ceremony* (1965), *Abstract Beings* (1967), *The Inside of the Law* (1968), *The Illness of Divine Origin* (1970), *The Vows of Poverty, Chastity, and Submission* (1972), and *Against the Beloved* (1975). She also published two children's books: *The Mast with Two Ships* (1969) and *Bobinocarians* (1969). In 1975, after a period of being harassed by the Secret Police for her relationship with a foreigner, she left for Sweden, where she settled with her partner, an editor of Belgian origin. There, she worked in publishing and wrote for the Swedish press. Melinescu started by writing in French and Swedish and published several volumes that brought her prestige: *The Father of the Lie* (1977), *The Children of Patience* (1979), *The Wolves' Rise to the Sky* (1981), *The Tree in the Wind* (1987), and *The Street Queen* (1988). She is also an author of short fiction—*The Bird Man* (1991), *Feather Molting* (1998); autobiographical writings (*The Diary of a Solitary Egotist*, 1982); and the poetry collections *The Fertility God* (1977), *The Smoke House* (1982), and *The Woman's Mirror* (1986). Beginning in 1990, the writer (whose works were censured after she left the country) reentered the Romanian literary world. Several of her anthologies as well as the books written in exile, a new volume of poetry (*Newborn Words*, 2002), and her *Swedish Journal* (vols. 1–4, 2000–2008) were released, the latter being considered one of the most important works of its kind. She is also a very prolific translator from and into Swedish.

A remarkable cultural figure and protagonist of a biography marked by numerous
dramatic turns (her father's suicide, the experience of exile, the unexpected death of
her husband), Melinescu produces an art of great depth and vitality in which one senses
"the boundless fascination that life exercises on [her]" as well as such recurrent themes
as love, fate, faith, and the act of creation construed as ardor and askesis.

FROM "TO WRITE"

When we write we must
keep a distance
from what took place
in words
as when you
save a man
from drowning—
you must hold him
tightly
but not too close
so that he can't pull
you down with him
into the deep.

The poem quoted above was published a few years ago in the volume *Newborn Words* and contains, in a simple form, my first perception of the creative act. An affirmation through negation.

The words resemble the sirens' songs, which Ulysses listened to, mesmerized, but bound fast to the mast of his ship, while the ears of his companions had been sealed with wax—so that they would not be seduced and pulled into the deep.

From the beginning, poetry did not seem to be about words. I had "a phonetic way" of perceiving creation—the world had been born not through word but through sound. All the tongues were sound—tone—in the beginning, and were to become sign—word—only later. Even the cries of the newborns were a pure, intense state of being, anterior to language. The affirmation of faith in all religions is not possible unless accompanied by a melody without words, through which it is precisely the primordial sound of the world—Aleph or Alpha, or simply *A*—that is celebrated.

"Newborn words" were a "secondary game," the transposition of sounds into signs, their power coming straight from a human commitment on the part of the one who uttered them—assuming that "the primary game" is existence, living, vital impulse, inspiration. The interiority of the word being the breath of any human act. And the message of any kind of communication is situated between inspiration and the creative process—the existence of a tension dressed in signs, in the process of being lived out. In religious terms, one could say about that initial breath or tone that "there is no place in which It does not exist."

Writing was not born on the writing table. As a prototype for the creator, the poet alone possesses the keys to his own voice—through voice he stands as a medium for an archaic element, a kind of embryo of phonetic light that rests at the basis of his voice. An embryo full of mystery that casts light onto the images and the forms of language. Poets depict differently the genesis of the inner voice, something that has overwhelmed them or has struck them all of a sudden in order to send out a message—as was the case with the prophets of the Old Testament—forcing them to speak in tongues or with their entire body, which had suddenly turned into "someone else's mouth."

I do not remember how I learned the alphabet. Perhaps by looking over my sister's shoulder while she attempted to write letters and words, articulating them as she did, giving them the melody proper to her level of vitality that would self-infiltrate into the words through an act of mutual possession.

Since I was "inclined to drawing" as a child, I immediately discovered the sounds in voices and the signs that—albeit mute—could be brought to life by a human being. My name seemed melodious to me, made of singing letters, and I considered it to be my first dictionary, with eight letters that could change places and engender other words—pseudonyms for the ludic artist in me. While playing, I derived other names from my own: Ariel, Eli, Gala, Lara and many others. Perhaps this initial inspiration, this "primary game," was an unconscious search for poetry, "a second game." Via a "phonetic mode" of creation, the poet in me—coming from outside poetics and aesthetic rules—was aspiring to express her state of being, intuiting poetry to be a solid settlement at the center of the human.

In school, I found out that writers existed. A beautiful profession, although it was not exactly a profession. A profession having the gift of renewing memory and the senses, a nourishment for eyes and starving ears. One of these writers used to live not too far away from our street, and his name was George Bacovia.[1] He was not well liked by the regime, being called "a bourgeois poet"—he was pessimistic and could not sing of the "bright future."

The poet had a garden with lofty dahlias that neighbored a service station where I was sent to buy lamp oil. Once, I caught a glimpse of him by sticking my head through the fence posts. He was old and ill but played the violin as if he had found himself on an island, alone with his violin and his garden. His violin expressed states of being beyond words, much like his poetry, pure, without linguistic experiments. I imagined that by playing the violin the poet beguiled inspiration for his poems, that state without words that made it seem as if his poems were being written on their own. As I did in the graveyard near our house, by listening to the rustle of the wind through the branches of large trees, or in the trees full of fruit, to the breeze resembling the language without language of the dead underneath.

The world I lived in was full of a politics and an ideology of which I understood nothing. Not long after I saw him, George Bacovia, the poet, passed away suddenly—impoverished and disappointed. His death made me think that it wasn't enough to live in order to express life, that there was another life that could save you from moral death when life stagnated—a life through art. Poetry, for instance, was a profound commitment, transgressing with its tone the aberrant states of being imposed by politics and ideologies.

Writing was related to reading. Through books you could become aware of the different ways of being human, you could reach out to the experience of other people, to their suffering. I would hide in the cellar in order to read—I could focus more easily there, I could hear the voices in the books, the primordial sounds of creation from before writing.

My father gave me old books of poetry, which one could not find in libraries and Stalinist bookshops. Some poets spoke of their ways of writing. They

1. George Bacovia (1881–1957), an important Romanian poet (see table of contents).

all depended on breath, inspiration, the phonetic embryo of light that infil-
trates words to stay in them and differentiate them from the words untouched
by breath. All the people could write words, but few were able to breathe life
into them from the abundance of their own lives. [. . .]

The fact that I write in two languages makes me separate them, and I have
two different times and two different inspirations for each of them.

In order to write in Romanian, I have to wake up early in the morning, as
if performing a ritual, to mentally empty myself of Swedish, to wash, to comb
my hair, to put on perfume, to wear a white shirt and blue pants, to throw
my red silk scarf over my shoulders, waiting for a sound, walking around the
writing table from where the lilies—called "tigerliljor" in Swedish—send me
their perfume and that white-pink color so loved by Nelly Sachs.

Many writers called writing "a spiritual profession," others "a calamity," "a
torture." Balzac considered writing to be a sacrament—he had to be clean and
chaste before the words. Each morning he would put on his cloak made of white
cashmere, using as a belt a thick tassel, evocative of Franciscan friars. The cloak
had large sleeves that no drop of ink ever stained. He would only drink water,
and as for eating, he possessed the frugality of an ascetic. For lunch he ate little,
mainly that onion soup he would prepare himself. To stay awake at night he
drank coffee—some say—eighty thousand cups of strong coffee in his life.

When I lose all hope of hearing a rustle or a ripple that would move the
branches in my brain and under whose guidance I could write again in my
native tongue, I consider my favorite writers in the process of writing.

For instance, I look at the photo taken by Tore Johnson of Ernest Hemingway writing, an image cut out of a newspaper and put on display on the
writing table. The writer was in a large room in his villa, Finca Vigía in San
Francisco de Paula, in Cuba. Hemingway would work standing up, writing at
a typewriter on top of a bookcase that came up to his waist. Behind him there
was a double bed on which one could find in a certain order-chaos the pages of
a new novel on which he was working at the time. Perhaps the novel in which
he was depicting a young woman's sadness following an abortion. When he
went out for lunch in a small restaurant nearby and suddenly his character
approached, in flesh and blood—a young woman with the purple, dark rings
of a hidden pain under her eyes—he stopped, perplexed, as though his own
fantasy had suddenly become incarnated into a human being. His hunger

vanished immediately, and he returned to his room, continuing to work as in a trance until dusk.

It is as if I was that young woman with a sad face encountering the creator who could put her pain into words, so that it could be metamorphosed into the intensity of life.

At night I find myself faced with another impossibility: that of writing in Swedish. Swedish is in the air that I inhale, and it impregnates my entire life. I can never get rid of it. For my efforts to write in this language, I received accolades but also blows. Some threats over the phone. Once, an anonymous voice prohibited me from writing about Karl XII, by saying that he simply was not my hero. I was struck silent, Carolus Rex was the world's hero, Voltaire's, he belonged to all who love history.

There is nonetheless another image that does me good. It is Nelly Sachs's fragile silhouette. I sometimes visit her grave at Norra Kyrkogarden, whispering some words in front of it. But at night her being is in a dark chamber. She is awake but her mother is asleep and Nelly cannot turn the light on. Not only because it would disturb her mother's sleep, but especially because it is risky for a Jewish woman who escaped the Nazis to keep a light on all night long. It is as if she feels threatened again by the Nazis who survived her to this day. But Nelly does not surrender, she sits straight up in her chair, with a pen in hand and white sheets of paper on her knees. She writes Swedish words in the darkness of night. Because it is not enough to live to express life, you must also commit your existence to words in order to save it from moral death.

The image of the poet's hand writing in the dark calms me by arousing my "creative intellect." Consciousness springs forth like lightning, and with it, words pour out in streams. Myself, I am writing in Swedish again, although I do not write more than a page of manuscript per night. Nevertheless, I am not filled with despair, thinking with a certain cheerfulness: as long as I am not hanged, I can write another page in Swedish.

Deep inside I feel the presence of all the languages that I know, more or less. But at night, more than ever, Swedish presses down upon all of them, coming out on top, once more impregnating the air I breathe with the exigencies and joys of the world in which I landed.

Translated by Raluca Manea

Andrei Codrescu

(b. 1946)

After his poetic debut in a number of Romanian literary magazines, Andrei Codrescu left Romania. From 1965 onward he made his home in the United States, where he published an impressive number of volumes of poetry, prose, and essays. He teaches English literature at Louisiana State University and collaborates with National Public Radio. He has also worked in film and was the screenwriter of *Road Scholar* (2004), a film in which he also acted. He is the editor of the online publication *Exquisite Corpse: A Journal of Books and Ideas* (www.corpse.org).

After 1990, Codrescu returned to the Romanian literary world by publishing a number of articles that were collected in the volumes of *Letters from New Orleans* (2006). In 2007 he also published the collection of verse *The Forgiven Submarine*, written in Romanian with the poet Ruxandra Cesereanu.

Belonging to Romanian literature more through origins rather than works (written almost entirely in English), Andrei Codrescu cultivates ancient myths and folklore in his writing, masking the ancient in the contemporary. (*Translated by Carla Baricz*)

BI-LINGUAL

I speak two languages. I've learnt one of them in a trance, for no reason at all, in a very short time, on horseback, in glimpses, between silent revolts. One is the language of my birth, a speech which, more or less, contains my rational mind because it is in this tongue that I find myself counting change in the supermarket and filing away my published poems. In a sense, these two languages are my private day and night because what one knows without having learned is the day, full of light and indelicate assumptions. The language of the night is fragile, it depends for the most part on memory, and memory is a vast white sheet on which the most preposterous things are written. The acquired language is permanently under the watch of my native tongue like a prisoner in a cage. Lately, this new language has planned an escape to which I fully subscribe. It plans to get away in the middle of the night with most of my mind and never return. This piece of writing in the acquired language is part of the plan: while the native tongue is (right now!) beginning to translate it, a big chunk of my mind has already detached itself and is floating in space entirely free. . . .

Ştefan Agopian

(b. 1947)

Ştefan Agopian began but never completed studies in chemistry at the University of Bucharest. He worked for a time as a technician and then as a proofreader for cultural publications. After 1990, he became editor for a number of reviews and head of a publishing house. He is known for his novels: *The Day of Anger* (1979), *The Velvet Man* (1984), *Notes from Sodom* (1993), and *Fric* (2003). Agopian constructs a picaresque and sensationalist prose, with fantastic elements molded on historical facts that he integrates into a space of Balkan ludism and theatricality. He is a refined stylist with a talent for vivid description.

from "Toward a Liberal Grammar"

Borges said: the irreducible part of literature is the letter, the alphabet. The library of all possible books through the combination of words into phrases, and of phrases into texts, cannot be greater than "what is." Something *greater* than this would be incomprehensible. However, that which is incapable of being understood is, nevertheless, the object of literature. Literature tends, through the novelty of combinations, toward the limit of this meaning beyond words. What prevents it still from crossing to the other side is the fact that what is incapable of being understood increases with each book. A written book enters not only into libraries but also into reality. The thirst for the real, it was said. But the real is both life and books, the life of texts and the text originating in the shadow of a life. The Library of Babel is a universe in expansion, like the universe itself. To see the real only through the hexagons of reality of the bee's eye would mean to pass over (but now the eye of the mind looks) the miracle that takes place in the honeycomb: the honey. That which is added onto reality. The imagination is (not) capable of producing something that does not exist, it causes to exist what it produces. Its irreducible aspect can no longer be the letter. The imagination introduces a criterion into the arbitrary and infinite game of Babel combinations. From all possibilities, it retains only the combinations that obey grammar. Subject, predicate, direct object, complement. Reality is not grammatical. In any case, it does not have the grammar of language. In the logic of reality, no text follows after death. In the grammar of language, hence in that of the imagination, anything can follow. A dream or a new life experience. Grammar is more liberal than reality. It allows me to write "fiery snow," but reality does not permit me to say "the sun rises every evening." That is why literature is not added onto reality as one of its mirrors, but as a perpetually renewed genesis. A continuous genesis. The writer writing is subject to other laws than man living. And the written man, the character, is subject to other laws.

A grammar of the imagination cannot be described. It can, however, be put to work. It is then judged after its works. It has been said of *Sara* that it is a poetic novel.[1] This is a sign that we do not have names for the works of imagination. Is *The Death of Virgil* by Hermann Broch a poetic novel? We have become used to no longer permitting to the novel what we allow in poetry: complicity with the mysterious. Today, textual exclusivity is practiced in prose, is understood as a miracle in itself, with the aim of explaining the miracle and passing, in this manner, from "mirroring" to the "autism" of texturing. Grammar, without a proper color of its own, without ethics or logic, seems to have become that which it had to be: *a body of laws.* Unfortunately, the zone of "that which is" is parenthesized. The true mystery of the making of the text is, however, the remaking of existence itself with the help of a grammar freed from any servitude.

Translated by Carla Baricz

1. *Sara* (1987)—novel by Ştefan Agopian.

Mircea Nedelciu

(1950–1999)

A graduate of the Faculty of Philology in Bucharest, Nedelciu worked as a night guard, tourist guide, and bookshop clerk. In 1990 he founded a Franco-Romanian association of editorial distribution and began to work as a journalist. Diagnosed with a grave illness (Hodgkin's disease), he underwent several surgical interventions and spent his last years in a wheelchair. The text included here was written a few days before he passed away and was published in a weekly journal in which he had had a column. Considered a leader of the '80s Generation, a personality of great human and literary force, Nedelciu published several volumes of short fiction—*Adventures in an Inner Courtyard* (1979), *The Effect of the Controlled Echo* (1981), *Amendment to the Instinct of Property* (1983), *Yesterday Will Be Another Day* (1989), *The 80s Generation Stories* (1998)—and the novels *Raspberries of the Plain* (1984), *Fabulating Treatment* (1986), and *Woman in Red* (written with Adriana Babeți and Mircea Mihăieș, 1990). The novel *The Sign of the Diver* (2000) was released posthumously.

Concerned with the technical renewal of prose, but equally interested in the valorization of orality and humor, Nedelciu made identity (in particular the identity of the young) and the difficulty of forming and maintaining identity in a world deprived of an "integrating valence" his pervasive theme.

Horizontal Man

In the end, God punished me for being lazy. I always had more ideas than I put into practice. I would just get up in the morning with an idea and, rather than nicely laying it down on paper, I would get dressed, go out, to work when that was the case, and, in the evening I would meet up with all sorts of guys and girls, ha-ra-hara, ga-ra-ga-ra, ha-haha, with a beer or with a walk . . . and time would go by. I would get home at night with other ideas, similar or even more interesting than the ones with which I had left home in the morning. Except that at this point I would have even less time or desire to put them down on paper: the exhaustion, the confusion!

In twenty years I only blackened about a thousand pages of printed paper: fifty pages a year—shameful.

So that in the end God said: "It's time for you to stay home and write!" And He took away my legs. Now I get up in the morning and I just can't believe that I am not able to take a single step. The notion of "step" has disappeared from my universe just as the notions of brother, sister, uncle, aunt, or brother-in-law disappeared from the Chinese universe. Since the regime prohibits them from having more than one child, you see why the above-mentioned notions have become meaningless to them. Same for me: from bed to wheelchair I don't take a step, I "transfer myself" with the help of my arms. The bipedal position is no longer available to me, in any way: I am a horizontal man. And if the elevator is broken for weeks, I can't even leave my house in the wheelchair. What is there to be done in this situation? The morning shows on television are extremely boring, the newspapers recount the few interesting things that I had seen the previous night on television. And so life goes. The books that you didn't read in your adolescence or early youth are no longer books, but objects of study through distracted perusing.

I have therefore nothing else left to do than to sit in front of the typewriter and somehow deal with the old sisters of my vigorous ideas from the time I was young. Such is the definition of the horizontal man: without hatred or favoritism, without regrets and useless anger, simply free up your ideas and allow them to take written form. If they are to be of service to someone, someday, who knows.

I know, time seems to be running out, putting down on paper everything that goes through your head doesn't really work either. Selections, fittings must be carried out, you must know to do the opposite of what the tailor does: to take the measurement once and to cut ten times, to eliminate, to suggest rather than to develop in detail. But these are things that one learns: in fact, one does not even learn them, they simply come on their own, under the pressure of time, which, as I was saying, gives one the impression of running out.

What is, in the end, has a hideous shape and looks at you incessantly. You knew even before that the figure was there, but all you did was to ignore her, to think of her as remote, to try to play your parts usually with your back turned to her, to mock her once in a while, well aware that she does not take you seriously either.

Not now, this can be no longer, the confrontation is inevitable, you must fight rather than run away from her. Remind her that she is ugly, while life is so beautiful, rely on the space that separates you still from her as on an extremely elastic space, expandable, divisible by a dozen means, among which writing, that is, the laying down of ideas on paper. The match has entered its nervous phase, alive, a phase in which mistakes are to be paid for twice, three times, four times over, which is enough reason for you to avoid making one. From this point of view, the position of a horizontal man can be seen as an advantage: you cannot fall down, you can only advance or retreat (strategically, of course).

We'll see where all this leads, but I can already tell you that I have discovered a few tricks (with some enemies, of course, it makes no sense to fight without tricks). For instance, to describe a healthy leg in detail, the toes that move freely up and down, the mobility of a slender ankle, the movement of the shins and of the thighs while dancing—all this puts my hideous enemy in a real state of uncertainty. My enemy knows already that my legs belong to her, but I speak of other legs: there are so many of them and there will always be more!

Translated by Raluca Manea

Ioan Petru Culianu

(1950–1991)

Graduate of the Faculty of Romance Languages at the University of Bucharest, Ioan P. Culianu completed his studies in the West (having sought political asylum in Italy) and obtained doctorates from the Catholic University of the Sacred Heart in Milan and the Sorbonne in Paris. He went on to teach Romanian literature at the University of Groningen, in Holland. Disciple of the historian of religions Mircea Eliade, he took up his mentor's post at the University of Chicago, where he taught the history of religions from 1986 to 1991. In May of that year, he was murdered on the university campus (the crime remains unsolved).

Culianu published a monograph, *Mircea Eliade* (1978), and an impressive number of studies in the history of religions and the philosophy of culture (in Italian, French, and English). Of note are his scholarly books *Eros and Magic in the Renaissance* (1987), *Out of This World: Otherworldly Journeys from Gilgamesh to Albert Einstein* (1991), and *The Tree of Gnosis* (1992). His articles and essays on Romanian themes were collected posthumously in the volume *Romanian Studies* (2000). He was also the author of the novel *Hesperus* (1982) and of short stories, which he wrote in Romanian, and which were collected under the titles *The Diaphanous Parchment* (1989) and *The Art of the Fugue* (2002).

Night

June 1972

The obsessive image of a *certain night* into which the character sinks without the possibility of ever returning reappears in many of my stories. One of these stories, unpublished like the others (with the exception of the first, whose title I do not remember, and which appeared in an obscure university publication not benefiting from a wide release), is called "Maia"; I found it by accident at the bottom of a drawer while looking for a lost manuscript regarding the problem of the heart in Giordano Bruno's work. I remember when I wrote it and some of the circumstances: I had come home to Iași from a symposium on orientalism (this is when I got to know Professor V.).[1] I accompanied a distinguished lady professor to the Mitropolie,[2] where she had reserved a room; more precisely, I carried her bags. During all this time, I was exceedingly polite and detached with everyone; I then spent a stunning morning, which strengthened even more my admiring respect and love for Professor P.

The story named "Maia" was banal right up until the end: a guy loves a woman, meets another one, leaves the first one, marries the second one (Maia), who is an actress; after a pretty harmonious coexistence, Maia dies, and he dreams that he is called up to heaven. He then *awakes* and realizes that the events took place in his sleep. This is the first part; it is odd for two reasons; *first of all, because everything takes place extremely quickly;* and second of all, because Maia, even though she is an actress, proves to be something of a housewife as well. I will recount the second part textually, even though it is lacking in any artistic merit:

> Oscar Ceria, holder of a college degree in mechanics, a young hope, awakes after this strange and unsettling dream. He feels like laughing. It must be late at night. He wants to make a bit of light and smoke a *Moon* cigarette. But his hand feels only the dark. For a moment he is horribly afraid; he does not know where he is. Everything is pitch black. He rises and walks: darkness

---

1. Iași—important city and cultural center in the northeast of Romania where Ioan Culianu was born and grew up.

2. Mitropolie—institution belonging to the Romanian Orthodox Church; hierarchically, it is superior to the "Episcopie" and inferior to the "Patriarhie," which is the national seat of the Romanian Orthodox Church.

arid landscape darkness. He touches the ground: it is as if it is and isn't; his fingers sink. He lies down again and waits to fall asleep, to wake up. He does not succeed. He rises, runs, his soul fancies lights in the distance, lights that do not exist. He calls out by name the other half of his dream: Maia! Maia! Pitch black of colors and sounds . . .

The first story on this theme, the published one, was written at the age of eighteen and was extremely condensed. It was only two pages, and though I do not remember the title, I can recall the rest of the details. It had as a *motto* the reply of General Simon de Montfort, who led the 1213 crusade against the Albigensians, to a soldier who had told him that there were many Christians among the captured: "Kill them all, God will recognize his own" (*Tuez-les tous, Dieu reconnaîtra les siens*). In some measure, the story was autobiographical; I felt myself lost in that *noche oscura* of the senses described by San Juan de la Cruz. A young man awakes in an eternal night "barren of color and sound" next to his beloved, who in sleep resembled a toad. He leaves that place and finds himself among "calcified ruins," battered by a beginning of the world wind, hearing strange harmonies. That was all. The image of this night, however, is not that of *la noche oscura* of San Juan. Rather it was a leave-taking of the senses, a frightening purgatorial desert that required one to always trust in the light. At the same time, it also represented a sort of *memento:* people are born, hope, love, and die with a stupid regularity; the reader must remember this at some point and shatter the illusion that he or she is a person steeped in complex occurrences, [and know that everyone is] driven by the same implacable law. A passage from the Bhagavad Gītā speaks of the wise man as he who transformed the day of all other beings into night and the night of ignorance into day (2.69: *yā niśā sarvabhūtānam tasyām jāgatim samyamī, yasyām jāgrati bhūtani niśā paśyato muneh*). Life in its full becoming toward death is unsatisfactory: it is the "living death" of which speak the Muslim dervishes and the Spanish poets, the mystics (San Juan), or the eroticists: Timoneda, Juan de Menesco, Duarte de Brito. In one of the sonnets from *The Heroic Frenzies*, Giordano Bruno says: "in living death dead life you live," making the same transition as San Juan toward the dying light: "My life lives dying; were it to die, it would live." And Timoneda, in *Sarao de Amor:*

"Are you, Juan, either living or dead?

—I am alive; alive only in dying."

Francesco de Sanctis discovers this point of view in the entire spiritual condition of Dante's epoch, it being the key to the *Vita Nuova* and *La Divina Commedia*. Some researchers observe in this point of view a radical Platonism, aestheticized and tamed in the fifteenth century by Marsilio Ficino's school; others attribute it to the Christianity of the ascetic orders; in Spain, it is spoken of as the influence of the Muslim mystics; others speak of a stoic influence, a hermetic influence, a Judaic influence, of the penetration of oriental ideas into the "healthy" trade and war-oriented society of the Latin-Germanic peoples. Others even attribute it to the most intimate observations of a universal man who comes to know himself and finds that he is impure and broken, who wishes for salvation from error and from fear of punishment.

I associate the image of the night with the *Rubaiyat* of Omar Khayyam, in a beautiful French translation; in the 125th quatrain is described the "Desert of Nothingness"; in another quatrain, which I do not find in the newer editions, the face of he who has departed from the world appears contemptuously, like "the beauty of the flowers and stars"; it is also tied to one of the Buddha's sayings and the realization of ignorance; to the incandescent *Nights* of Novalis; to the other German Romantics; to a poem by Valéry; to a summer with the bloody reek of love near the lofty and placid smell of the sea; to a Damascus knife with an *alpha* carved into the blade; to my favorite poet, John Donne, who runs after a shooting star. Resurrecting all of these memories, I feel them in my soul like a painful *magical net* that urges me to run toward new horizons; simultaneously, I feel that a heavy mystery readies to burst, delaying in a place of minute suggestions and melancholia; that it will not burst, after all, if I follow the path of the life I have lived until now. A great weariness overtakes me, I throw myself into sleep in order to be—for the longest time possible—clean, like a newborn rocking in his mother's womb, eyeing with one laughing eye the heights from which he sets out and with a tearful eye the abyss to which he proceeds: from living night into dying night.

Translated by Carla Baricz

Alexandru Vlad

(b. 1950)

A graduate of the Faculty of Philosophy at the Babes-Bolyai University in Cluj, Vlad occupied various positions, including rural high school teacher, owner of an antique bookshop, art gallery guard, and typist. From 1990 onward, he was editor of a literary magazine. He has published in a prolific manner, both in the literary and the daily press; a number of his articles have been collected in the volume *The Glass Lamp* (2003). He is an author of short fiction, including *The Gryphon's Wing* (1980), *The Way to the South Pole* (1985), and *My Life in the Service of the Country* (2004); two novels (*The Cold of Summer,* 1985, and *The Double Rainbow,* 2008); and travel literature (*Athens, Athens,* 1994). He is also known as a translator.

Cautious and demanding of his writing, subjecting each piece to successive rewritings, Vlad creates a fiction of the everyday. He selects, however, those events that allow him to reveal or suggest, under the guise of apparent banality, the enigmas present in one's life or the sedimentation in one's psyche.

FROM "I AM ALWAYS BEHIND"

In the old days, when I would get my hands on an English magazine, no matter what it was about, I would read everything, including the ads. In one of those magazines, under personal ads, a lady looking for a husband demanded the following qualities: "Intellectual, between forty and forty-six years old, with a liking for traveling and conversation. *No writers.*" Thus, under no circumstances was he to be a writer. The only condition posed by the lady. Beyond the aura, of whose consequences the lady in question was probably aware, I say to you that the writer is an individual always in crisis. He may appear to you smiling nonchalantly, but the wrinkles, before appearing on his face, are engraved upon his soul—otherwise they don't appear at all. So the writer is an individual whose existence is in crisis. When he is younger and more enthusiastic, he cannot watch a sunset without realizing that he will have to describe it at the height of feeling. He is always in competition with the height at which he feels the world. There is always in him the one who perceives and the one who tries to match in words what he has perceived. And whenever he finds a pretext not to write, he is happy not to write. I would like to confess that when I turn the light on an empty, standard sheet of paper, my stomach hurts. And if I can, I do not write on it. I only write when I know that time has run out. I have to turn in an article the day after tomorrow, but there still is tomorrow. When tomorrow comes, I pace frantically around the house, I fight with my children, I look for excuses not to write, I tell the others not to answer the phone and only after that do I start writing. I am always behind; in my own feelings, in my own projects, and in what I have promised to the journals that do me the honor to solicit work from me. When you write a good book, you are told that it is good so late that you do not even recall what book it is: "Did you like it? Which one? That one? No, not that one, the other one." You become detached. To the extent to which a book is finished, it leaves you, it ceases to belong to you. There remain rudiments for a while, then they too disappear. And so it should be, the slate must be wiped clean in order for you to be able to write on it a second time. You are never certain that, if it was a success one time, this will be the case a second time, that it can come out at the same level of quality which interests you. There are professional writers in the West, scriptwriters. They are not interested in quality.

They are only interested in the reader's response. Of course, the reader can be easily manipulated. If I told you: "He entered from the cold outside, with light surrounding him, throwing his hair back in one move," you would see him, right? But I did not tell you whether he was blond or dark-haired, if he had a moustache or not, if he was old or young, I did not tell you any of this. One can form a visual image almost without any visual information. There is of course a "craft," but I am interested in whether I too feel something when I write. If not, we turn off the light and put it off until tomorrow or, if possible, until the day after tomorrow. [. . .]

These years after the Revolution have put us yet again in crisis with ourselves. [. . .]

The writer says that a crisis takes place with respect to his place in society. It is true, because the entire "underground" in books used to consist of a kind of conspiracy of the author and the reader. The wretched trip to Deva described by Mihai Sin in one of his novels is in fact an image of society.[1] Now, when I read it, it seems to be just that, a wretched trip. A political metaphysics had been buried here. No novel holds up if it does not have two-thirds below, in implications. Now, this political metaphysics no longer resides in the complicity between author and reader, of a "we know what we meant to say there, we know what this refers to." You may now say these things out loud, in the visible, "upper" third of the book—but what happens to the other two-thirds? This remains to be discovered, which is the reason why I wait to see and readjust; it is not easy, anyone can come and say, "You have not put out a book in so many years." And this is the reason for the translations I now do from my favorite writers. [. . .]

Translated by Raluca Manea

---

1. Mihai Sin (b. 1942)—Romanian novelist; Alexandru Vlad is referring to his best-known work, *Knock and You Will Be Let In* (1978), whose plot is based on a day trip spent on a bus with a dictatorial driver.

Gheorghe Crăciun

(1950–2007)

Graduate of the Faculty of Philology of the University of Bucharest, Gheorghe Crăciun taught Romanian in rural areas until 1990, when he began teaching at the University of Braşov. At that time, he also became an editor of a literary magazine and director of a publishing house. One of the literary stars of his generation, the so-called '80s Generation, promoter of postmodernism and constant literary renewal, Crăciun was the author of the novels *Original Documents / Legalized Copies* (1982), *Composition with Unequal Parallels* (1988), *The Bodiless Beauty* (1993), and *Pupa Russa* (2004) and of the journal *The Body Knows More* (2006). He also published volumes of essays, including *With the Open Guard* (1997), *The Postbellum Literary Experiment* (1998), and *Downgrading* (1999). To these creative undertakings he added two volumes of literary theory, *Introduction to Literary Theory* (1997) and *The Iceberg of Modern Poetry* (2002).

Crăciun often focused on two themes in his writing: corporeality and scripture. In his last novel, *Pupa Russa* (a Romanian rewriting of Flaubert's *Madame Bovary*), the two themes entwine, illuminating a universe in which vitality and beauty are eroded by decadence, neurosis, and the threats of an aggressive quotidian.

FROM *THE BODY KNOWS MORE*

MARCH

I am not a writer driven by the search for the exact word, for that which the French call *le mot juste*. I was not granted this happiness. Neither precision nor exactitude is my problem, but the total sum, totality. A first handicap: I cannot get past the multiplicity of the real. A second: I do not know how to see essences. Actually, they do not interest me, because I am not convinced that they exist. The motivation for and the fissure in my writing are of an ontological nature, and I do not think that this happened from the beginning, from the moment in which I knew that I wanted to be a writer. I had to experience many failures and desperate situations to come to this point. In the beginning, I thought that language was everything, that truth, the credibility of the world, rested in language. I thought that language had a poor structure, that it had to be remodeled, even syntactically. It seemed to me that two languages existed; the second, the literary one, being hidden within the first, the everyday one, but only as potentiality.

In the poetry that I made until I was about twenty-five or twenty-six years old, I did seek, it's true, the exactitude of the world, its denotative strength, but also a syntax of actions, of gestures, a procedural syntax. At the time I was missing substance, I did not really know what to write about. Sensation seemed enough. Everything that was in my near vicinity, everything that was related to the crass banality of my existence satisfied me. I expected that revelation would spring from this space. I thought that in that space hid truths that no one had seen which could not be discovered or understood through thinking, but only through poetic speech. Not even now have I made much progress regarding the things about which I feel that I must write. However, I discovered at a given moment that I would like to make of my craft a mode of exhausting that which comes into contact with me. I use the word *exhaust* in its full, definitive sense.

Nevertheless, writing shows me that literature cannot be about precisely this, that literature is implacably a purification, a metonymy. And then I have a tendency to retreat into spaces such as this notebook, sheltered from the shortcomings of imagination, of description and narration. A certain fatigue in the construction of subjects and in the delineation of spaces of exploration becomes evident. It is not as if I do not have the patience. To me, it would seem pointless from the start. My books up until now express, when you come down to it, an inability. The real, much like the imaginary—which is nothing more than a real constructed somewhat more freely—is indestructible, is invulnerable. Its variety and processes cannot even be touched. Not to speak of the full realization of these features!

The prosaists of the French New Novel have proposed to themselves the dismantling of the real in a manner that is much more technical than I have ever attempted to be, in texts of a horrifying consistency and power of aspersion. The result? A literature of sad futility, the proof of a crushing defeat.

That which the world admires in a writer is his power of self-destruction. *How could he have written something like this and not have died?* When a writer dies, the apparent regrets hide, in fact, a satisfaction: *It finally happened. He wasn't an Übermensch!*

Double-dealing, cowardice, duplicity, dissimulation, in order to be understood, all require the existence of those who write. They shouldn't marvel too much that the writer is a monster. He is precisely the monster hidden in every man. Only the writer is capable of finding our secret identity. As for the fictionality of writing, this is a convention that is necessary to make the monstrosity acceptable. [. . .]

I write in order to seek some limits, but writing has no limits. I write to replace my continuous interior nebulosity, but writing cannot be replaced by anything. I write so as not to be a mechanical brute, but writing scours my instincts. I write in order to protect myself from my own pulses, but writing brings me an even more painful frustration. I write, and I can no longer regain my lost teeth. I write, and I feel more and more ugly, more immoral, more irresponsible. Nothing pleases me while writing. Writing is insatiable, is a horrible wish to surpass the human, to palpate something of the monstrosity of your own being. I write so as not to hide, and I dress in veils, allusions, thick strata of untruths and speculation. I write because death is coming; I foresee it and in some states I desire it. I write also because I can no longer love or because I am ashamed of myself. I write so as to be able to be silent and more; and in fact, I stir about me a barren din, of no use to anyone. I write because often I feel like an idiot, incomplete, a guy who does not deserve his punishments, a guy annulled by others' books. I write so as to repossess life, but life is not repossessed through writing.

I write to her, to a woman. You can only write to a woman. The rest is desolation and literary history. "I write so as not to go mad," "I write so as not to forget," "I write because I fear," "writing is physiologic," "writing is the only thing left that allows a minimal authenticity"—pop songs. I am afraid of my obsessions, that's why I write. I don't even know what a true obsession means, that is why I write. I am not capable of risking everything for an obsession and so I fool myself writing. I write and my youth is definitively lost. I write so as to show that this is unbearable. Writing never saved anyone. But the refuge found in its illusion gives me a feeling of betterment, of more safety every time. Yes, tens of thousands of pages can be written throughout life, but only about one subject: you, yourself. I do not write in order to be myself. Such a thing is impossible through writing. Writing is scattering, destruction, vanity, illness, sleep, trance. But also an attempt of the body to unite, at last, with the mind. [. . .]

Translated by Carla Baricz

Floarea Țuțuianu

(b. 1953)

Graduate of the Nicolae Grigorescu Art Institute in Bucharest, the painter and draftsman Floarea Țuțuianu has published a number of volumes of poems: *The Woman Fish*
(1996), *Libresse Oblige* (1998), *The Marcu Lion* (2000), and *The Art of Seduction* (2002).

Utilizing "words razed with a thin ankle" but also straightforward speech, Țuțuianu
attempts to capture the image of the woman "with a thousand and one faces," of the
woman capable of play, handling with pleasure and ambiguity all manner of scenes
of seduction and eroticism, though also aware of suffering and of the possibility of an
authentic religious existence. (*Translated by Carla Baricz*)

THE ART OF SEDUCTION

Ear doesn't hear me. Eye sees what it believes
Tongue doesn't obey. Time is against me

Somebody comes leafs through me goes away.
Somebody else comes
Tramps all over me waits. The last to come
shall also be the first who:
Puts a finger on his tongue then riffles through me
Page by page: only sophisticated words with a model's legs
He sees in color everything moves. Let him lead us on

I prolong it through words. Only milk and honey
He squeezes me between pages. He wants to know so much more
I pour a little poison. Just enough to. O bathe it in words
I stay on his brain on his tongue. I spew fire and pearls from my mouth

Loneliness gets transmitted from me through oral contact

He turns pensive. Sees blue. Is someone else
Wants to capture me alive. Skin me
I scream discreetly disappear with easy elegance between the lines

Ear doesn't hear me. Eye sees what it believes
Tongue doesn't obey. Time is against me

LA FEMME POISON

Tarted up
and dragged down by thought
secretly polishing a solitude of dreams
Yes. I'm a body who flings herself at words

The fresh smell of paper, ink
makes me giddy. When I read
I can multiply by means of spores

Pencil in my hand I caress you
and take your breath away
(so flower-like yet carnivorous)

Even now you won't leave me
with my face washed by words on the knife-
edge of the tongue—
when the last verse loses its way

Translated by Adam J. Sorkin & Irma Giannetti

Alexandru Muşina

(b. 1954)

A graduate of the Faculty of Philology in Bucharest, Muşina worked as a French teacher at a school in a rural area. He also grew and sold flowers. In 1990 he became editor of a literary journal and a professor at the University in Braşov; and in 1997 he founded a publishing house in the same city. His incisive and polemical writing in the press is partially collected in the volumes *Synapses* (2001), *The Letters of a Pheasant* (2006), and *The Letters of a Marine Genius* (2007). He is also the author of insightful works on poetics: *Where Poetry Stands* (1996) and *Essay on Modern Poetry* (1997). His main literary activity is that of a poet: *104 Castle Street* (1984), *The Things I Have Seen* (1992), *3 Mimosa Alley* (1993), *The Tomography and Other Explorations* (1994), *Personae* (2001), *Even Animals Are People* (2002), *Hinterland* (2003), and *King of the Morning* (2009).

A promoter of the poetry of the everyday, Muşina places ordinary scenes in a hyperreality populated by fantastic or nightmarish figures. Under the influence of postwar American poetry, Muşina employs the form of the long biographical poem, in which the lyrical voice oscillates between elegy and sarcasm.

The Poetry of the Everyday

1981

Let's face it, we have grown somewhat wary of oracular poetry. The gods in whose name it claims to speak do not exist. We have grown wary of mercenary poetry, the poetry of buffoons who sing of the peasant and wheat fields from cafés and editorial offices in Bucharest; of the poetry of the pranksters who drive around in a Mercedes but claim to know the value of a 100-lei bill; of "hermetic" poetry, a product of the incapacity to feel and express emotion, as well as of that of the *proletkultists* who "converted"—for good? one wonders—in order to keep themselves in the cultural moment as much as possible. A sclerotic poetry that has become a token of presence or a shiny trifle in exchange for which one demands all the goods of the earth; a poetry in which—beyond the transparent film of words—the blood of everyday life does not pulse.

That is why I propose that we talk about the poetry of the everyday. That is, a poetry about our ordinary life which, at the same time, can also express the poetry in this life. Modest as it may be, tiring and always too short, but the only life we have or will ever have.

Of course, one may write in any way about anything; personally, however, I cannot understand poetry in any other way than as an attempt to give meaning and beauty to my life in the here and now. Of which 99 percent is represented by the banality of the everyday. The historical event itself is only the keystone of a "building" made up of thousands of ordinary moments, it is a social nexus, a "hotspot" of collective existence, which does not necessarily coincide with the high points of individual existence. But poetry deals precisely with our poor being, with inner events.

Such poetry also represents, if you will, a revenge of the spirit against the haphazardness of birth, which favors, socially speaking, some over others from the start. It is an intrinsically democratic reaction—on an existential level—of affirming the absolute that is to be found in each human being, beyond the inequalities which force, opportunism, and social structures generate.

It is, at the same time, an anthropocentric reaction of recuperating the integrality and coherence of the human being—a being "scattered" by the techno-scientific revolution and the numerous fanaticisms born out of the unilateral treatment applied to its victories.

The departure point for the poetry of the everyday will inevitably be the rediscovery of one's own corporeality, the control—through words—of one's own sensations. Which are not the same as those of our forerunners. The victories of technology caused an expansion of our various senses, a change in the relations among them; the pace at which one perceives exterior stimuli as well as their nature changed rapidly over the last fifty to one hundred years. We live in a world of sensations, a world that we are barely beginning to know. Words themselves no longer designate the same sensorial realities, which is why they need to be "retested," together with their contexts.

It should not come as a surprise, then, the strong sensuality—sensoriality, one could say—in the poems of the most gifted young people, a sensuality that sounds vulgar, even obscene to more "refined" ears. There is here, in this pan-sensorialism, a need for authenticity, because any imaginary construction risks appearing insipid and fastidious in the absence of a fresh sensorial "basis."

Automatically, there comes a reverse determination: the poet must write about the immediate reality because we cannot know sensorially anything outside our objectual field. Hence, it strikes me as normal that the metaphorical-objectual system of the poet—who generally lives in the city—comprises "the concrete with trolley buses" rather than "the field of flowers."

Talent matters, of course, and Eminescu is still Eminescu, but we must not forget that he wrote a poetry of his existential universe, of his time; we ought to think about our time. The chance of eternity passes through the ephemeral and the particular. And, in the end, what matters is what you want: to be called a poet or to express as much and as poignantly as you can what you think and feel?

A poetry of the contemporary world will be, implicitly, political, because interdependences have become infinitely more united and more complex. A decision taken by a certain individual one hundred or ten thousand kilometers away can directly and almost instantaneously determine my "intimate and personal" life. It will not be about bellicose declarations, which belong to a submissive rhetoric, but about an almost visceral rejection of everything and everyone who forces their way into your soul.

The poet can no longer ignore anything that takes place around him; at the same time, one can no longer invest the poet with a special status, from the outside. The poet will only speak in his name; he no longer is, a priori, a representative. He may perhaps become an exponent, who expresses as well as he can what his fellow beings are also feeling yet cannot express as well. A cure of modesty after which poetry will recapture its force and its bygone social status.

A poetry of the everyday means, at the same time, also the "poetry" in the everyday, the miraculous concealed in the banality of everyday life. The modern individual lost his "imaginary paradises"; he can no longer believe in the sacred time and sacred space that oriented and valorized the existence of individuals with an archaic mentality. But to sacralize means to valorize, to signify; and man cannot exist outside these, he is horrified by formlessness, by chaos. The sacred does not disappear, it melts, it hides in the profane. Under the crust of habits, of routine, of worn-out words, there bubbles a wondrous world of sensations and feelings, "a spellbound reality"; the poet will discover (or stage) true epiphanies of the banal. All of these exist in us. At sixteen, while strolling with a young woman, did we not indeed have spiritual sensations—and not just spiritual—that were infinitely bigger than the ones we have at twenty-six (or at thirty-six, forty-six, etc.) when we make love, even to the most beautiful woman?

However, the everyday is, you will argue, often dirty and shallow. That is because we cannot see beyond our own exhaustion or indifference. A true poet of the everyday will show us "the suspended gardens" in the utility closet of a blasé soul. More so, by not ignoring or condemning it, but by trying to understand and valorize it, the poet humanizes the super-technologized world we live in (and which, quite honestly, no one would give up), he tames— by naming them—"demons" with strange names—Alienation, Monotony, Reification, etc., etc.

How to recognize the poetry of the everyday? It is quick, ironic, inventive, "sincere" and direct, deprived of prejudices but not of a secret prudishness, unpredictable, above all: an image filtered through fresh sensors the lucid and hot minds of the world in which we are learning how to live. [. . .]

Translated by Raluca Manea

Marta Petreu

(b. 1955)

Graduate of the Faculty of History-Philosophy of the University of Cluj, Marta Petreu (born Rodica Marta Crişan) taught high school. After 1990, she was editor of a monthly magazine and of a publishing house. She is the author of a number of philosophical studies: *Unfinished Theses* (1991), *The Games of Logical Mannerism* (1995), *An Infamous Past: E. M. Cioran and the Rise of Fascism in Romania* (1999), *Ionescu in His Father's Country* (2001), *Caragiale's Philosophy* (2003), *Parallel Philosophies* (2005), and *The Devil and His Apprentice: Nae Ionescu–Mihail Sebastian* (2009). She is better known for her poetry: *Bring the Verbs* (1981), *The Morning of Young Women* (1983), *Psychic Place* (1991), *Imprudent Poems* (1993), *The Book of Anger* (1997), *Apocalypse after Marta* (1999), *Phalanx* (2001), and *Jacob's Ladder* (2006).

In a convulsive and anguished medium of revolt and self-deprecation, the poet often speaks of love, longing, and a God who cannot protect those who believe in him. As any great poet (she is considered one of the most important Romanian poets alive today), Marta Petreu seeks out and unflinchingly descends into her own self, though never at the expense of the sidereal heights she explores to write a poetry of "ferocious beauty."

The Ladder

I descend. It is an abrupt almost vertical ladder
There is the sea. The sea is the color of blackberries
the sea is the color of tar
I descend. Step by step
sucked into the depths. I descend
Feeling with my sole the narrow stone stair

I descend. I descend against my will
Against my wish and my reason
I descend. Suffering I descend into my own vision

I no longer remember what is above. I know that down is dampness
blood and tar. Down is the absence of forgetting
and so of forgiving
From horror
the fleshy muscle of the heart has balled up like a hedgehog
from horror
the fleshy muscle of the heart is heavy like a stone

I descend. I have nothing more to wait for—I tell myself:
The ladder that reaches to heaven descends for me

Night Letter to Tame My Beloved

In order to still be able to tell myself something,
I must do it under the masked form of verses
and even then it's not certain that what I write will reach you
(the experience with the manuscript of *Psychic Place* was telling
isn't that so?)

(In any case, your reaction to my volume remains stupefying:
even if one poem offended you and another wounded you
you had before you a volume of poems
the book of a poet—poet free of quotation marks
and free of your supposition that I was somewhat delirious
even now as I write on this typewriter these lines that irritate you

and which are neither poem nor letter

You didn't love my *Verbs* and you didn't love my *Morning* written always
     for you
you can't stand the *Psychic Place* in which I find myself
and from which—if I will escape—I will have to escape by my own wit
And if *Psychic Place* will appear I will dedicate the first copy to you
But only after I will have glued all the pages together with bone glue
nontoxic of course
so that you won't be able to read one verse of those wonderful verses
which—all of them—I wrote for you

about you
about me through you
so that you will never be able to read me like I am
     poet-in-love-to-the-death-with-you-like-I-am
And if I leave go ahead and glue your own book
like you glue envelopes and stamps: minutely, delicately, with care
with no shadow of impatience
I hope your hands won't tremble)

As for the poem to Castalia it doesn't exist any longer: I assassinated it
on that Thursday anniversary
I ripped it into tiny tiny shreds the size of your stamps
Because: even if all the good poets in Romania
decided to write verses only for you
you still wouldn't have the right to hit me: like a professional boxer
with bad intentions: meaning in the full light of my eyes and of my
     woman-in-love's devotion

And even if I now write these lines to you on the typewriter
with my tears fogging my glasses and trickling finely pulverized
on the keys:
everything means the same thing
(I could write you a verse in a hurry
about how everything comes to dust
even love
But it would be a lying verse because my love is not over
and I have come to dust but not it)

A woman who loves must be a great pest
for the beloved man whose love has gone to the devil
isn't that so?
Who traces your skin with her hands? I asked myself one day
sitting in a sort of straightjacket (comfortable, in fact)
and with a wall before me

But the wall is between us
Everywhere there are only poorly painted well-built walls
good night
marta

Translated by Carla Baricz

Ion Mureşan

(b. 1955)

After graduating from the Faculty of History-Philosophy at the University of Cluj, Mureşan taught history in a rural school before becoming a newspaper and journal editor. Reserved in terms of editorial appearances, Mureşan has published only two volumes of poetry, *Winter Book* (1981) and *The Poem That Defies Understanding* (1993), and one volume of essays, *The Lost Book: A Poetics of the Trace* (1998), all very well received by critics. A poet and visionary often likened to Rimbaud, Mureşan experiences poetry as a form of madness or damnation, likening it to a "rabid bitch" or a "skinless woman." The damned, demonic power at work in the poet pushes him toward nightmare, hallucination, apocalypse, or extreme satire.

LIFE UNDONE BY POETRY

Poisoned verse, slow-worm, sing of how you've glued your repulsive
lips to my lips.
Your words scoured by scabies, smothered by lice,
your whore words
bite the breasts of young ladies, bite the grizzled hair
on men's chests,
bitch pups, you've maimed my loves,
you've sapped my life, you've scattered the honey of my days
on the tongue of the shameless!

Not the critics, not the literary reviews, not the subtle scholars
will get you,
but the dog catchers, the exterminators, the Department of Health, the
        Secret Service
the dermatologists, gynecologists, for them,
one by one, you will become a means of fulfilling work.
As for me
you've sapped my life, you've scattered the honey of my days
on the tongue of the shameless.

THE POEM THAT CANNOT BE UNDERSTOOD

I am working on the poem that cannot be understood.
It is a black and shiny stone
from which the coarse hair of thirty-three beasts
suddenly begins to grow;
It is the green swamp that stretches out across the town square—
from its reeds howls softly, fawningly a lonesome fox;
It is the wooden bride (a wonderful bride
of wood!)—the hunted dress,
the mouth of herbage,
the whimper covering the window like a white muscle;
It is the grotto in the sky and the cloud of blood that growls

in the grotto in the sky;
It is the murder of crows that circles with delight
around the forehead,
the black hoarfrost of my forehead: the tongue in my mouth is cold
like ice, and almost brittle
like a decoration awarded by God
to the prophets;
It is the wine that turns to sand in your mouth.

O, times when our home flowered on the shore
of a slippery language!
When words issuing forth from speaking tree hollows,
would climb the walls like snails . . .
Then the mild, dusty archives of the madhouse,
where I examined the marks invented by madmen,
where I compiled one of their great histories,

which I was never able to read,
having written it just so, in those dry marks.
That is why I have included it in the poem
that cannot be understood.
I see the head, round like a gold balloon
pulling away over the tall shelves.

I hear the waves of the sea crashing against the walls
of a tall and yellow warehouse
and almost old, almost bowed over,
with the halo folded under my arm,
I get in line, after hundreds and hundreds of people,
to be able to see, maybe now, toward the end of my days,
the healing poem,
the poem that cannot be understood.

Translated by Carla Baricz

Magda Cârneci

(b. 1955)

Following the completion of university studies in art history in Bucharest, Cârneci
worked as a curator and then as a researcher at the Institute of Art History, publishing
a number of monographs consecrated to important Romanian painters. After 1990,
she received a doctorate in art history in Paris, which is at the origin of her influential
book *Fine Arts in Romania: 1945–1989* (2000). In 2001 she settled in Paris, where she
worked in higher education as a lecturer of Romanian. Since 2007 she has been the
chair of the Romanian Cultural Institute in Paris. As a writer she used the pseudonym
Magdalena Ghica until 1990, at which point she returned to her real name. She is a
promoter of postmodernism in Romanian literature—her essays and programmatic
texts being collected in *The Art of the Eighties: Texts on Postmodernism* (1996) and *Poetrix:
Texts on Poetry and Other Essays* (2002). She is also the author of the poetry collections
Hypermatter (1980), *A Deafening Silence* (1985), and *Chaosmos* (1992). Cârneci writes a
type of poetry that combines the pathos of lucidity with acute sensitivity, a poetry that
takes as its starting point everyday life and which, while seeking "to cast light onto the
bloody insides of today" leads toward a cosmic, visionary state put in the service of a
relentless spiritual quest.

I Am Not So Sure

For a while I thought that writers from Eastern Europe held a type of capital or monopoly on suffering over their colleagues from the West. First, on historical suffering—that goes way back, given all the empires and the wars that continuously fragmented and reconfigured this unstable and uncertain territory, with its flexible geometry and variously assigned names, based on opposite and contradictory geostrategic logics. Then, a monopoly on political suffering, more recent—for were these writers not the subjects of a bizarre totalitarian experiment on a continental scale, the patients of a well-known social engineering practice that wanted at all costs to produce a "(very) new man" and even managed it? This recent man, without memory, without history, the man subjected down to his very cells to fear and party imperatives, the man lobotomized by censure and self-censure, hypnotized by the "bright future" and the dross of the everyday to the point of forgetfulness and loss of self. Finally, the monopoly on moral suffering since, while exposed to this far-reaching as well as brutal and primitive pressure, the writers from the East often felt betrayed and forgotten by the more fortunate writers from the West, with respect to whom they developed ambiguous complexes of inferiority and superiority related to their supposed sacrifice for a noble and idealist vision of Europe. Now I am no longer sure about this monopoly.

It is rather strange to claim a superiority of suffering, be it quantitative, of intensity, or qualitative. All people and all societies have their share of suffering in forms difficult to compare and at distinct, unexpected times, but the final sum is probably almost equal for all. It is the slag of painful internal and external constraints, the corrosive acid of tensions among contradictory determinants, individual as well as collective. Is recent suffering superior to the suffering of the two world wars and of previous wars on the old continent? Is collective suffering superior to individual suffering or vice versa? What about the suffering endured in a passive, helpless, and cowardly fashion when compared to the active and reactive suffering, a consequence of one's resistance to injustice, of a defensive action, the result of a legitimate reaction? And how can unconscious suffering be construed in relation to that which passes through the filter of reason, through the necessity of recognizing, acknowledging, and taking responsibility?

If Europe had an expectation from its eastern part, it would consist in the realization of the specificity of our suffering in a lucid and mature manner, its rendition through an adequate and profound language; it would be the transformation of this suffering from a regressive and often paralyzing cultural obsession into a well-structured "cultural subject" with resonances in today's world, into an "object of understanding," of committed action and of everyday mental and psychic vigilance. All in a manner comparable to that in which the terrible experience of the Holocaust was transformed into a painful yet necessary constant of lucidity in the European psyche, through decades-long efforts made by numerous Jewish and non-Jewish writers and intellectuals. Will the writers of Eastern Europe be capable of being persuasive when it comes to the ontological evil that the experiment of the "new man" really produced in utopian European humanism, will they be able to propose a manner of surpassing it? Will they be capable of convincing the societies to which they belong that there is always a need for anamnesis, as difficult as it is salutary, so that an important clarification over human nature may be definitively secured in the European psyche? I do not know, I am not so sure.

For a while I believed that Eastern European writers held a type of monopoly of the soul or of the spiritual over their Western colleagues. For in the world we come from it is not yet ludicrous to speak of "the soul," it is not yet ridiculous or anachronistic to invoke "the spirit." The religious still has its place in the emotional economy of Eastern Europeans. As is the case with the empathetic link with nature and the universe, as of yet unevacuated from the cyclical rhythms of individual and collective life. "The care for one's soul"—for the soul that is hurt, humiliated, destroyed by political and social forces that are too large, but also the care for the soul that is capable of opening itself to states of exceptional grace, to superior functioning levels, to the cosmic vibration—this care seems to remain a constant of Eastern European writing, more so than in Western European writing. But I am no longer sure of this monopoly.

In a way, it is strange and impossible to believe that, from now on, great European literature will not let itself be nourished, circulated, fertilized by an involved trade with the emotional. It is only the temporal progress in a civilization that wishes to become more independent from nature, only a more pronounced stringency in rationalizing the processes that constitute us individually and those that bind us to our peers which can give the impression of a "forgetting of the soul," of its transformation or its loss. Then, perhaps, what we see in the case of Eastern Europeans is a temporary or an enduring desynchronization due to historical circumstances vis-à-vis an ongoing, apparently inevitable evolution of the European human state toward a more rational form of existence and functioning: an Eastern-phase different from the present turn of Western evolution, with its obvious dangers of "losing oneself" through social bureaucratization, hyperstress, professional mechanization, and the mass production of the "mass Übermensch" in a Nietzschean sense, fallen and corrupt.

If there is a phase difference with regard to "the emotional," "the soul," or "the self" between the eastern and the western parts of the continent, then the cultural mission of Eastern European writers would be to convince anew their western peers of the necessity of the spiritual for our fulfillment, suffering human beings that we are, and for a coherent and communicative collective metabolism. This mission would consist perhaps in having Eastern European writers demonstrate through their writing the possibility of a superior form of the emotional, decanted through reason and yet productive on a profound psychic level, replacing the religious but quenching nonetheless our thirst for spiritual fulfillment. Something along the lines of what the Czech philosopher Jan Patočka was saying with regards to the necessity of the "care for one's soul" and the resuscitation of the "spiritual man" through a "large philosophical metanoia, without precedent, of the European elite"; or, in the manner in which the Romanian philosopher Constantin Noica spoke of the constitution of a "cultural eschatology," a form of "transcendence without transcendence," in which cultural creativity is seen as a "secular esoterism" and a modern version of sacrality. Will Eastern European writers be capable of resisting the pragmatic, skeptic, secular media, and the materialist sirens, singing from the Atlantic Ocean of a humanity liberated from the slavery of feeling, of emotional reactivity, of religious protection, of spiritual quest? I do not know, I am not so sure.

It is all a matter of nuance but also of force, of perspective and of relativity, of individual synthesis and of personal, creative irruption. The mere fact that I am posing these questions probably shows that I come from Eastern Europe. If there is an expectation, it is double: it is not only the European expectation of Eastern European creativity, but also, mainly, our expectation of ourselves, of what we can and should extract, distill from our own individual and collective history, filled with suffering and spiritual quests. And perhaps this triple or multiple expectation has come into being already, with the fast-paced globalization that we are witnessing and in which we inevitably participate, for we will have to compare our traumas and our spiritual victories with ever-evolving historical experiences, with exotic spiritual traditions, with distant cultural codes. Perhaps more so than conforming to a European expectation, we will soon have to muster the courage to develop a consciousness, a perspective, a global vision of ourselves and of the world. And, who knows, even a cosmic perspective. Will we be capable of one, mentally and psychically, scripturally and stylistically? I do not know, I am not sure of it yet.

Translated by Raluca Manea

Mariana Marin

(1956–2003)

A graduate of the Faculty of Letters at the University of Bucharest, Marin worked as a
teacher in a country school as well as an editor for journals and publishing houses. She
is the author of the poetry collections *A Hundred Year War* (1985), *The Secret Wing* (1986),
The Workshops (1990), *The Mutilation of the Artist as a Young Man* (1999), and *The Golden
Dowry* (2002). Exhibiting strong criticism of the totalitarian regime, the collection *The
Secret Wing* was severely censured and could only be released after the lyrical voice was
re-attributed to Anne Frank, the teenage victim of Nazism. In addition to social themes,
Marin frequently uses eroticism, showing that both society and eros can generate
despair, "a ferocious solitude," and the inability to communicate. Her work expresses
itself forcefully through the pathos of confession and through a simple yet vibrant
language.

KITTY (OR THE GREAT FEAR HAS COME)

I never cared much for objects, dear Anne.
Even though I am a "Diary" and my name is
Kitty because you decided so.
And I never understood in living beings
the feeling of dominion over objects.
I live, I am alive, but above all I am an early riser.
And toward evening, here, in the attic,
where, in turn, I am not allowed to make a sound
when you talk to me,
I hear small steps about the guillotine
which, I know, could be waiting for you beyond the window.
Then I jot everything down
and know that someday I will speak.

Translated by Raluca Manea

Mircea Cărtărescu

(b. 1956)

A graduate of the Faculty of Philology at the University of Bucharest, Cărtărescu worked as a teacher in schools in the suburbs of Bucharest, as editor of a literary journal, and, beginning in 1990, as professor at the Faculty of Letters at the University of Bucharest. He published vastly both in the daily press and in literary journals; some of his articles appeared in *Forever Young, Wrapped in Pixels* (2003), and *You Baron!* (2005). He is the author of the collections of poetry *Headlights, Shop Windows, Photographs* (1980), *Love Poems* (1983), *Everything* (1985), *The Levant* (1990), *Love* (1994), *Double CD* (1998), *Pluriverse* (2003), *Fifty Sonnets* (2003), and *Nothing* (2010). He has also written short fiction and novels, including *Transvestite* (1994), *The Dragons' Encyclopedia* (2002), and the trilogy *Glaring (Orbitor)*, comprised of *The Left Wing* (1996), *The Body* (2002), and *The Right Wing* (2007). He has published two volumes of his *Journal* (2001 and 2005) as well as the studies *The Chimerical Dream* (1992) and *Romanian Postmodernism* (1998).

A complex figure in contemporary Romanian literature, Cărtărescu enjoys a very warm reception from the critics. What contributes to this status is his unusual talent in employing all registers of the Romanian language (from the lowest to the most refined), his exceptional (visionary, oneiric, ludic) imagination, his capacity to scrutinize the abyss of the human soul, as well as his ability to rise to the metaphysical projections of the individual (all born from a desire to penetrate the meaning of "the most enigmatic word there is, *myself*"). In the universe of this work one finds a strange and unique mix of extreme vulnerability and vivid perception and expression.

A GIANT DROP OF WATER REFLECTING A CHIMERA

JANUARY 25 [1990]

The only four forces that can lead to a real book: suffering, solitude, paranoia, hysteria. Among them, I have not practiced paranoia, and everything pushes me to do it in *Orbitor*. Everything but the fact that . . . I am not paranoid. The other ones I know all too well.

AUGUST 17 [1990]

The writer is the only one who uses his life entirely. Nothing gets thrown out. And, at the same time, he meditates on its usage and the circle closes.

FEBRUARY 3 [1991]

When I write poetry I employ what could actually be called a technique of self-hypnosis: I focus my gaze (the word is a metaphor) in a way I cannot define toward a precise area inside my skull, more toward the occipital lobe. Thence comes—when it comes—the stream of image/word. I visualize configurations in space that sublimate instantaneously into description.

JULY 25 [1992]

Two successive blows have destroyed, almost entirely, the world of my writing. The first is marriage, adulthood, which are in turn a kind of symbol for something deeper, as if literature had been a mistress that I had cheated on, despised, and abandoned. In fact, solitude, unhappiness, and erotic frustration were the engine of the poetry "of my youth" and of my prose pieces (to a smaller extent). I am no longer alone and unhappy. I can no longer be that. When I wrote of poetry "let it go to the devil, I am more important than poetry" the spine of my writing suddenly fractured. Exactly at that moment, two or four years ago, I matured, I left my bloody adolescent skin to dry out in the dust of the road. *The Levant* and *Lulu* (it's stranger with *Nothing*, it does not feed on the energy that emanates from the place where rejected adolescence and assumed maturity intersect rather immaturely on an extremely thin, ironic, and cynical edge—a knife's edge; since there is a maturity of adolescence and a puerility of maturity) have their origin in a different area, since you can rescue yourself—fully, though?—and, by eluding the central source, rescue the pearl from between the valves of the shell. If solitude, unhappiness, and frustration—which are all three shadows cast by frustrated sexuality, barred through ugliness and neurosis—would be the only ones capable to invoke the state of self-satisfaction of the writer, then I would have to resign myself and never write again. But, on one hand, the suffering that comes from a not entirely satisfactory life did not disappear completely, but was only attenuated through the routine of life as a couple, and, on the other hand, there is in the depth of my mind a past wound—that went, it's true, into a latent stage—but not scarred at all, because the latter is still me in a way. And third, there is a literature of adulthood, less dramatic than the former, but more powerful, etc., etc. Thus, perhaps the first blow, albeit more serious, is not decisive and lethal but turns my writing from pain and boundless history, as in *P.d.A.*,[1] into a lace of nerves and veins, sketched out with slight, calculated, blasé, but not entirely gross mannerism.

About the second blow, elsewhere.

APRIL 12 [1998]

For three months now I have not written or thought about anything. The only awareness of my presence between these hard and colorful surfaces, through which I cannot put my hand—the hand: another hard and colorful surface—is the fear—not too dramatic in turn—that comes over me at times: in fact, what do I do? What is happening with me? I have given up for years (years, really!) everything that used to make me real. I have deliberately suspended my vital functions: for a few years, I have been in fact in an affective, intellectual coma and what's more: in a psychic coma that can be irreversible. Sometimes I am afraid, and then I suddenly see myself: a middle-aged man, dragged toward a different life and from there to another, a man with a closed life, who does not have to fight for new territories any longer, but only to preserve the old ones, contested by others and often wrested away.

---

1. *P.d.A.*—abbreviation for Mircea Cărtărescu's *Love Poems* (1982).

SEPTEMBER 20 [1998]

I have never written my life. I was always the enemy of the autobiographical. What I wrote was everything that I could imagine to be more distant and disconnected from my life. Sometimes I got so far, however, that my writing, curved like Einsteinian space, caught up with my life on the other side of the hypersphere and became one with it. A few pages from my journal and from *Orbitor* are written life and live writing.

DECEMBER 13 [1999]

The most important thing (perhaps even of the last decade) is that I have an unusual desire to write. I can hardly wait to start over again and for those two or three mornings a week—when I have quiet, coffee, my notebook, and my pen in front of me—to come. In November I suddenly felt that *Orbitor II* was taking shape—I am approaching the first hundred pages—and was starting to steam up out of a bit of madness, with a drop of the universe sprinkled on top like powdered sugar. I want to make this book, which is now *ce seul objet dont le néant s'honore* in my life and the steel lung out of which only my head comes out.

MAY 4 [2000]

Perhaps in focusing on writing, unable to think of anything but the books to come, we are like a pilot who means to keep the airplane on the runway as long as possible, another hundred meters and then another, faster and faster, but without ever thinking to pull the gear at last so that the plane can take off. Thinking solely of redemption through writing, we miss on the true chance that was perhaps given to us; we live in two dimensions, incapable of conceiving of a third.

JUNE 25 [2001]

Just as others are afraid of death and incurable diseases, I am afraid that I will fail *Orbitor*. I wake up with this fear and I go to bed with it. I know that *Orbitor* is only a book, that it is not my entire life, and yet the thought that I will not be able to bring it to an end is unbearable.

JANUARY 14 [2003]

Paste, glue, grease, a heavy and shameful cloacal dejection have lately been soiling the ventricles of my mind. Demons and aborted creatures appear to me. I cannot repress abject thoughts, an unworldly weight pulls me down. I can't understand what comes from there, from below. From my angel, from his large, white skirt an enormous caterpillar is hanging, with festering skin. I try to be myself, I put my iridium sword (my angel has a sword) through the flesh of the hairy rings. Blood springs forth, but the pincers do not let go. It is just like this: when I do not write, the hell inside me swells up and breaks loose. I would write so much and so efficiently in order to empty it all out, to get to the bottom of the pit, to clean it like a glass, to make it into a newly painted house in which I can live.

FEBRUARY 4 [2003]

I am at the most dangerous point in my life as a writer: the results of so many years of work and solitude rush over me from all directions, bringing me down with them, as if I would suddenly gain one hundred kilos. This makes my bones crack and my kidneys swim in fat. To take action without wanting the results of that action—but how can you defend yourself against those results? At a given moment you are pulled out of your corner and exposed to the public: a spider as big as a gorilla in an iron cage. All I can do—for as long as I can—is to hold onto my wits. If I curse a lot, all day long, I am angry and tormented.

SEPTEMBER 22 [2003]

The more rarefied life is, the heavier it gets because it fills up progressively with blanks. I try to pull myself up like a wounded boxer. I walk around in autumn trying to recover, not chasing after images like Allen (Julian sent me an autographed copy of *Howl*, which I will be careful not to give in turn to just anyone) but chasing after reasons to live. I have a happy family, a truly wonderful little boy, a lover increasingly close to me, I have a world that has not harmed me too much so far, although it will kill me eventually (*But cloudy, cloudy is the stuff of stones*). If I were not an author ("may they write my name on the tombstone . . ."), I would be one of the most accomplished men. Why is it always that which you love the most that sentences you to unhappiness?

Translated by Raluca Manea

Răzvan Petrescu

(b. 1956)

A graduate of the Medical School of Bucharest, Petrescu works as a doctor in hospitals around Bucharest and in dispensaries in the countryside. Since 1990, he has also been employed as a journal editor. He has collaborated on various reportages, essays, film critiques, fiction, and translations for several journals in Romania and abroad. He is an author of short fiction—*The Summer Garden* (1989), *The Eclipse* (1993), *On a Friday Afternoon* (1997), *Small Changes in Attitude* (2003), *Foxtrot XX* (2008)—and theater: *The Farce* (1994) and *Spring at a Bar* (1995).

Interested in the typology of fragile and outcast individuals, in the subject of failure, and in the theme of constraint and violence, Petrescu constructs a powerful and tense literary universe, impregnated with what one of his characters calls "an obsessive state of unrest."

To Write in Despair

I gave up my career as a doctor, ripped up my diploma, threw it in the trash, gave my tensiometer and sterilizing drum to some people who thanked me, and decided to start writing. Attempting to study another type of despair. Because by reading books, at least, no one expects to have their whitlow, their tuberculosis, their wife disappear, no one expects to be saved. At best, books can only irritate. I learned on my own how to type using the 1927 Blanche method. With ten fingers. I destroyed the typewriter. I bought a new one. To write. How to. Do it in a moment of crisis. As if the entire world were under siege. As if everything were to disappear in an hour or the following morning, at the latest, including the cactus on the desk that you have forgotten to water, your wife's photograph, taken on the shore of a lake, the city, the leaves and the sand in your mind. To write in despair. With stresses on each vowel, in bold, Kierkegaard font, size twenty, and especially with death before and behind you, watching, smiling like a supermodel, with time on the table—ticking, maintaining tension through small, white spaces, laced through ellipses, gradually rarefying the text in order to compress it later in a vise, to make it scream, giving it a fast tempo, *allegro molto e vivace*, panting in a traumatizing crescendo. Not to protect your reader, to make him suspicious, to make him sick, to leave marks on his face, his back, his eyes. Without pity. To keep scattering. It does not matter what, just keep scattering. To scrape. To bite, to break little metal pipes, pencils, to rip up pieces of paper, which you are to make into balls of paper and throw from your balcony at the heads of the children who aimlessly go to school and who look at you and curse. You should curse back, taking aim at them with empty yogurt jars. To write with determination, with fury, with hatred. Clenching your teeth. Cursing. Suffering from ulcers, digestive bleeding, neurosis, the Spanish flu, hemorrhoids, duodenal tubing. Delirious. To become delirious. And without showing it, to write with love, masking it with ten liters of ketchup thrown on top. *Hunter.* To write out of sheer, intermittent madness. Like a hunter. Out of exasperation. Writing. Freezing. Meanwhile losing sunsets, friends, beautiful women, foreign countries. Once I wanted to throw myself off of something, head down, I found a bridge, it was a bridge built by the Germans during the Second World War and left by the Romanians to fall into ruin, and a peasant with whom I had shared a bottle of grappa saved me by taking hold of my coat collar. He yanked it off. And I haven't bought another coat since. And my wife, who doesn't understand why that is. Why do I cry at old movies that nobody else cries at, why do I laugh when there is nothing to laugh at, why do I get drunk when the world is so beautiful? All around me.

Why am I always looking for something else?

Translated by Raluca Manea

Matei Vişniec

(b. 1956)

Graduate of the Faculty of Philosophy and History at the University of Bucharest, Matei Vişniec was a history teacher in a rural primary school. He began his literary career by publishing three volumes of poetry—*Tonight It Will Snow* (1980), *The City with a Single Dweller* (1982), and *The Wise Man at Tea Time* (1984)—and went on to write theater that could neither be staged nor published. In 1987 he left Romania and sought political asylum in France. He took up residence in Paris, where he worked as a journalist for Radio France Internationale. With the exception of the novels *The Pas-Parol Coffee House* (1992), *The Panic Syndrome in the City of Lights* (2009), and the volume *Ulterior Poems* (2000), Vişniec dedicated himself entirely to theater, writing both in Romanian and French. His plays have gained critical acclaim and are performed and studied both in his homeland and in France. He is known for *Clown Hiring* (1993), *Seer, Don't Be a Snail* (1996), *The Spider in the Wound* and *The Hole in the Ceiling* (1996), *Decomposed Theater: About a Woman's Sexuality—Battleground in the Bosnian War* (1998), *The History of Communism Retold for Mentally Ill Patients* (2001), *The Parisian Mansard with a View Toward Death* (2005), and *The Man with a Single Wing* (2006).

Influenced by Beckett and Ionesco, Vişniec cultivates hyperbole, parody, and tragic farce, combining fantasy, humor, the bizarre, the absurd, and the literary in order to depict the fragility and loneliness of the human being in love and in faith.

The Falling Crumbs

The falling crumbs from the poet's table of work
sometimes make a deafening noise
shouts are heard, thuds
an old woman faints on the curb in front of the poet's house
a man dies crushed under a rainy car

from the table of work of the poet
sometimes fall enormous crumbs, inadmissible
when the poet is tired the city itself goes mad
the artesian fountains freeze, the trams crash into walls
words themselves become rarer, harder to understand

before the word, silence is made an enormous tail
attention, there will not be enough for everyone yells the poet
even before the word *love*, which was over a long time ago
wait a few irreducibles, a few groups of tired tourists

perhaps these traces of blood
lead to the word *loneliness*, says the poet to himself
having gone out himself for a walk through the city riddled with absences
perhaps before the word, man are left to circle
only dogs

Like Clothes Grown Too Large

There are days when the words sicken
  of man
  of man's brain, of
  his mouth that bites at nothingness
  even of the word *man*, which
  whatever might be said
  is the source of all words

angered at their own source
words thus become unusable
like clothes grown too large
like the word *body*, which
becomes useless
with the burial of the body

sickened by what they are forced to say
the words all bury themselves in the ground
in the hot ground, swarming
from man's mouth

Translated by Carla Baricz

Carmen Firan

(b. 1958)

Graduate of the Department of Mathematics of the University of Craiova (1981), Firan taught math in rural primary schools and later worked as the editor of a newspaper. She was the executive secretary of a national cultural foundation, and in 1997 she became assistant director of the Romanian Cultural Institute in New York City. She moved to the United States in 2002 and is director of development of the New York branch of a Romanian patrimonial foundation. She has written theater, screenplays, novels (*Closer and Closer,* 1991; and *Farce,* 2002) as well as short stories (*The Heater Repairman and the Wife of the Hermeneutist,* 2005). However, she is best known as a poet and has published a number of critically acclaimed collections of verse: *Illusions Tried on One's Own Skin* (1981), *Paradise for Monday* (1983), *Tamer of Stolen Lives* (1984), *Clear Nights for You* (1988), *Purely Black* (1995), *Place to Live Alone* (1997), *Afternoon with Angel* (2000), and *In the Most Beautiful Life* (2002). Firan writes confessional poetry that centers on love and combines disquiet and anxiousness with irony and playfulness. (*Translated by Carla Baricz*)

FROM "THE POWER OF WORDS"

They say you sometimes dream your faith on solstice nights or following long stretches of meditation and spiritual initiation, or simply when the turmoil of searching becomes unbearable. At that time, I had no inkling I would become a writer. I was studying mathematics, which I gladly would have changed for stage directing, but the communist Eastern European world we were living in did not encourage dreams. The words imposed by the dictatorship would take up only two dictionary pages: empty slogans, preciosity with stiffener, political slogans, tortured syntagmas, emptied of meaning, the censorship of freedom of expression, and the like. A linguistic nightmare from which everyone escaped as he could. Artists would hide behind metaphors; ordinary people would murmur and curse. Some would make peace with the system and become megaphones of ideological emptiness; others would assume the loneliness of their own thoughts awaiting, more and more hopelessly, a liberating miracle.

We lived a double life, each in a different language. We talked in a certain way in public or when being watched, and differently among ourselves. Paradoxically, we were still *communicating*. Through that communication, we were surviving culturally and keeping mind and soul sane. Language had become a living animal, which would insidiously squeeze inside our cup of milk, inside our walls, and penetrate the design of our rugs. It flew—simulating freedom—from one window to the next, condensed, profound, intense, alert, and we cherished each word as our only hidden treasure.

What could be easier than talk; what is more natural than rolling words about your mouth? Nevertheless, we had become aware that what normalcy was for those beyond the Iron Curtain was a stance of vertical resistance for us. We were stealing words and carefully protecting their mystery and sanity. We couldn't afford to pauperize them; neither could we let them emerge at random. We each had only one life to live, and the obsession to leave something true and authentic behind translated into the importance of communication.

Paradoxically, again after the fall of the Berlin Wall, when the live animal was freed from the cage that imprisoned him for decades, words woke up confused and disoriented. They sprang up unchained and unclear, sniffing the new reality, adjusting their step and making unnatural leaps over abysses and lost history. The faucet was fully open, the fences torn down, the barbed wire was broken. Only the newly found freedom was difficult, and too few knew how to live it. It was there to stay, with all its fears and uncertainty, with the wild roaming of the language freed from official control. Some started to swim although afraid of water, some learned to fly although afraid of heights, others started to imitate the Western world we had so much longed for, swallowing its rules automatically, randomly, without chewing, wishing only to catch up and be like them. Language, kept for so long in the dowry chest and suddenly freed, lost its core and often its beauty as well. Communication became pragmatic and efficient for some, trivial for others. Now there was need for a different resistance on another aesthetic level, to avoid falling into another noisy inferno of emptiness, this time the emptiness of consumer society.

It seemed to me that the challenge being a writer now, just as then, was most inspiring, the perfect theater where the grace and pleasure of handling words and preserving their meaning changed to a tormenting duty. The roots of the tree would go deeper and deeper into my dream's soft soil; their tentacles would reach far into the guts of Earth, hiding small shiny rocks, traces of clouds, blue and purple molecules in which life was endlessly resurrected. You only had to dig, push the soil away. [. . .]

For more than thirty years I lived in the opaque world of communism, where time meant nothing. In the absence of any real dialogue within its social and political structures, all we had left was talking among ourselves. In that Balkan atmosphere, our conversations, sometimes brilliantly lit by a ruined "little Paris" on a molded sky, were delightful, baroque, a never-ending chatter, spectacular and useless, over full ashtrays and cheap alcohol, nightlong discussions and hung-over mornings when it would start all over again. We weren't in a hurry to get anywhere. We had no place to go. The dictatorship seemed permanent. To keep our sanity we only had words, the language, airy imaginative phantasms, grim existential critiques, fable-making, hairsplitting. Brilliant ideas or dashing banalities. Survival. Words were powerless to change our destiny, but therapeutic in keeping us sane. The Soul? No one mentioned it, but it was there all along, in the arabesque of our lamentations, in the last cigarette butt crushed at sunrise against the background of a hideous smoking factory on the outskirts of the city.

Time is everything in America. It is sold at each deli and hot-dog cart, on TV and by insurance companies, on slot machines and with Staten Island ferry tickets, in the *Have a nice day* greeting everyone utters automatically only to get rid of you quickly. Using concentrated formulas of conventional language does not stem from emptiness, but from fear of lingering too long in a syntagma that is not likely to bring anything new when weighed against *Have a nice day! Time is money.* The Soul? It is lying somewhere on a shrink's chair, or in the schedule of TV talk shows.

While inside the whale's belly, I quickly sketched the steps of loneliness: from the *chosen* isolation, where you have the revelation of your own interior beauty, to the *imposed* solitude, where you look at the tops of the buildings and can't see the stars because of the roofs; from *seclusion*, where a good book still keeps you warm, to *estrangement*, where the language becomes a power-less being, swallowed by the first carnivorous flower; and even further on, to *alienation*, where words lose their meanings and weight, the godly effort fails on a computer screen or in a cell phone you use only if there are people around to hear you.

Let's take this word that is overused in America: *love*, repeated until all that is left of it is a white bony phalanx pointing to the abyss. Over here everyone loves, from dawn to dusk, and no one is shy about publicly showing his or her love. Before hanging up the phone, after speaking with a close one, automati-cally out comes "love you," meaning actually more "talk to you soon." Love extends to objects, dishes, landscapes, and situations. People are often saying, *Oh, my God, I love this, I love that* . . . without nuance, ignoring the existence of synonyms (between *like, value, be attracted by,* and *love,* there is not only a difference in intensity but also a temporal one). And while the mouth fills up on the vowel *o,* the word disappears, its weight is canceled, the meaning lost. Love repeated carelessly and continually all over the place becomes worthless. Tolstoy probably would turn in his grave and give up throwing Karenina in front of a running train. Perhaps he would send her to a shrink and launch into an endless tirade on the harmony between *mind, body, and soul* in search of the *interior child.*

I can remember how difficult it was to articulate love words in my adoles-cence, the crazy pirouettes taken by our sentences, the way we weighed their intensity, graded their emotion, using an entire linguistic allusive arsenal. We were convinced that our inhibition was due to education and that it would be indecent to dispel the mystery and force of the strongest word by just randomly saying it, or that once said, we would awaken exposed and vulnerable, or we would strike pathetic chords. And what if, once uttered, the love words hit a wall? Of all humiliations, ridicule is the most shameful. Furthermore, we lived in a closed society where discussing sex was taboo, contraception was interdicted, and love was confounded by the Communist ideologues with either the party or reproduction. I feel like all this happened a hundred years ago. . . .

How easy it is today to deal with a sex party, although what a huge abyss separates sexes in big American cities, where having a career and/or *single* status are so highly regarded. At the end of the day, independent and liberated women and successful men sniff at each other, sitting in bars, exhausted from a harrowing workday, drinking cocktails and beer, laughing out loud, maybe too loudly, only to start this game all over again the next day. The chat is often very strident. What you say doesn't matter, only being heard, leaving the impression of detachment, sufficiency, self-confidence inside a solid system. If you look closer and put your ear to the words, machined-gunned from one to the other under the pressure of communication by any means, the loneliness is overwhelming, only the surface casing of motivations is shiny, only the polish blinding. *Love* is reduced to sterile linguistic automatism, incapable of sustaining the elevation of the divine word. *To love* becomes a common verb, said without any special emotional participation, an expired ingredient randomly peppered among ordinary recipes, without any savor.

Translated by Alexandra Carides
English editing by Maurice Edwards

Bogdan Ghiu

(b. 1958)

A graduate of the School of Philology at the University of Bucharest, Ghiu translates abundantly, mainly from French literary theorists. His published poetry includes *The Author's Handbook* (1989), *The Poem with a Meter-long Side* (1996), *The Art of Consumption* (1996), *Grams* (1997), *Archipelagos* (1997), *Trousers and Shirt* (2000), and *(The Cardboard Poem)* (2006). In 2008 he published *I, the Artist*, a collection of essays. The dominant theme is writing itself, pursued in the manner of its unfolding as well as in the dramatic nature of a total existential implication. Each poem is, in an ambivalent manner, both the safest refuge, the sole body of the writer, and the antechamber of death: "I write a poem with a meter-long side / from which I can jump."

"MADNESS" AND THE ART OF WRITING

Recently, in the context of a conference in Cluj concerning an author, Michel Foucault, whom I have worked on (primarily in translating him), a somewhat younger colleague of mine, Caius Dobrescu, usually thoughtful in his comments, drew a connection—in a serious, yet markedly pejorative and dismissive manner—between the French writer's dominantly critical, infinitely suspicious, and even "apocalyptic" views on modernity and the so-called critical paranoiac method of Salvador Dalí. Yet it seems to me that "critical paranoia" is—to put it bluntly—the source itself, the pulse and the impulse of *creation:* if certain malefic configurations of reality did not "come" to you, and if you did not also suspect the malicious existence of their "authors," why would you even step out of line and start writing, painting, shooting film, becoming yourself an "author" who seeks to be taken seriously and to impose a true reality? Without fear and indignation there is no *step toward creation* and no sign ("thorn," "nail," "gadfly") or possibility for art either, that is, the possibility to elaborate minute techniques, as efficient as possible, to "reestablish the truth." In our idealizing and disembodying purism, which has become an aesthetic means of pleasing—to which the de-virilization, de-empiricization, de-sensorialization, phobic de-sensitivization vis-à-vis the "impurity" of the *political*, imposed by communism, contributed infinitely—we ended up forgetting—and despising, by way of exclusion—the details and the "accidents" that push (awaken) us to creation. We would then lose, in this way, the very roots that art has in reality, in the "paranoid" revolts of true creators, always "angry at life."

The persecution that Leo Strauss was talking about, more than half a century ago, in *Persecution and the Art of Writing* does not exist—and ought not to be regarded as existing and ought not, consequently, to be left or expected to arise—solely under the guise of the persecution practiced, through censure, by the political. In order for us to hope that we will elaborate art, that is, techniques of efficient countercommunication, we have to "politicize" ourselves on our own, without waiting for the political to take the initiative. All the great authors of literary or philosophical works got started (on their work) and were supported in their toil by various "persecutions": "something" in their contemporary world was not working as expected and was not giving them peace, it was "persecuting them" by directly interpellating them and making them, in turn, interpellate their fellow beings. The decision and the capacity to let yourself be *affected* first—im-pressed toward ex-pression and, of course, publication—and, then, at length and as coherently as possible, to let yourself be "persecuted" by the world in which you live and the will to "reestablish the truth" with respect to the world—starting nonetheless from the immediate—constitutes the original (and *material*) motor in the process of creation. If he had not felt himself, *paranoically* so, to be directly targeted by the false heroism propagated by "chivalric literature," so well liked by the audience, Cervantes would not have set out to write *Don Quijote* [. . .] that is, to stage the weak, comfortable, sedentary fictional madness, which runs rampant on television today. We do not have to wait, as if ailing, the instauration of some totalitarianism or the fall into tyranny—or seek, unsatisfied, with hope for salvation, that others or catastrophe mobilize us!—in order to start to elaborate some calculated and inventive arts of communication "between the lines" of the actual state, of truth as it presents itself to us today. Great creators do not wait to be *driven mad*, they *drive* themselves *mad*, and *the construction* always begins with—and is sustained by—a counter *reaction:* the epistemic reaction, given that in all cases we are talking about truth. One cannot create without a goal-medium-support, by taking advantage, through infinite detours and "theatricalizations," of an existent and virulent force. Hence the impression of *vitality* and *good health* that the reading of great classics, who were all *combatants*, exudes. Literary technique is a technique of war. Otherwise we risk being driven mad by silence and dying of inutility. Non-revolted at what his fellow beings—"bewitched" by the mirage of "reality," which is staged, perhaps, by a Cartesian daemon—do not see, the writer does not take action, and his art (cubed, "matching words": among them, to reality and to the audience) eminently and generously *polemical* in a visionary way, stands apart from our arts of living, through which we manage to not go mad in life. The writer is a good therapist even based on the fact that he *identifies* and *proposes* causes for "the unraveling" of the world, mobilizing our hopes and giving us the impression that we can and have to fight, that we can take action.

Translated by Raluca Manea

Cristian Popescu

(1959–1995)

Scarred by the death of his father when he was a teenager, Popescu graduated from the Faculty of Philology at the University of Bucharest after irregular studies. He worked as a night guard at the Astronomic Observatory and, after the fall of the Communist regime—during which he felt "like an entire country (almost), one with the wooden mannequins on display in shop windows"—he became an editor at a literary journal. Suffering from a psychiatric condition (during his crises he "went to Hell"), he died unexpectedly in February 1995. Considered an exceptional poet of remarkable originality, Popescu published the poetry collections *Forward* (1988) and *Popescu Art* (1994). *Notebook for Reading and Calligraphy* (2003), consisting of materials from the manuscripts he left behind, was published posthumously.

The author used the form of the biographic prose poem, in which everyday life oscillates between two types of experience: a demonic one, involving nightmarish apparitions ("proof to my demonization, the vomit of sin") and a strong religious experience, thirsting for light and redemption, in which the human being addresses with desperate familiarity a protective God. The dramatic aspiration of this poetry is to depart from Rimbaud's formulation ("I is another") in order to regain something akin to the identity of divine nature ("I is He who Is").

GRUELINGLY SQUEEZED LIGHT

[. . .] (This is why I write: to wed myself, to conquer and ravage my loneliness, to embody it, so that it no longer exists as such; so that I no longer exist as such; so that something without person, gender, and number exists. I write for the same reason the world exists.)

I also write literature with the intention of forming myself (as much as possible), of cleansing myself (one step at a time) of the daily amassed sin; when you write for an entire life in order to leave the ballast, the dirt, and the filth of sinfulness on spiritually hygienic paper, "images" are often times *punishments:* sanctions that I alone apply to myself: imprecations of prophylactic distaste that trickle from the corner of my mouth down my chin. [. . .]

SELF-CONFESSION. I am guilty and sinful. I think about this and feel the yellow light of the lamp trickle into my eyes like yellow piss in urinals. This is all that I deserve. (*Here the readers break into thunderous applause. Cheers.*) My guardian angel fell from the skies, not because he had sinned, but because I was born. He is now my ghost that haunts the other world. And I am his ghost, who haunts this place, our place. I do not have the right to meet with him except in the visiting room of the poem. That is why I write. This is all that I deserve. (*The readers applaud for a long time. They chant: Po-pes-cu-Po-e-try! Po-pes-cu-Po-e-try!*) I will end up a mad and near-analphabetic hag, who goes to the National Library every day, asks for all of my books, lights a candle at their head and conducts masses for the absolution of their sins. A hag who does not even have a tomb on which to light a candle. I will end up a mad hag who believes that when she cut off her finger with the bread knife, my great-grandfather's finger grew back on; and who believes that she is Veronica Micle from the waist down.[1] This is all that I deserve to become: death. The mad hag to whom all graves are distant relatives, but who does not have any one grave as mother, grandfather, grandmother or father. (*Here the audience chants, after the well-known patriotic tune: Po-pes-cu, peo-ple, Ro-ma-ni-a / Po-pes-cu, E-mi-nes-cu, Po-e-try*). This is all that I deserve. And when I engage in these exercises in self-mutilation, I am proud because I engage in them. God, flush the water! Flush the water of Your tears over

---

1. Veronica Micle (1850–89)—poet; Mihai Eminescu's famous beloved and muse.

me! God, may the whirlpool of Your tears pull me to the bottom! The devil's chortle deafens me. This is all that I deserve. [. . .]

It is almost impossible for me to describe the vicious circle of doubt—motivated, for those around me—that a certain deed, gesture or look of mine, or a certain tone of voice is not produced by me alone, but also by my condition. I cannot examine myself enough to know how much of what I write is proof to my demonic possession, vomit of sin, of the contact with evil, and how much of it is light gruelingly squeezed from the struggle with darkness. I sometimes think that the "artistic value" of my texts is of no significance at all under theses circumstances. But what can one do? Society demands value, and the madman is—by definition—an asocial person. Therefore: "Let's go, Popescu, give us something of value."

I think it is hard to understand, for healthy people, what it is like to go through ten days and ten nights without sleep. Pure and simple: just as astronauts see the dark side of the moon, by not relaxing your mind for some time you reach—willingly or unwillingly—the unseen part of the mind. For a poet, for an authentic intellectual, the 4 percent out of what we generally use of our brain (through constant mental effort and contemplation) intersects in some way or another with the rest of 96 percent, generally left unused. In the case of the madman, in my case, these two regions intersect each other chaotically. And this happens particularly when I am having a crisis. (I have had three crises until now: one in 1981, another one in 1991, and yet another one in 1994—forgive me God Almighty and merciful, I was in hell three times. Take pity on me.) [. . .]

SUNDAY. Luminous night. The idea came to me (it came to me, I did not produce it) that I copy in my notebook, at the beginning of each "work" night—after I jot down date, time, and place—a psalm. In 150 nights, all the psalms would pass through the nib of my pen. And then I would start over. How gentle, how calming (but also profoundly taut in itself) is a copyist's toil! This morning-night I transcribed the first psalm. May God help me continue night after night! It is also a means of marking the everyday (regardless of the fact that the latter is, paradoxically, nocturnal to me). [. . .]

WEDNESDAY. A night of deep, deepened silence. My bone marrow is made of fresh honey, cold, invigorating. I am thinking again about the yellow or red vermouth that curdles in crystals. I wrote about angels last night. I read about the Eucharist. Now it is morning, but still dark out. It's past five. Outside the window electric lights are flickering all of a sudden, the lightning sparks of tramways. One begins to hear the city.

There is a cup of cocoa next to me. It's quiet. I almost pulled my dried, deformed mother's belly up to my chin. As usual, in the morning, after a night of work: the fugitive's guilt, the irritating sensation of desertion: I go to sleep as the city rises.

Translated by Raluca Manea

Ruxandra Cesereanu

(b. 1963)

A graduate of the Faculty of Letters of Babeş-Bolyai University, Cesereanu is a profes-
sor at the same university as well as editor of a literary journal. She is the author of the
poetry collections *Live Zone* (1993), *The Garden of Delights* (1993), *Fall over the City* (1998),
The Schizoid Ocean (1998), *The Woman-Crusader* (1999), *Venice with Violet Veins* (2002),
Kore-Persephone (2004), *The Forgiven Submarine* (with Andrei Codrescu, 2007), and
Coma (2008). She has also published several works of fiction—*The Purgatories* (1997),
Trikephalos (2002), *Nebulon* (2005), *The Birth of Liquid Desires* (2007), *Angelus* (2010)—and
essays: *Voyage to the Center of the Inferno, The Gulag in Romanian Consciousness* (1998),
Panopticon: Political Torture in the Twentieth Century (2001), *The Violent Imaginary of
the Romanians* (2003), *December '89: The Deconstruction of a Revolution* (2004), and
Romanian Vices (2007).

Practicing the lyric theme of masks (the woman-crusader and the courtesan being
among her favorites) that allows her to stage emotions, Cesereanu is interested in
excess and extremes, delirium and violence as means of attaining the "live zone," the
blood zone that alone is construed as authentic.

THE FLOODED SUBMARINE

2006

To me poetry is the condition that comes closest to the state of trance. I believe it is the only genre in which I try to cultivate—without artifice, coquetries, or rhetorical bite—a state of trance. That is to say, from inside the state of trance that ultimately has to do with delirium (hence the *deliriumism* that I theorized), my feeling is that, as a poet, I can become a kind of conduit through which the unconscious gurgles and a series of networks of communication with the world get established. But here, I will have to speak, one way or another, of the way in which I later attempted to build an image in order to make sense of my own poetry, to know why certain mechanisms exist in my poetry. The key image for the poetry that I write is that of the submerged and flooded submarine, a submarine that also has something to do with reason—the latter is not absent, it exists, but only as secondary to those alluvial and gurgling conduits of the unconscious. You will have to imagine this submarine submerged and flooded, with water first breaking through the exterior compartments, then getting to the center and eventually, the crew, drowned in its entirety, floating in the submarine. The idea of division and fragmentariness—when prose poems are not at stake—is probably very important for the transcription of this trance, which is ultimately a kind of scribe for delirium. Is this delirium a form of exorcising our incompatibility with the world, or our alienation, is it a form of communing with the world to which we belong, is it a form of therapy? I believe it is a bit of each. I am thinking, for instance, of a book of mine translated in the U.S. in 1997 and published in Romanian in 1998, *The Schizoid Ocean*. In this volume I found the formula with which to express myself via various characters in a hospice—the neurotic, the hysteric, the psychopath, the maniac, and so on. After I published this volume, someone made the following remark to me: in order to be authentic, in order for us to be certain that you were real when you wrote this book, you should have been committed to an asylum at the time, since only then would you gain credibility for what you did. In fact, this is not how things stand, and it is a mistake to conceive of them as such. I do not believe that we need to be interned in an asylum in order to be able to write about alienation, suffering, anxieties, neuroses, or psychoses. The fact that in real life we try to control these things through our will and to appear in front of others, in our visibility, as normal, is an entirely different matter. It does not mean that we do not have traumas or, as I was saying, neuroses. And it is perhaps through the state of trance (at least as far as I am concerned) that I express myself best, this trance being a bridge toward the reader, the most adequate passageway for me to channel what I have to say, more precisely, my three main themes, which are equally important: love, faith, and death.

Translated by Raluca Manea

Simona Popescu

(b. 1965)

A graduate of the Faculty of Philology at the University of Bucharest, Popescu worked as a Romanian language teacher in a rural school and as editor at a publishing house. She is currently an assistant professor at the University of Bucharest. Esteemed as one of the most important writers of the last decade, Popescu publishes poetry, including *The Xylophone and Other Poems* (1990), *Juventus* (1994), *Night or Day* (1998), and *Works in Green or My Defense of Poetry* (2006); fiction (*Exuvii,* 1997); and the essays *Volubilis* (1998), *On Surrealism and Gellu Naum* (2000), and *Clava: Critifiction with Gellu Naum* (2004).

The obsessive theme of the author is *juventus,* construed as a unique state that combines timidity and fierceness, fragility and unsuspected force in a young individual; according to the writer, it is only by investigating youth that one can reach the "fluctuating fog of one's multiple being" or arrive at the "core of the brain where states, images, voices unfold their nerve endings."

The Pact with Yourself: Opus or Life?

[. . .] The Opus! Such fascination . . . The Opus—devouring, colossal chimera that ruins lives. So many people haunted by indistinct torments, searching for immortality. Pseudonyms, heteronyms, characters, identities, selves, parts, words—a whole mechanism of illusion. The Opus—self-mystification, substitution, alienation. The Opus—lugubrious word: it comes in the place of life where the latter will have ended. Tombstone.

Life? Which life when speaking of a writer? Life according to résumés, dictionaries? The one recounted by the mouth of a stranger? Everyday life? Sleeping life? Life unfolding before witnesses? Without witnesses? That volatile substance that your senses and mind seize once in a while, could it be that? The rare sensations of perplexity when everything comes into focus? Or the moments when domestic happiness makes you as transparent and fresh as morning air? The life that is expressed or the tacit one?

There are human beings who make the connection between the chaos of metamorphic life and its crystallization into words. They take on the word "I"—the most mysterious, most disquieting of words. I thought a lot about the statement of a contemporary Romanian poet who used to say that "the poet, like the soldier, does not have a personal life." I believe that things are quite different, that the poet, rather, like the soldier, *has* a personal life. Unique, irreplaceable, specific, distinct. And, moreover, that he not only possesses the tragic awareness of this ephemeral singularity but also the torturing need to find expression, to see himself—the unknown, the unseen—to see himself regardless of what he would discover. However, what "personal life" means, what one understands by it, is to be found in books. For some—everyday meetings, stomachaches, gossip, trifles recorded in disillusioned journals. For others—fuzzy states, dreams, visions, confusions, everything that partakes of what Keats called "negative capability."

I never understood the advocates of the impersonal style, even the subtlest among them. One day I happened upon a sentence from Nabokov that touched me in the way in which (in my case, at least) only statements of a personal nature can: "Over and over again my mind has made colossal efforts to distinguish the faintest of personal glimmers in the impersonal darkness on both sides of my life." [. . .]

Writing—the pact with yourself, torturing and anguishing. You do not know if you rescued or lost your soul through it. A form of seizing, as through the dark, something to resemble you, as in a dream, where you join a being that appears to be you. But also a way of losing yourself. Unbearable thought, even now, as you are writing.

Translated by Raluca Manea

Filip Florian

(b. 1968)

After attempting a degree in geology and working on and off for the press and radio, Filip Florian quit his job and left the capital in order to devote himself for a number of years to the writing of *Small Fingers*. The book appeared in 2005 and was followed in 2006 by the autobiographical novel *Băiuţeii* (*Alley Boys*), written in collaboration with his brother, Matei Florian. *Small Fingers* was received enthusiastically and praised both for its author's refined stylistics and for the profundity with which he treated the theme of memory. In 2008 Florian published a novel, *The Days of the King*, to great acclaim.

WRITING AND THE CULINARY PREDILECTIONS
OF MY GRANDFATHER

I write in a mansard room, less than ten meters wide, of whitewashed plywood, through the middle of which passes the ample paunch of a chimney gathering the smoke of five fireplaces. This area is just below the tin roof, so I can hear to perfection the drumming of the wind and rain. I am surrounded by old photographs, by icons and watercolors—among which lie a demure nude and many silent objects. I have no doubt that the spirit of my grandfather passes often through here, for after all, he was the one who transformed a corner of the attic into this room of which I speak. Perhaps he comes down the chimney, perhaps he sits under the awning, I don't know. When I look out through the small window, after having seen the forest for a lifetime, I find myself looking down on six construction sites, dragons of sorts, four villas and two hotels in full construction. The circular saws, the drills, the dump trucks, the bulldozers, and the swears of the workers resemble neither the blackbird's song nor the squirrels.

Writing, as I see it, is not a team sport, but a strictly personal illness, noncontagious, with varying symptoms. I think that it is each author's duty to follow his obsessions, his goals, his voluptuousnesses and voice. Each writer should be at ease in his own skin.

As I was saying, I am often visited by my grandfather's spirit in the room in which I write. So, one summer, when I could not speak to him, it so happened that I wrote a minuscule novel in four parts, which I christened *The Culinary Predilections of My Grandfather*. It sounds something like this:

1. Auntie Frosa, Truffles, and Sherbet

With downy cheeks, with dimpled chin, with a chest powdered to the décol-letage of the dress and a beauty spot somewhere in close vicinity, just above the brooch (as I remember from a small painting, a portrait in oils with a gold oval frame), Auntie Frosa went to play rummy on Thursday. And Thursday, when she played cards, she took care early on in the morning to order a carton of confections from Nestor's, nicely wrapped at her insistence in wax paper, after which, before lunch, with her white hair and lofty look (from the same painting), she would hide the package in the wardrobe and lock the door with a key. An Aunt Banty, whose cat had not been in the pantry, and who carried an umbrella and wore veiled hats to shield herself from the sun, Eufrosina as she was called, possessed a keen sense of danger; she knew all too well what children meant in a household of young professors and would often exclaim: "les barbares!" Back then, bizarrely enough, my grandfather was a little boy. And little boys have always been blessed with a keen sense (not precisely olfactory) of knowing when chocolates, cakes, or shortbread cookies secretly appear under their very own roof. Mircea Chiril, ignorant of the flowering of the generation of '27 and of the blossoming of the economic crisis of the 1930s, would enter his aunt's room immediately after her departure for town, would crawl under the bed, behind the draperies, in the linen trunk, or through the clothes covered in mothballs, would hear her returning steps, sense her moving about, would guess from her movements where the shiny package was hidden, would wait for her to finish and lock up, to wander away, and would then issue forth from his corner and search silently, undo the ribbons and the wax paper, and fill his mouth with two or three truffles at once, would pass his fingers through the charlottes and lick them one at a time, comparing and swallowing, the thin cocoa powdering making him cough, but he would refuse to cough, and then at last, like a lazy, glutted tomcat, would attempt to tie the colored ribbons as they had once been tied. Lord, how Auntie Frosa would blush Thursday evening during the rummy matches, when her confections were served!

Once, not on a Thursday, on another day (for obviously there were six other days of the week to be had), the little boy who was to become my grandfather discovered a jar of sherbet, wrapped in a chemise. He emptied it in peace, sprawled on the ample, sailing-ship-like bed of his septuagenarian aunt, and after having finished, overtaken by boredom, caught a few of the flies thrashing about against the windowpane and shut them in the jar. Frosa bustled into the salon in the afternoon, exclaiming: "Fulvi, my dear, those blasted flies ate all of it! And then they croaked. . . ." Fulvia (her daughter-in-law and Mircea Ciril's mother) laughed with one eye and with the other gave the little boy dirty looks. He was drawing a rooster.

2. His Artillery Army

Those were times of war. Hard times. But not as hard as they could have been, because my grandfather (having become a man, as the inexorable laws of time decreed) had married soon after the fall of Odessa and then, instead of being sent to the front lines, had been admitted (through the intervention of a general, an uncle of my grandmother from Iași) to a school for artillery officers. During some maneuvers taking place east of Turnu Severin,[1] he was visited by his young wife (who turned more heads than any luxury automobile) and received permission to spend the weekend with her, in a village close to the military encampment. Like two doves they dreamed of crêpes, cooed in the

1. Turnu Severin—port city on the Danube, in southeastern Romania.

country kitchen, fluffed their wings a little, and by and by set the fire going. The batter in the pan bubbled and smoked, but nothing set or goldened. After some time, the old woman who had taken them in told them, pityingly: "Won't you put some flour in that milk, dearies?"

3. The Summer Miracle of the Işalniţa Combine

In the first years of the new republic, my grandfather's clock of personal history struck slowly and faintly, so as not to disturb the striking of the great horologe of collective history. As the brother of a political prisoner and the son-in-law of an industrialist, the engineer Mircea Chiril (who had once been a little boy) worked on isolated construction sites, which rarely acquired their employees' dossiers because of the clouds of dust, approximating maps, and impenetrable roads that stood in the way. During the construction of the radio relay station on the peak of Coştila, he ate polenta with marmalade for months, and in his travels through fog and drizzle toward the railway on Jepi,[2] in Valea Mălinului or in Valea Albă, he gave away his cigarettes a number of times (all of the cigarettes he had in his knapsack); he gave them to men with beards and guns, men without uniforms, who never unclenched their lips to tell him anything, but who always saluted and thanked him by nodding.

Later, when the ticking of the clock slowed down somewhat, when my grandfather's two little girls began to flit through the schools of central Bucharest, and when he worked on sites tied to some road or railway, the nature of meals changed. At Săvineşti, where a poster taped to the wall of the apartment building said that "It Is Illegal to Grow Pigs in Your Bathtub!," he would receive fresh eggs—not from the countryside, but from someone's balcony. And at Işalniţa,[3] returning home one morning in July, his roommate filled his plate with chicken borscht. "Mister engineer," the other asked him, "do you remember last week's soup? It had soured real bad so I gave it a good boiling and made a nice borscht . . . Did you like it?"

2. Jepi—natural plateau in the Carpathian Mountains.
3. Işalniţa—small town in southern Romania, known for its chemical plant.

4. Salami from the Fireplace

In the later years, when the horologe struck more and more hoarsely and my grandfather was more and more my grandfather (for I had been born, had babbled, learned to walk, speak, write, kiss the girls, recite patriotic poems, and even solve equations), he, who no longer worked on construction sites but on Calea Grivița in a designing institute, had the idea of renting the mansard room to a woman who worked in a sausage factory.[4] He did not ask her for money because money was becoming increasingly useless, nor for sausages, because they had long become abstract notions due to the retired generation, who hid them in cellars, in caves and grottos, even in holes dug behind apartment buildings in the dead of night. Instead, the young lady paid her rent in slabs of salami, six a month, which she would fearfully sneak out through the main gates of the factory by stuffing them under vaporous and sweat-stained rayon blouses. In the summer, when he didn't make a fire, my grandfather kept the salami in the fireplace.

Translated by Carla Baricz

4. Calea Grivadei—principal avenue in Bucharest.

Florina Ilis

(b. 1968)

A graduate of the Faculty of Letters at the University Babeş-Bolyai, Ilis chairs the Department of Bibliographical Research at the Central University Library in Cluj. She debuted in poetry with *Haiku and Calligrams* (2000, with Rodica Frenţiu), after which she published the novels *The Descent from the Cross* (2001), *Matthew's Calling* (2002), *The Children's Crusade* (2005), and *Five Colorful Clouds in the Eastern Sky* (2006). She is also the author of *The Science Fiction Phenomenon in Postmodern Culture: Cyberpunk Fiction* (2006) and the theater volume *The Arithmetic Lesson* (2006).

Ilis creates memorable characters and captivating stories using broad themes (faith, creation, love, fate, etc.), which she minutely renders through the pulsating filigree of common gestures and thoughts. Her fiction, received with great enthusiasm, distinguished itself via its ability to present the image of Romania today, that is, of a paradoxical land: vital and suicidal, struggling with its own fears and filled with projects and phantasms, incapable of precise plans and full of creativity, a tragic and jocular country.

How Should I Write?

[. . .] *How should I write?* I ask myself again. It would perhaps be more appropriate to begin by describing *how I write*. I care immensely about the way in which a book is constructed. I do not start to write before organizing the structure of my novel in detail. Then, I do not put down a word until I feel the rhythm of each sentence, so that I can transcribe it, like a musical phrase, into notes. And, third, I do not begin to work on a project until the characters that are formed in my mind have revealed their secrets to me and tempted me with the ways in which they will surprise me when I write. The rest, the details, come naturally.

I should add a few things that pertain to the practice of writing itself, for instance, the fact that, from the very beginning, I have gotten used to writing directly at a computer and making the necessary corrections on the initial text. When I start to work on a new novel, I have the entire book in my head, from the first to the last scene. That is why, when I sit down to write, I only transcribe from memory what was previously created in a region of my mind that is difficult to map. I take breaks from writing only in order to do supplementary research on the "secret" and "unseen" life of my characters. I should also add that I work only in the daytime, especially in the morning, a detail that may or may not be related to the fact that I do not see anyone before noon, and that, sometimes, if the phone doesn't ring, I do not get to utter any words out loud. From the moment when the book that I am about to write takes shape in my mind, writing flows easily. The latter is a kind of transcription of that which is already in my mind. The unconscious writing that takes place day and night is translated into conscious writing. Nevertheless, this does not mean that I do not edit the text, that I do not make changes until I find that the text is ready to go to print. Conscious writing is not easy, but it constitutes my contribution to creation.

However, I haven't said anything, again, *about* writing. I only spoke of *how* it is that I write.

I could talk, of course, about *what* I write. I have written poetry, haikus to be exact. I was fascinated by this type of poetry because of the mathematical rigor of the lines, but also because of the ineffable, which the poet, using dense syllables, must render tangible and visible. With her calligraphy, Rodica

Frențiu (the author of the calligrams) helped me evoke, in an *authentic* manner, a world so distant from us, that of the Far East.

I have also written poetry. *The Children's Crusade* (2005) is the third novel of a trilogy that begins with *The Descent from the Cross* (2001) and continues with *Matthew's Calling* (2002). The three novels do not constitute a trilogy in the strict sense of the term; they do not share a common plot, and, with a few exceptions, they do not have the same characters. Nevertheless, considering the unitary conception that generated them, I believe that these books can be construed as a trilogy. I conceived *The Descent from the Cross* as the novel of the creator, of the artist who can be found in a state of permanent confrontation with his own creation. *Matthew's Calling* is the novel of the self, which faces the insufficiently explored territories of virtuality as well as its seductive temptations. *The Children's Crusade* constitutes the novel of the world, a world confronted with itself or, rather, with its own dilemmas, which the innocence of children, like a faithful mirror, reveals. Moreover, taking as a point of departure the style of the three books in which I have repeatedly made use of the comma—as a sign of expression lacking in stylistic constraints—I called this imaginary trilogy *The Trilogy of the Comma*. Starting with my fourth novel, *Five Colorful Clouds in the Eastern Sky* (2006), I entered a new stage of creation, which I can call, taking into account the same orthographic criteria, *The Stage of the Period*. In this novel I sought to capture the tangential points that exist between the traditional Japanese world, with its pervasive semiotics, and the contemporary world, in which technology becomes the individual's second nature.

Naturally, I have also written theater. I have published three plays in which I tried to capture, in a manner more direct than prose, the way in which the individual behaves when he steps forward and faces a type of manifestation of fate that he, as an actor involved in the events, cannot perceive consciously; a manifestation that the spectator, identifying with the actor, can observe and which leads the former to question his own identity.

Perhaps it would be easier to say *what* writing is to me. I take writing to be one of the highest forms of knowledge. I believe that, through art, something of the invisible beauty of the world becomes manifest to our senses in a form in which they can *bear* its presence without *losing* themselves. To participate in this manifestation of beauty in art is a form of knowledge. I would never give it up. I have dedicated my entire life to the quest and transcription of this beauty. When I think of what literature and art mean to me, I am always reminded of Nietzsche, who, in one of his moments of extreme lucidity, said: "We have art so that we shall not be destroyed by truth." This statement is one of those in which Nietzsche manages to oppose two terms that do not find themselves, from the perspective of signification, in a situation of mutual exclusion. Art does not represent in any way for Nietzsche the equivalent of an illusion or a mystification but, as I see it, *another* truth, a truth that can correspond to a level of reality other than the one that is given, *actualized* in existence. Thus, art, through its very essence, acquires the ability to reconstitute a truth of a different nature, a truth *superior* to the *immediate, murderous* truth that is expressed through common sense in life. However, the individual usually perceives existence within the limits of the immediate truth. The tragic nuance that is manifest in Nietzsche's statement consists precisely in this inability of ours to free ourselves from the murderous melancholy to which reason, led to its own limits when faced with existence, brought us, rendering Being fragile and dissipating the spell. Art, in its essence, manages to hold us under a spell of suspension, guarding us against murderous truth, developing in us the capacity needed to *surpass* the tragic consciousness of an existential void. Literature gets to represent today not only a way of understanding the world, but the unique opportunity of *accommodating Being* to the crisis of consciousness. An accommodation which I call a *soft accommodation*.

Translated by Raluca Manea

Doina Ioanid

(b. 1968)

A graduate of the Faculty of Letters at the University of Bucharest, Ioanid worked as a teaching assistant in higher education. She is currently an editor with a prestigious weekly cultural journal in Bucharest. She has published the collections of poetry *The Marzipan Little Lady* (2000), *It Is Time to Wear Earrings* (2001), *The Book of Bellies and Solitude* (2003), and *Poems of Passage* (2005).

In her choice of the prose poem and of a language of elegant simplicity, which translates real force and inner depth, Ioanid is a poet of impressive originality, endowed with a voice of feline and generous femininity that speaks of love, vulnerability, fear, and death.

The Path to the Other

It all started as a game, when I did not even know the alphabet. I nevertheless wrote on the walls of my home, with chalk, with pencils, with whatever else. I drew made-up letters, amalgamated letters, just as they had stuck in my mind after glancing at the storybooks that my family read to me. In time, they made me unlearn this habit, they sent me to school, where, to my surprise, we started to make little canes, horizontal lines that made no sense to me; I wanted letters, I was waiting for them. And I waited for them for so long that, when I finally learned them, they had nothing of the mysterious air of the letters I had once drawn. Writing became drudgery, a duty for school that I carried out quickly; consequently, today my writing is unsightly and unstrung.

Since at that age one endeavor is quickly replaced by another, I discovered that it was more interesting to play with words. This time, not made-up words, like those of most children, but words that I knew quite well. I would repeat them ad nauseam, until they became so bizarre that they no longer signified anything. It amused me. Until one day. I was alone in our summer kitchen and was feeling so lonely that my ears were ringing. I kept looking around but could not find anything to play with, so I started to name each thing: lightbulb, chair, table . . . I started naming them faster and faster until I became dizzy and my tongue staggered. As I was stubbornly continuing to utter their names, I was getting increasingly sick. And when I realized that between words and things all ties were broken, I was utterly frightened, so frightened that I got the hiccups, like those of a hysteric frog, that resounded in the whole house. I had been left out of language, while the world had turned upside down, deprived of meaning. I no longer remember what I said when my grandparents returned, but I was delirious. I remember that they rubbed my temples with camphor and put me to bed. I laid there for two days without daring to utter another word, for fear that my sickness and my fright would return.

When I went back to school I refused to read, and the teacher, who was a complete stranger to my fears, without even suspecting them, started to fill my grade book with bad grades. I kept at it for a few days, maybe a week, but to me it appeared much longer. One evening, before going to bed, my aunt came by with a beautiful, illustrated book. She opened it and started to read to me. I closed my eyes, thinking that the sickness would return and that the endless void would reappear. But none of these things happened. The words flew smoothly and seemed to be in their right place, opening up a whole universe. It was *The Happy Prince*, by Oscar Wilde. Then she read to me *The Nightingale and the Rose*, a story that I liked even more and with which I have been "in love" to this very day. From that evening onward, things went back to normal and everybody was content. Except that I wanted to reach on my own that whirlwind of feelings spurred on by words, and so I began to write composition upon composition. It seemed that I had made peace with the world of words. But this didn't last long, only until the fifth grade. I had a final exam in Romanian literature. We had to relate the story of Sadoveanu's *A Poor Man,* and I rejoiced since I had already done so for homework and was content with it. To my great surprise, this didn't happen on the final exam, as if the account I had written for homework stubbornly continued to stay in the homework notebook. At that point I experienced the terrible feeling that the world of words is a fragile and unrepeatable place.

As a teenager I started reading more, chaotically, without any guidance. I would go to the library and randomly take books off the shelf. That's how I read a lot of nonsense, but also books such as *The Flowers of Evil, Madame Bovary, Anna Karenina, The Brothers Karamazov,* and *Vegetal Dream* by Magda Isanos, which helped me better understand what was happening to me, to understand the darkness in which I was floating and all that was fermenting indistinctly in me. Other people's writing was of great help to me. I no longer had to get through that difficult age on my own; my grandparents had no time for existential crises nor would they have understood them, laid-back, God-fearing farmers that they were, and in the communist world nobody was going to explain to me what was what. Then it occurred to me that I could write about what I was experiencing. Enthusiasm soon left me though, when I realized, to my despair, that I was producing nothing but deplorable, syrupy effusions. And so I learned another lesson: nothing that I experience is important unless I find the right word for it. I didn't write for years after that, so disappointed was I in myself. On the other hand, I started to read more closely, trying to discover how it was that great writers managed to arrive at those personal, sublime, and fascinating worlds. At university I took up writing again: it was slight and bad. I burnt everything. Then, without realizing how and through what alembicated and strange process, when I least expected it, I found my way to words. All I know is that I was no longer in a rush. I carried inside me vague sensations, images, until they leavened, fermented, and then found their own way out—a story, an expression, or the right word.

Beyond this trajectory, writing was to me an exorcism, a mode of survival: the world with all its senselessness, its merry-go-round and madness became ordered and gained in meaning. The mere fact that I could express myself [. . .] helped me get over a lot, over the madness in my disunited family, over the break with the world, over the loss of my dear ones, over the dross of the everyday. Nonetheless, therapy through writing has no literary value if it does not go through other filters. In order for writing to become relevant, it is not enough to express yourself; what you express must become powerful, new, seductive. That is, if you want to have readers. You can write exclusively for yourself, but only in an initial phase, as a naïve teenager. I know of no writer who wrote only for himself. Anyway, I wouldn't believe him. As far as I am concerned, I write to share with others my loneliness, my sadness, my fragility, my love, my doubts, the fear and the joy of finding myself, that is, all that is human. In fact, I believe that every writer remakes, in his own way, this path toward the other, in the attempt to reach him, to shatter his solitude with one sentence. Many writers have lifted the burden of solitude from me, and I would like to be able to do the same in turn, even if only for one reader.

Translated by Raluca Manea

Dan Lungu

(b. 1969)

Graduate of the School of Philosophy of the University Alexandru Ioan Cuza in Iaşi, Dan Lungu is assistant professor of sociology at the same university. He has published the volume of poems *Edges* (1996); the collections of short stories *Collection of Phlegm* (1999), *Prose with Detail* (2003), and *Gang Guys* (2005); and the novels *The Paradise of Chickens (False Novel of Hearsay and Mysteries)* (2005), *I Am a Communist Granny* (2007), and *How to Forget a Woman* (2009). He has also published a play, *Wedding on the Ground Floor* (2003). He is the author of a number of sociology studies, including the volume *The Construction of Identity in a Totalitarian Society: A Sociological Study of Writers* (2003).

Dan Lungu writes about the post-Communist Romania of today, choosing characters from diverse backgrounds, ranging from frustrated and aspiring children and young members of gangs to discontented workers adrift in a changing political environment.

How I Did Not Become a Genius

I was twenty when the Romanian Communist dictatorship collapsed. I cannot say that at that time I was already a mature writer, though I was an insistent aspirant. I assiduously frequented the literary world. I sought with ardor and shyness the companion of consecrated writers, of "great writers." The first fully fleshed authors whom I admired were, evidently, those from my hometown and its surroundings. I did not admire many because the town was small and provincial. None of them had been included in the school books, but all of them dreamt of becoming part of the history of literature. On the other hand, from among the deceased, a few were quite famous. One was even the greatest Romanian poet, the quintessence of the history of literature. Grand commemorations were organized on these individuals' account, lots of wine was imbibed, much was prattled, and the same conclusion was systematically always reached: that in those realms genius felt at home. It irradiated from the depths like a sort of magnetism that impregnates those born there in the very fibers of their hearts. This sounds like a secret promise to all those who had learned to hold a ballpoint in their hand, the promise of a sure future, without any doubts, bright. I presume that each community of small-town scribblers, from anywhere in Romania, was convinced that it populated a blessed earth of magnetic waves of talent-in-itself. It's strange how such a backward mysticism of creation, talent, and genius could exist in an epoch that preached atheism.

And so, I completed my apprenticeship both under the masters in the library and the classics in situ. From the latter bunch, I learned a ton of initiatory things that you can't find in any manual. For example, that there are two types of authors, those who "have balls" and those that do not possess such a thing. Symbolically speaking, of course. Those in the first category are talented, strong, expressive, while the others are mere epigones. Well, the classics in situ always decided at some bar counter who were those "with" and "without," and the lists varied depending on obscure criteria. It was moreover implied that women could not aspire to the accessories of masculinity, perhaps only in absolutely exceptional cases, which had something to do with natural anomalies. But the most awesome were the abundantly gifted, the ripe geniuses, meaning those blessed with two pairs of balls, though these were rare cases—for example, Eminescu and Nichiţa Stănescu. Happily, the writers with three pairs never came up in our discussion. And yet I did find out that there is some inexplicable connection between talent and alcohol tolerance. If your own performance is modest, it is more honest to put down the pen since you will be fated to be no more than a measly epigone—or, if you are not genius material, it's not even worth writing. The geniuses, with one or two pairs of you-gentlemen-and-ladies-know-what spontaneously, rapidly, as in a trance set down on paper their verses, for they are, after all, inspired. From their hands pour only jewels, masterpieces. Any editing of the text, any ulterior intervention, constitutes a sacrilege. After a session of inspiration, it is strongly encouraged that the author refresh himself with a beer. Surrounded by friends or accompanied by a woman. It is indicated that this latter *persona designata* always be different, for habit and monotony may be hazardous to talent. To top it all, I found out, moreover, that poets are truer writers than prosaists, who are a sort of second-class citizen of literature. The literary critics are nothing more than hapless failed writers, who survive dissecting what the geniuses have written, but with whom, unfortunately, it doesn't hurt to be on friendly terms. Very little is said about playwrights. In any case, it was clear that the true poets must grow their hair long, while the true prosaists must be solid and "have a hard ass," in order to be able to endure long sitting sessions. The prosaists of weak constitution can kiss the history of literature goodbye. The most they can become is literary critics. Etc.

Of course, I meditated upon everything I heard.

One fine day, after a period of bitter doubts, I rose—obliterated—from the writing table, forcefully telling myself: "That's it! I am not a genius, and that's it!"

No matter how much goodwill I put into interpreting the facts, it was clear that inspiration didn't strike me out of the blue. The magnetic waves of talent-in-itself stubbornly avoided me. There you had it, the writing went slowly, erringly, and in its wake remained tons of corrections and cuts! Sisyphic labor of a graceless serf. Studying myself in the mirror, I was almost overtaken by tears. Short hair, with schoolboy bangs, was the antithesis of the Emniscian curls in the textbook picture. *How could you write poems when they forcefully cut your hair at school?* I told myself resentfully. I lifted my shirt and carefully examined the prominent ribs and deep sternum. Disaster! It became clearer and clearer that I didn't have a chance even as a prosaist. Never had

Sadoveanu, the Ceahlău of Romanian literature, looked so scrawny and raw-boned.[1] Nothing more was left to me but to become a literary critic, which seemed horrible. Some time later, I began writing again, fully conscious that I was not a genius. And it seemed, maybe, to go better . . . It's true, I had also put on a little weight.

Two or three years ago I was asked again the banal/complicated question, why do you write? I thought long and hard, but I did not succeed in identifying only one reason, strong and clear, for doing so. I write for multiple reasons, which change with time: because I like to, because I'm used to doing so, to amuse myself, to surprise my friends, not to disappoint, from boredom, from curiosity, in order to get to know myself, because I feel like I'm going crazy if I don't, etc. And probably each time the words arrange themselves a little differently on the page.

Translated by Carla Baricz

1. Ceahlău is the name of a mountain peak in the eastern Carpathians. Mihail Sadoveanu (1880–1961), a novelist of epic force and author of dozens of volumes—including a number of masterpieces such as *Ancuța's Inn (1928)*, *The Axe* (1930), and *The Golden Branch* (1933)—was nicknamed "the Ceahlău of Romanian prose."

Bogdan Suceavă

(b. 1969)

Suceavă is a graduate of the Faculty of Mathematics at the University of Bucharest, where he worked for a time as an assistant professor. He holds a doctorate in mathematics from Michigan State University. He settled in the United States, where he is a lecturer at California State University, Fullerton. He has had a vast publishing history with literary journals in Romania, and he edits an online journal. He is the author of the poetry collections *Legends and Superstitions* (1995), *Visions and Portraits* (2001); the short story anthologies *The Fear of Sunset* (1990), *The Empire of Ancient Generals and Other Stories* (2002), and *Grandfather Returned to French* (2003); and the novels *Under the Sign of the Orion* (1992), *It Came from Sharp Time* (2004), *Miruna, a Story* (2007), and *Vincent the Immortal* (2008).

Regardless of whether he is writing about love, power, madness, or memory—some of his favorite themes—Suceavă oscillates between the comic and the tragic, valorizing the strangeness (be it peaceful or explosive) of everyday life.

from "The Secret Code:
Notes for a Literary Confession"

One of the questions I get asked increasingly often is, "When did you start
to write in English?" Such a question rests on the premise that for every
Romanian writer it is only a matter of time—once he has crossed the western
border of his country of origin—until he can aim for a full repudiation of
the supposedly unfulfilled Romanian identity. Common sense seems to ask:
don't we all want this? Construed in such a way, Romanian identity appears
unwhole, if not a hindrance. If we leave Romania, if our formal education
goes through the formative pattern of another culture, if this culture exerts a
strong influence upon us, would it not be expected that we adopt it fully? [. . .]

Things were different for me. I left Romania in 1996. I have since lived in
Michigan, Arizona, and California and written several books of literature
in Romanian. I do not plan to change my literary language. For more than
a decade I contributed to several cultural reviews in Romania. I had the
opportunity to carry on numerous dialogues. I participated, a number of
times, in conferences or literary events as a Romanian writer. I received—as
a Romanian author—solicitations to write for publications that come out in
other places around the world. Very many things happen to me as if I did
not live near Los Angeles, but in any one of the places where I used to feel at
home—Bucharest, for instance. Furthermore, I chose to write fiction about
Romanian realities. I wrote about Romania as it was before 1989 and after.
I also write about Romania in the future, as much as I can construe it . . . I
should start from the beginning. I wrote my first short story at seventeen. It
was no good, and I am proud to have realized that rather fast. I did not cause
any harm; no one saw anything. Later, I specialized in prose, after a long time
during which I experimented with various poetic formulas, without convincing myself of capturing the essence of any of them. I had moments when
I was happy that I expressed a certain image or a certain idea, but, despite
all this, it seemed to me that the entire edifice was insufficient. The optimal
literary formula is one that allows you to state the essential, to eliminate the
ballast, to access a truth concealed beyond the cosmetics of reality, beyond
the lies that we are inclined to believe or follow. I learned this in mathemat-

ics: this is what mathematics aspires toward, this ideal liberated of repetitive affirmations or commonplaces toward which mathematics instructs us to be heading. At the time when I was writing poetry, before the age of twenty-four, I discovered several things. In a poem, even when you write in a jesting tone, you do not feel like lying, you do not want to approximate, you do not want to mock, you do not want to look for excuses or to content yourself with half-measures. Concision is part of the game. On the other hand, I discovered that as a domain, short fiction is just as honest. I think the best moments for short fiction were 1994 and 1997, when I wrote five or six texts each time. I waited for almost a decade for those texts to be collected in a volume. I wrote in the apartment in Bucharest, in a house in the countryside—when I was still in Romania—in the Michigan State University Library when I was a student and did not yet own a computer, in my office at the Department of Mathematics; and one of the short stories was written at an airport, when I had to wait too long between two flights and the fever of writing had reached the upper limit. But neither statistics nor locations are of interest. All this information does not go into the text; it is ballast, it is décor. As I was saying, the criterion is different: Did any of these texts manage to say something important, to decode a message concealed in the ambiguous sphere of reality? Belonging to a culture does not manifest itself through the location where the text is written, but through the manner in which one tries to essentialize the literary act. You pursue an idea in a style that is meaningful in the context of a certain cultural perspective. This perspective is usually influenced a lot by the culture of origin. In Romanian culture the important things, the ones from which we select our literary themes, always seem different from the ones in other cultures. We select our themes in a different way, which we discover only when we see that some of the things important to us are not important to others. This somewhat different perception of what deserves to be told and nuanced renders difficult the translation of several texts that established themselves long ago in Romania.

For me, another rule of the game in regards to short fiction is that not even two out of the total number of stories resemble each other. To write a four-hundred-page novel based on a classic literary solution, to follow a beaten path, pursued sometimes by others—for instance, the literary solution invented by Camil Petrescu or the one invented by Jules Verne—seems facile. I believe that the great effort resides in imagining for each new story a normal, natural yet distinct solution, whose particularity can solicit the reader, in unveiling a new mode of communication, a new discovery, a cavalry charge. It's been known for a long time that each text contains its own poetics. I don't think that an experiment of limited use would be of interest, but rather a whole solution—mature, accomplished, published after due consideration. Ideally, in each text the author should be persuasive, the theme interesting, the effort of the original construction meaningful. The problem presents itself as such: you have ten pages at your disposal and a story. Behind this story there is something essential, a truth for which you would be capable of fighting in a duel. It does not matter if you have written three thousand pages or ten pages until then. It matters that the synthesis that you put forth be profound. [. . .]

Here I will allow myself to evoke one of my texts of short fiction, the one in which I consider that the attempt to synthesize was most successful. The idea came to me in February 1999, while I was attending a class in differential geometry. The topic of the class that day had no connection with the literary theme of the text that I was going to write a few hours later and in which I set out to capture Bucharest—a whole city synthesized through a story that would encompass it in a single metaphor. I was in one of the conference rooms in Wells Hall, at Michigan State University, in one of those advanced classes that only four or five students attend. All of a sudden, while I was follow-ing a proof, I had the vision of a large, vibrating drum, on which lay, at the crack of dawn, the city where many of my friends live, with its extravagant architecture, with fragments of buildings left over from bygone times. And I wrote, in a single work session that lasted six hours, a short story that I considered at the time to be the text that best captured my literary voice. Five years later, I used that narrative point of view when I wrote the novel *It Came from Sharp Time*. For me the literary act had become a struggle to synthesize and express the essential, just as in mathematics you strive to cover all the cases in the proof of a theorem. I choose my characters in such a way so that they capture—through their own literary construction—the key to a world. Who could have been the most appropriate witness through whose eyes the Romania of the 1990s, Romania in transition, in transformation from one world into another, could be seen? The image that haunted me for so many years was that of a strange old man, half-vagabond, half-scholar, who had audited our math courses at the University of Bucharest at the beginning of the 1990s. At one point, years ago, I had sat next to him in a classroom at the other end of the world and we had audited together a course in which a similar theorem and proof were being discussed. Beginning with his image, the passage of years had allowed me to see the emergence of a literary character. Here is the construction I proposed when I wrote about

> the old man whose given name was Saint Peter, whom I saw for the first time in Roman Plaza in the summer of 1988,[1] wearing a ragged coat, with loose pockets—filled with holes and books—carrying in dirty one-leu bags all kinds of torn registers, wondrous treatises, textbooks, or apocryphal editions of the *Philokalia*. Imagine the most peaceful citizen of the world, an old man feeding only on bread (he would start on it in the morning, at dawn, and toward evening, still chewing, would get three-quarters into it and that would be all he ate), spending his entire time either in the technical courses in architecture or in the Polytechnic, or at Măgurele, in physics, or, at other times, in math. He lived somewhere close to the intersection of Polonă with Mihai Eminescu, in a little-known corner, where the initiated claimed that one could find—in an underground bunker reminiscent of the bomb shelters from the war—the biggest library in Bucharest, significantly superior in volume count to the Library of the Academy, which would rank—according to statistics from the Library of Congress—ninth in the world. He had imagined his own system of cards, of classification, of ordering and searching for volumes, so that he was never lost in the infernal database. That underground was a particular space, with ample ramifications toward the sewers, and each corner was filled with folders, coverless volumes, photocopies, forgotten editions, all of them signed by many, very many authors that no one had ever heard of, as though his library had come together as a plausible alternative to the entire universe. That space was both a laboratory and a reading room (you would have found it too uncomfortable, but to him it didn't matter), a place for meditation and a praying chamber, with its walls covered—where there were no shelves—in icons.

Putting aside the ironic nuances that such a description implies, this passage is important to me because—as far as I was able to see—in Romanian culture the most valuable contributions were made by those living on the

---

1. The Roman Plaza—central square in Bucharest.

margins. The number of those discovered or thoroughly understood much later, or after their death, is too large not to make one wonder.

I was interested in writing about Bucharest, in capturing the "essence" of this geographical space, also because I do not want to avoid responding to the provocation. I do not believe in the existence of distinct criteria for the literature of exile. I no longer believe in the "dramatic" experiences of exile today, nor in the soppy, syrupy, pathetic tone that still makes itself heard at times. Those who left Eastern Europe after 1990 did not suffer in the same way as those who were forced to leave their country before the fall of the Iron Curtain. I am not prisoner to my fate: I can travel and live wherever I want. I am responsible for what I choose, and my gestures are not impelled by an irreconcilable political situation, as was the case with other writers before 1989. I live a fate that I chose for myself, just as I choose the books that I read, and I try to read just for pleasure. Nevertheless, it is true that our motherland remains forever the place where we opened our eyes, of our childhood, that illusory and levitating universe to which we always happen to compare the one in which we live. Yet I know very well that the space in question no longer exists. We remember, however, that feeling of plenitude and the carelessness we only had at seven or eight. That feeling opens up the gates to capturing the secret code of a geographic space, of a world. We see and we imagine through the eyes with which we once saw—without knowing that this is happening to us—the ideal space, the happiest age of all.

Starting in the mid-1970s, I took many trips to all the corners of Romania. By the end of the 1980s I had gone almost everywhere. There are cities that I know in detail and I remember as they were before the transformations in the '80s, when a lot of historical city centers were destroyed in an architectural effort that aimed to prove the superiority of socialism. There were transformations that altered—unfortunately—the historical identity of some places. I preserve these types of memories that others from our generation no longer have in general. With no intention of exaggerating in any way, I dare say that I know Romania very well. In the fall of 1985 I watched in grief as the old center of Târgoviște was demolished, one house after another. One evening I gazed for hours on end at the falling walls. There were thick, brick walls in which the mortar had turned to sand and from which the mold gave off a fetid smell. Such scenes come to inhabit you, they get deposited in successive and distinct layers of memory and end up haunting you, popping up in your mind when you have long since moved to another world and occupy yourself with other things. They haunt you even when you would like to be other. And the truth is that you cannot be other as long as you carry with you this memory that is also the premise and substance to the way in which you understand the world.

On the other hand, you are aware, as a writer, that fiction in a realistic register, based on a particular, concrete reality, can only be written if you live there, only if you are well immersed in that reality. Czesław Miłosz said it. Inevitably, sooner or later, if you don't live in a place, its contemporary evolutions will surpass your perceptions. You end up obsolete, outdated, if you persist in themes and directions for which interest is dwindling down. The most beautiful stories that we imagine expire, even if we don't enjoy admitting it. Evolutions—which no one can anticipate and which have to be lived in order to be understood—take place.

Literature can propose to research and understand, to explore the possibilities of reality, to continue this reality, to prolong it, expanding its resources of the imaginary in the directions suggested by the necessity of meaningful synthesis. We are not talking about either pamphleteering, or propagandistic literature, but about something else, which does not serve any cause in this world. The ethics of such a literature does not allow for materialization—meaning, more precisely, that it does not allow for any equivalent in the practical space, of the political. It does not allow for *applications*. On the contrary, it has multiple possibilities for confronting the political space, although literature may very well find inspiration and take characters from the strata of this world. In any case, it is not about a mere imitation of reality, but about finding the ultimate consequences of certain events, with real roots. [. . .]

It may so happen that fiction succeeds in identifying a substantial theme, which is to become visible only when it is illustrated in a novel or short story, although those events never took place as such. It can be that such a prose piece captures the essence in a way in which the mere transcription of our biography does not. In Romania, during the period after 1990, information of a documentary type interested people for many years. After the historical type of information from journals and memoirs was assimilated, an important part of the audience turned their attention toward fiction.

Thus, the defiance continues as it always has: the starting point is reality, but we know very well that what interests us lies beyond it, in that space of general ideas, of principles, where the enunciation of our discoveries can be synthesized at times in concentrated formulae that aim to reach—for a brief moment—lucidity.

Translated by Raluca Manea

Florin Lăzărescu

(b. 1974)

A graduate of the Faculty of Letters at the Alexandru Ioan Cuza University in Iaşi, Lăzărescu worked as an editor for a journal and a publishing house. He is currently a freelance writer. He has authored the volumes of short fiction *Mistletoe Nests* (2000), *Six Ways to Remember a Horse* (2003), and *The Tube with a Hat* (2009) and the novels *What We Know of the Panda Bear* (2003) and *Our Special Envoy* (2005). He wrote the script for *The Lamp with a Fur Hat* (directed by Radu Jude, 2006) and is the scriptwriter (together with Lucian Dan Teodorovici) of the TV series *Animal Planet Show*, an animated political parody.

In Lăzărescu's fiction the construction of reality includes, along with observations regarding the everyday, exceptional events and characters, often characterized by the nightmarish and the metaphysical.

OUR SPECIAL ENVOY

"Yo, are you writing? Are you writing? Write!" my father would say, checking on me.

"I am writing."

He walked agitatedly around me, rummaging somewhere in the depths of his memory and then dictated. I wrote:

Call me Joseph!

"It's a good start. I like the way it sounds. Keep writing."

A few years back . . .

"When, Father?" I would interject.

"It doesn't matter when. Shut up and write."

. . . being left with little to live on or, rather, completely broke . . .

"But how did you end up broke?"

"Why won't you shut up? Write!"

. . . and not finding anything of particular interest on land, it occurred to me that I would try out being at sea for a bit . . .

He would then stop dictating, dissatisfied.

"You know what? I don't really like this story. Let's forget about it."

I had written the beginning to dozens of stories that we never continued. Ever since he had taught me how to write, we would do this almost every day. As much as I enjoyed listening to his stories, it was tiring when I had to write them up. I couldn't understand why he wouldn't write them up himself, why he was also bothering me.

Sure enough, writing was not at all among my favorite games. I had been born a warrior, I didn't have time for nonsense. And, when Father didn't have his eye on me, I prepared to defeat the head of the Huns. At the time of the evening call I asked the watchmen if they had caught a glimpse of him. They never answered me, but I knew that they had seen him. They did not want to scare me, which was silly, because I wasn't afraid anyway.

I had learned from my father how to set a trap for wild beasts. Holes, spikes, loops of all sizes—I had become a master at it. The rabbits fell in great numbers. Sometimes even a wild boar. My father cut them up himself and smoked their meat. We were gathering reserves for winter, when we would go deep into the caves of the citadel and do nothing but sleep, eat, and chat around a blazing fire. We were retreating like bears to our lair, as Father used to say.

Only once did we get close to catching a bear, but the rope didn't hold up. Anyway it was not good to eat. And only once did we catch a wolf. A silly cub that fell into the hole covered with branches and leaves. I wanted to keep it, but my father didn't let me. The she-wolf came every night and howled next to the citadel. I released the cub out of pity.

So . . . I was thinking: Why couldn't I catch the head of the Huns with a loop or a hole craftily prepared? I was already seeing myself running up to

Father full of pride and asking him to come quickly to see the head of the Huns impaled on the spikes at the bottom of a hole. Alas! I had encircled the citadel with holes, and I think I would have caught him if Father hadn't gotten angry at me and covered them all up. Once, when he was visiting, Friar John fell into one of them. He was lucky I had not had time to place the spikes in it, otherwise he would have been gravely injured.

I am telling you, brother, the kind of life I had then, you wouldn't believe. I would have gone on living like this forever, which I thought was going to be the case. That is, in a way, I knew from my father's stories that we were going to die, but I imagined we would find our end at the same time, him as king, me as a little prince, without growing old. One day, we would be chatting around the fire, in our lair. Father—on the throne of the immortal one. Me—on the bed. He would tell me a story and I would fall asleep. He would keep going for awhile, then bend over to throw some logs into the fire, and then we would both fall into a sleep from which we would never awaken.

But it wasn't meant to be.

Lately, Father had become quieter. I wasn't aware of it then because I was used to his moods. Only later did I understand what was happening. Sometimes he would not talk to me for an entire day. He would lock himself in his room. I would eavesdrop and it seemed to me that he was moaning, crying. As I was saying, I had gotten used to not minding him much.

Then, one morning he woke me up by shaking my hand. Fearful, I opened my eyes. I was even more scared when I saw his face. It had completely changed: a terrified look, red eyes, dark circles large like plums. His hair and beard had turned white. I almost failed to recognize him. My bow and arrows were hanging from his neck. He had mud traces on his cheeks.

"My son, today the train goes by!"

My father, the king, had told me a lot of stories, but I had no clue as to what a train was.

"What is a train?"

He gave me a strange, reprimanding look.

"I went through so many pains with you for nothing. You didn't understand anything. You didn't pay attention! I have been preparing you for so long for the big moment, and when it arrives, you forget everything."

What was I forgetting? I didn't have the slightest clue as to what he was talking about.

He grabbed me forcefully by the arm and dragged me after him. I burst into tears, partly due to the pain, partly because I felt that something terrible was happening.

"Don't whine like a woman. You are like one of those palefaces set against the stakes of boiling cauldrons! Hold on to me!"

I was too frightened to cry. He dragged me through the undergrowth into the woods, farther than we had ever gone. Only a few hours might have gone by, but it felt like years to me.

I could no longer recognize my father. He was yelling at me. He even hit me over the head a couple of times.

Once in a while he stopped and crawled, advancing slowly through the bushes, advising me to do the same.

"Be careful not to crack a branch! It is important that you not make a sound!"

Sometimes he made a sign with his hand for me to stop. He lifted his head and sniffed the air like a wolf. Then a terrifying howl came out of his throat.

"The coyote's howl. You must remember the coyote's howl. This is how you notice if anyone is around. You do it now, like I taught you."

It's true that I felt like screaming, but certainly not like a coyote, since I didn't even know what a coyote was at the time.

"You don't want to listen to me, is that it? You are not listening to your father! Nothing will ever come of you. I struggled to teach you—and for nothing."

We stopped at last near a path that was crossed by two train tracks. Naturally, I didn't know what they were. I was waiting to see what Father was going to do.

He left me to watch from a cliff and approached the tracks on all fours. He put his ear to one of them. He jumped and howled victoriously like a coyote. He told me to come down to where he was. He showed me the tracks and said happily:

"Listen!"

I glued my ear to the train tracks.

"Can you hear?!"

I could hear nothing but the creak of the trees.

"I told you that the train would come today! And we will plunder it! Firearms, blankets, women! Everything will be ours!

"Why?" I asked him with a whimper.

"Because it's in our blood, as Indians. I said so!"

I started to cry, with my ear glued to the train tracks. I do not recall how long I stayed like that. At a given moment, Father lifted me up and stroked my hair. Although he was completely changed, I recognized the king's gaze in his eyes.

"Don't cry anymore. Run and get Friar John!"

I ran away as if that was all I had been waiting for. Skipping from one stone to the next, like a madman. I got bruised all over, I hurt my knees, I got lost in the woods, but still I reached the friar's cell. I didn't have the strength to talk to him. I dragged him by the hand to the train tracks. I found Father lying next to it, all shriveled and stiff.

John lifted him on his back and carried him to the citadel, without a word. We buried him close to a wall, in a trap I had made for the head of the Huns.

When we were done covering up the trap, the friar took me in his arms and said:

"Henceforth you will come live with me. Forget these places."

I grabbed the young unicorn by the reins—in fact, the colt whose horn never grew—and I went down the hill. I remember that I turned my head and looked at the soldiers who were guarding the walls. All of a sudden I realized that they were no more than rag dolls mounted on wooden crosses. Scarecrows . . . [. . .]

"Yo, are you writing? Are you writing? Write!"

I have been living for more than thirty years in this world that equally fascinates and frightens me. And each day the fascination diminishes, and the terror grows. I have the feeling that I haven't understood a thing.

"Hey you, are you writing? Are you writing? Write!"—this still rings in my head, in the voice of my real father, although he never addressed this injunction to me. But I like doing it, going by one of his sayings, which he uses when he does not see a way out of a situation. He shakes off the burden and suddenly becomes optimistic:

"Don't worry, we'll figure something out!"

I get up from my chair, go to the window, open it wide, and howl.

Translated by Raluca Manea

Ana Maria Sandu

(b. 1974)

Graduate of the Faculty of Letters of the University of Bucharest, Ana Maria Sandu is a journalist. She has published the volume of poems *From the Reminisces of a Scald-Pate* (2003) and the novels *Girl from the Boxcar* (2009) and *Kill Me!* (2010).

Sandu is interested in the feminine universe seen from a perspective that combines candor with cruelty, investigating the different ages of an abused and unfulfilled femininity.

A SORT OF JOGGING

For a long time I thought that writing wasn't something palpable. Only the books that I read succeeded in gathering and solidifying the gold dust. My words would not allow themselves to be brought to the surface so easily. Great writers resembled two-headed dragons who could easily have filled countless pages had they been in my place and had they been assigned a composition for homework. I detested them for this ability.

The afternoons passed slowly; I desperately lay in wait for words to fall into the trap so that I might then see them flow down the page. Most of the time I would end by pestering my parents for help. My words were not ready to show their faces. Not yet.

During high school, I had to walk an ugly stretch of road, about two kilometers long, each morning. I would walk while still in a state of semi-wakefulness in which the books I had read late into the night, the fear of death, and the sensation that what I was then experiencing could not possibly repeat again the next day all jumbled together. I would translate my fears into pompous words that made me more tipsy than any drink. Real writing came later. I tame it every day and still do not know which of us is stronger. Perhaps that is the reason why there are so few moments when I feel truly comfortable.

The story that made me dream more than any other is a true one. My novel *The Girl from the Boxcar* had just come out. A reader-friend who lives in Paris was eagerly awaiting it, so I had rushed to the post office to mail it. The days passed, we would continue to communicate by email, but the book had not yet arrived. I verified the address a number of times, there had been no error, there was no rational explanation for the loss of the book. A month and a half passed. My friend went to the post office where she receives her correspondence a number of times and asked whether there were any Romanians working there.

After we had lost all hope, one day the book appeared. It seemed to have been thoroughly read, my friend told me that its pages had been marked attentively. Someone in this wide world had violated my correspondence and "subtilized" (*subtilizat*) my book for a time. He or she read it and passed it on. I wish with all my heart that he or she had written a line or two so that I might know whether he or she had liked it or not.

I have thought countless times of that copy lost in some post office, or perhaps in some warehouse filled to the brim with packages; of that unknown reader who made me dream of "the power" of this profession as the critics never could have. When I doubt my reason for writing, I invoke that reader. That illicit gesture helps me.

Another time, I was sitting at a table with a writer friend. I was recounting my foreign "literary" experiences, speaking of how desirous the public is to attend readings, to see authors in flesh and blood, to ask them any number of things. My friend had participated in many events of this sort, and because we had both passed though Vienna within a space of a few months, we could compare the public, the sensations.

Since that had been the first time I had done something "live," in front of a real audience, I was nervous, afraid that no one would come on a Wednesday afternoon, especially in a city in which there are, on average, a hundred cultural events per day.

And yet about thirty people showed up. I felt good; well behaved, I listened to Katharina Stemberger, a very nice actress in vogue at that time (I had seen her the evening before in a movie I watched on television in my hotel room), who read in German some ten pages of my novel. After a time, it seemed to me as if I almost understood, as if the words sounded familiar even in a language completely unknown to me.

After the Viennese discussion, I somehow arrived at the theory that you write as you are. You cannot hide.

As if a chemical formula is responsible for the way in which you choose words and put them together. A formula similar to the one responsible for the smell of your skin, just to give one example. I am speaking about something that has traditionally been called "style," though it is much more cruel and unforgiving.

I have asked myself countless times as I read about what hides behind certain texts. Some individuals write haughtily, while others write like suicides, as if they would throw themselves into space without a safety net. Then there are those whose words stink, those aged ones, crazy and cunning, fearful, flamboyant, those who would do anything to show themselves off, those who sneak into the folds of the text. . . .

Maybe there is no logic to my theory, but I don't think it's ever played a practical joke on me. Every time I have read someone else's text and then met the author, it has been proven that he was precisely as I had imagined him. He had a certain "air" that I had found even in his writing.

I have now reached a point where I write as if I were jogging.

Every day counts. I imagine that I am serene and motivated, like any runner in this world. Perhaps that is why writing is the only moment in the day during which I feel that I become pulverized and that nothing truly touches me any longer. I lose my ties to the purest and truest reality.

My muscles tone themselves and tire simultaneously. I move and so do not reveal my age and do not detect any new cellulose. I can easily remove the nests of white strands and do not need to cut them out with the little scissors only to discover, each time, that there are more. . . .

Translated by Carla Baricz

Lucian Dan Teodorovici

(b. 1975)

A graduate of the Faculty of Letters at the Alexandru Ioan Cuza University in Iaşi, Teodorovici worked as an editor for a publishing house. He is the author of the collections of short fiction *The World Seen through a Hole the Size of a Joint* (2000), *96.00. Stories* (2002), *When I Slapped Him Twice* (2004), and *The Other Love Stories* (2009) and the novels *A Little While before the Aliens Descended among Us* (1999) and *Our Circus Presents* (2002). He also writes plays (*Zero Audience*, 2003) and film scripts; he is the co-author (together with Florin Lăzărescu) of the TV series *Animal Planet Show*.

In his exploration of everyday life, the writer underscores its grotesque and absurd aspects. He is also interested in its meditative states and in its parables, which he employs with humor and irony.

Character

Just like that: first, like a dove. The heat twirls the air into waves moving forward, toward the horizon, and the dot leaps among these airwaves, like a dove. Later on, it grows while I, the observer, am unable to say why that is. It grows and takes up a larger space from the horizon to the canopy of the sky, but this is not a problem; this canopy is utterly gigantic, and, for the most part, it stays blue. The dove, although it has grown substantially, is so insignificant compared to the immensity of the blue that one could not say that it stains it. But it grows. It keeps growing until it becomes so clear that it gets inscribed into the line that moves from the horizon, a line that most people call a road, and which I call a gray snake that wraps itself around fields, tight and suffocating, up to the place where the earth meets the sky. Finally, it grows until, under an aura made by the sun, the dove becomes an eagle, then the eagle becomes a beast hunting after its prey, and at last the beast turns into a bus emerging from the smoke of the exhaust. We continue: the bus, once it is sketched out, resembles a toy at first. After a few moments, the toy no longer resembles something that could be handled by a child, but is rather like a toy into which a child could climb. Eventually, the vehicle acquires the normal dimensions of a bus only when it gets very close to me.

I am a writer. The fields around me are green and fertile, the road resembles a snake stretched over the fields, the sun comes down with its burning rays over the place where I stand, and the bus goes by and moves away.

Just like that: first, like a bus. Then like a toy into which a child could climb. Naturally, it soon becomes a toy that the same child could handle. It's strange: although some might think that the car then gets to resemble a beast hunting after its prey, I notice that it stays a bus. One whose characteristics I can no longer make out, but which I can imagine. Even stranger: it is no longer an eagle, it no longer turns into a dove, although it already reached the other horizon and one can no longer clearly say that it follows that line which most people call a road, and I call a snake coiled up over the hills, curved and shiny. At last, the bus is lost beyond the point where the earth meets the sky, and I stay on the road, surrounded by green and fertile fields, by hills splashed in the sun that lowers its hot rays over me, by the blue and unstained canopy.

I am a writer. You are a reader. Together, we did something wrong. Distracted by the landscape and the description of the bus, we lost sight of the fact that the man who interests us all, the protagonist of the present piece, has just gone past us. He was on the bus.

Translated by Raluca Manea

Permissions

GABRIELA ADAMEŞTEANU. Excerpt from "Literature as Religion and Fear," in *The Encounter*. Iaşi: Polirom, 2003. Translated by Raluca Manea. Reprinted with the permission of Polirom.

ŞTEFAN AGOPIAN. Excerpt from "Toward a Liberal Grammar," *Amphitheater*, no. 5, May 1988. Translated by Carla Baricz. Reprinted by permission.

TUDOR ARGHEZI. "Cuts on the Arm of the Pen," in *Ars poetica*. Cluj: Dacia, 1974. Translated by Raluca Manea. Reprinted by permission.

GEORGE BACOVIA. "Gloss" (1946) and "Enough" (1926), in *Works*. Bucharest: Minerva, 1978. Translated by Carla Baricz. Reprinted by permission of Daniel Bacovia.

GEORGE BĂLĂIŢĂ. Excerpt from "The Raft on the Crest of the Wave," in *Dog on a Leash*. Viitorul Românesc, 2004. Originally in *Dilemma*, October 1995. Translated by Carla Baricz. Reprinted by permission.

CEZAR BALTAG. "Existence Starts to Gain Density," excerpted from an interview with Florin Mugur, in *The Writer's Profession*. Bucharest: Albatros, 1979. Translated by Raluca Manea. Reprinted by permission.

ION BARBU. "Notes from a Literary Confession" (1932), in *Poems, Prose, Compendium*. Bucharest: Minerva, 1997. Translated by Carla Baricz. Reprinted by permission.

LUCIAN BLAGA. "To My Readers" (1924), "Self-Portrait" (1943), and "Biography" (1929), in *At the Court of Yearning: Poems*. Translated by Andrei Codrescu. Columbus: Ohio State University Press, 1989. Reprinted with the permission of the translator.

ANA BLANDIANA. Excerpt from "Fear of Literature," in *Corridors of Mirrors*. Bucharest: Cartea Românească, 1984. Published by Editura LiterNet 2003. Translated by Carla Baricz. Reprinted by permission.

MAX BLECHER. Excerpt from *The Lucent Den*. Bucharest: Vinea Press, 1999. Translated by Carla Baricz. Reprinted by permission.

NICOLAE BREBAN. "Why Do I Write? What Do I Believe In?" *Journal of History and Literary Theory* 32, no. 3, 1984. Excerpted and translated by Raluca Manea. Reprinted by permission.

EMIL BRUMARU. Excerpt from Letter 56 to Lucian Raicu, in *The Coffee Beggar*. Iaşi: Polirom, 2004. Translated by Raluca Manea. Reprinted with the permission of Polirom.

MATEI CĂLINESCU. Excerpt from *Writing and Reading or Vice Versa*. Bloomington, September 2007. Translated by Carla Baricz. Reprinted by permission.

ION LUCA CARAGIALE. "Some Opinions" (1876) and "Letter" (1909), in *Works, Prose, Verses, Journalism, Letters*. Bucharest: Minerva, 1971. Translated by Carla Baricz.

MATEIU I. CARAGIALE. "Remember" (1924), in *Remember: The Kings of the Old Court*. Bucharest: Minerva, 1988. Translated by Carla Baricz.

ION CARAION. Excerpt from *The Syllable Hatter*. Bucharest: Cartea Românească, 1976. Translated by Carla Baricz. Reprinted by permission.

MAGDA CÂRNECI. "I Am Not So Sure," *Contrafort* 6, no. 152, 2007. Translated by Raluca Manea. Reprinted with the permission of the author.

MIRCEA CĂRTĂRESCU. Excerpts from "A Giant Drop of Water Reflecting a Chimera." January 25, August 17, 1990; February 3, 1991; July 25, 1992, from *Journal I, 1990–1996*. April 12, September 20, 1998; December 13, 1999; May 4, 2000; June 25, 2001; January 14, September 22, 2003, from *Journal II, 1997–2003*. Bucharest: Humanitas, 2001, 2005. Translated by Raluca Manea. All reprinted with the permission of Editura Humanitas.

NINA CASSIAN. "The Immigration Department," in *Call Yourself Alive? Love Poems*. Translated by Andrea Deletant and Brenda Walker. Boston: Forest Books, 1988. Reprinted with the permission of the author.

PAUL CELAN. "Partisan of the Erotical Absolute" and "Perhaps One Day" (1947), in *Romanian Poems*. Translated by Julian Semilian and Sanda Agalidi. Copyright © 2003. Reprinted with the permission of Green Integer Books, www.greeninteger.com.

RUXANDRA CESEREANU. "The Flooded Submarine" (a text prepared for a meeting with the students of the School of Philology in Cluj, 2006). Translated by Raluca Manea. Reprinted by permission.

E. M. CIORAN. Excerpt from "Advantages of Exile," in *The Temptation to Exist*. Translated by Richard Howard. Translation copyright © 1968 by Richard Howard. Reprinted by permission.

ANDREI CODRESCU. "Bi-lingual," in *Alien Candor: Selected Poems, 1970–1995*. Copyright © 1996 by Andrei Codrescu. Reprinted with the permission of David R. Godine, Publisher, Inc.

RADU COSAŞU. "My Art Was Born from Fear," in *The Work of the Novelist*. Bucharest: Cartea Românească, 1980. Translated by Carla Baricz. Reprinted with the permission of Polirom.

GHEORGHE CRĂCIUN. Excerpt from *The Body Knows More*. Piteşti: Paralela 45, 2006. Translated by Carla Baricz. Reprinted with the permission of Editura Paralela.

IOAN PETRU CULIANU. "Night," in *The Art of the Fugue: Stories*. Bucharest: Polirom, 2002. Translated by Carla Baricz. Reprinted with the permission of Polirom.

LEONID DIMOV. "The Noble Fool of Totality," in *Argument, Spectacle*. Bucharest: Cartea Românească, 1979. Translated by Raluca Manea. Reprinted by permission of the author.

VIRGIL DUDA. "The Story of a Title." Translated by Carla Baricz. Reprinted by permission.

PETRU DUMITRIU. "Cognitio incogniti," *Apostrof* 5. nos. 1–2, 1994. Translated by Raluca Manea. Reprinted with the permission of Biblioteca Apostrof.

MIRCEA ELIADE. "On Writing and Writers" (1934), in *The Road to the Center: An Anthology*, edited by Gabriel Liiceanu and Andrei Pleşu. Bucharest: Univers, 1991. Translated by Raluca Manea. Reprinted by permission.

MIHAI EMINESCU. "The Personality of the Creator" (1870), in *Of Culture and Art*. Iaşi: Junimea, 1970. Translated by Carla Baricz. Reprinted by permission. "To My Critics" (1876), in *Poems*. Translated by Leon Leviţchi and Andrei Bantaş. Bucharest: Minerva, 1978. Reprinted by permission.

CARMEN FIRAN. Excerpt from "The Power of Words." English translation by Alexandra Crides. English editing by Maurice Edwards. Reprinted by permission.

FILIP FLORIAN. "Writing and the Culinary Predilections of My Grandfather." Translated by Carla Baricz. Reprinted by permission.

BENJAMIN FUNDOIANU / BENJAMIN FONDANE. Excerpt from "A Few Wild Words" (1930) in *Privelişti / Landscapes*. Translated by Dan Solomon. Bucharest: ICR, 2004. Reprinted by permission.

BOGDAN GHIU. "'Madness' and the Art of Writing," *The Literary Daily*, no. 133, December 4–10, 2004. Translated by Raluca Manea. Used by permission of the author.

PAUL GOMA. Excerpt from "The Colors of the Rainbow," in *The Colors of the Rainbow: The Earthquake of the People*. Oradea: Biblioteca Revistei Familia, 1993. Translated by Carla Baricz. Reprinted by permission.

VINTILĂ HORIA. Excerpt from *God Was Born in Exile*. Translated by A. Lytton Sell. Copyright © 1961. Reprinted with the permission of St. Martin's Press, LLC and HarperCollins Publishers, Ltd.

FLORINA ILIS. Excerpt from "How Should I Write?" Translated by Raluca Manea. Reprinted by permission.

DOINA IOANID. "The Path to the Other." Translated by Raluca Manea. Reprinted by permission.

EUGÈNE IONESCO. Excerpt from "When I Write" (1958), in *Notes and Counter Notes: Writings on the Theatre*. Translated by Donald Watson. Copyright © 1964. Reprinted by permission of Georges Borchardt, Inc. for Editions Gallimard.

PANAIT ISTRATI. "Preface to *Adrian Zografi* or the Confessions of a Writer of our Times" (1933), in *The Life of Adrian Zografi*. Bucharest: Minerva, 1983. Translated by Raluca Manea.

NORA IUGA. "Prisoner or Master of Language?" *Literary Romania*, no. 22, June 7, 2000. Translated by Raluca Manea. Reprinted with the permission of *Literary Romania*.

MIRCEA IVĂNESCU. Excerpt from "The Text Writes Itself," interview with Titu Popescu, *The Earth*, no. 11, November 1983. Translated by Raluca Manea. Reprinted with the permission of Mircea Ivănescu.

FLORIN LĂZĂRESCU. Excerpt from "Our Special Envoy," in *Our Special Envoy*. Iaşi: Polirom, 2005. Translated by Raluca Manea. Reprinted with the permission of Polirom.

GHERASIM LUCA. "Tragedies That Must Occur," *The Immediate Life*, December 1, 1933. Translated by Raluca Manea. Reprinted by permission.

DAN LUNGU. "How I Did Not Become a Genius." Translated by Carla Baricz. Reprinted by permission.

MARIANA MARIN. "Kitty (or the Great Fear Has Come)" (1986), in *The Golden Dowry*. Bucharest: Museum of Romanian Literature, 2002. Translated by Raluca Manea. Reprinted with the permission of Editura Muzeul Literaturii Române, Bucharest.

VIRGIL MAZILESCU. "preface" and "honey on the tongue" (1979) in *Poems*. Bucharest: Vitruviu Press, 1996. Translated by Carla Baricz. Reprinted by permission.

GABRIELA MELINESCU. Excerpt from "To Write." Translated by Raluca Manea. Reprinted by permission.

FLORIN MUGUR. "That Which Remains," "The Dance with the Book," and "Stanzas," in *Sketches of Happiness*. Bucharest: Cartea Românească, 1987. Translated by Carla Baricz. Reprinted by permission.

ION MUREŞAN. "Life Undone by Poetry" and "The Poem That Cannot Be Understood," in *The Poem That Cannot Be Understood*. Târgu Mureş: Arhipelag Press, 1993. Translated by Carla Baricz. Reprinted by permission.

ALEXANDRU MUŞINA. "The Poetry of the Everyday" (1981), in *Sinapse*. Braşov: Aula, 2001. Translated by Raluca Manea.

GELLU NAUM. Excerpt from *White of the Bone* (1947), in *Poetize, poetize*. Bucharest: Eminescu, 1979. Translated by Carla Baricz. Reprinted by permission.

MIRCEA NEDELCIU. "Horizontal Man," in *Formula AS Magazine* 9, no. 371, July 1999. Translated by Raluca Manea. Reprinted with the permission of the author.

OCTAVIAN PALER. "The Second Love," in *Poems*. Bucharest: Albatros, 1998. Translated by Crisula Ştefănescu and Emily Chalmers. Reprinted by permission.

HORTENSIA PAPADAT-BENGESCU. Excerpt from "Autobiography" (1937), in *The Woman before the Mirror*. Bucharest: Minerva, 1988. Translated by Carla Baricz. Reprinted by permission.

CAMIL PETRESCU. Excerpts from footnotes in *Procrustes' Bed*. (1933). Bucharest: Minerva, 1976. Translated by Raluca Manea. Reprinted by permission of Mrs. Florica Ichim.

RADU PETRESCU. "Ill from Unwritten Books," from June 28, November 10, 1949; October 7, 1858; January 17 and 27, 1959, in *The Catalog of My Daily Movements: Journal 1946–1951 / 1954–1956*. Bucharest: Humanitas, 1999. Reprinted by permission.

RĂZVAN PETRESCU. "To Write in Despair," in *Small Changes of Attitude*. Bucharest: Allfa, 2003. Translated by Raluca Manea. Reprinted with the permission of Editura Allfa.

MARTA PETREU. "Night Letter to Tame My Beloved," in *Psychic Place*. Cluj: Dacia Press, 1991. Translated by Carla Baricz. Reprinted by permission. "The Ladder," in *Jacob's Ladder*. Bucharest: Cartea Românească, 2006. Translated by Carla Baricz. Reprinted with the permission of Polirom.

CRISTIAN POPESCU. Excerpt from "Gruelingly Squeezed Light (1990–1993)," in *Notebook for Reading and Calligraphy*. Bucharest: Vinea, 2003. Translated by Raluca Manea. Reprinted by permission.

SIMONA POPESCU. Excerpt from "The Pact with Yourself: Opus or Life?" in *Volubilis*. Pitești: Paralela 45, 1998. Translated by Raluca Manea. Reprinted with the permission of Editura Paralela.

MARIN PREDA. "The Writer and the Word," in *The Impossible Return*. Bucharest: Cartea Românească, 1971. Translated by Carla Baricz. Reprinted by permission.

LIVIU REBREANU. Excerpt from "Confessions" (1943), in *Literary Confessions*. Bucharest: Minerva, 1971. Translated by Raluca Manea. Reprinted by permission.

ANA MARIA SANDU. "A Sort of Jogging." Translated by Carla Baricz. Reprinted by permission.

MIHAIL SEBASTIAN. Excerpt from "The Curse of Writing," in *Essays, Annals, Memorial*. Bucharest: Minerva, 1972. Originally in *Rampa*, February 1935. Translated by Raluca Manea. Reprinted by permission.

ALEXANDRU SEVER. "Assyriology (The Library of Clay Books)," in *The Inventory of Circular Obsessions*. Cluj: Biblioteca Apostrof, 1999. Translated by Raluca Manea. Reprinted with the permission of Biblioteca Apostrof.

MIRCEA HORIA SIMIONESCU. Excerpt from "Wanda, or the Interpretation Syndrome," in *A Half Plus One*. Bucharest: Albatros, 1976. Translated by Carla Baricz. Reprinted by permission.

ION D. SÎRBU. Excerpt from "Not to forget . . ." (1973), in *Letters to the God Almighty*. Cluj: Biblioteca Apostrof, 1998. Translated by Raluca Manea. Reprinted with the permission of Biblioteca Apostrof.

MARIN SORESCU. "How to Be a Fakir" and "House under Surveillance," in *Censored Poems*. Translated by John Hartley Williams and Hilde Ottschofski. Reprinted with the permission of Bloodaxe Books, Ltd.

NICHITA STĂNESCU. "My Soul, Psyche," in *The Book of Rereading*. Bucharest: Cartea Românească, 1972. Translated by Carla Baricz. Reprinted by permission. "The Poet, Like the Soldier" (1971), in *Bas-Relief with Heroes: Selected Poems 1960–1982*. Translated by Thomas C. Carlson and Vasile Poienaru. Tennessee: Memphis State University Press, 1999. Reprinted by permission.

BOGDAN SUCEAVĂ. Excerpt from "The Secret Code: Notes for a Literary Confession." Translated by Raluca Manea. Reprinted by permission.

OCTAV ŞULUŢIU. "An Inner Daimon," *Facla*, no. 1321, June 20, 1935. Translated by Raluca Manea. Reprinted by permission.

LUCIAN DAN TEODOROVICI. "Character." Translated by Raluca Manea. Reprinted by permission.

DUMITRU ŢEPENEAG. "Praise of the Anonymous," *Literary Romania* 4, no. 23, January 1969. Translated by Carla Baricz. Reprinted with the permission of *Literary Romania*.

CONSTANTIN ŢOIU. Excerpt from "The Team Passing through the World," *Literary Romania*, no. 18, May 2, 1991. Translated by Raluca Manea. Reprinted with the permission of *Literary Romania*.

FLOAREA ŢUŢUIANU. "The Art of Seduction" and "La femme poison," in *The Art of Seduction*. Translated by Adam J. Sorkin and Irma Giannetti. Bucharest: Vinea, 2002. Reprinted by permission.

TRISTAN TZARA. "It Evenings," translated by Julian Semilian and Sanda Agalidi, and "Introduction to Don Quixote," translated by Julian Semilian, from *Born in Utopia: An Anthology of Modern and Contemporary Romanian Poetry*, edited by Carmen Firan and Paul Doru Mugur. New Jersey: Talisman House, 2006. Reprinted with the permission of Julian Semilian.

MATEI VIŞNIEC. "The Falling Crumbs" and "As Clothes Grown Too Large." Translated by Carla Baricz. Reprinted by permission.

ALEXANDRU VLAD. "I Am Always Behind," in *The Glass Lamp*. Cluj: Grinta, 2002. Translated by Raluca Manea. Reprinted with the permission of the author.

Writers / Works Index

NORMAN MANEA left Romania in 1986, spent a year in West Berlin, and arrived in the United States in 1988. He is a Francis Flournoy Professor of European Culture and writer in residence at Bard College, and his literary work has been translated into more than twenty languages. He has received, among other awards, Guggenheim and MacArthur grants in the United States, the Nonino International Literary Prize in Italy, and the Prix Médicis Étranger in France. He is a member of the Berlin Academy of Art and was honored by the French government with the Ordre des Arts et des Lettres of highest rank.

SANDA CORDOŞ is Associate Professor in the Faculty of Letters at Babeş-Bolyai University in Cluj-Napoca and head of the Department of Romanian Literature. She has contributed articles and essays to prestigious literary reviews in Romania and is the author of the volumes *Literature between Revolution and Reaction* (1999), *Alexandru Ivasiuc* (2001), *In the New World* (2003), and *Why Should We Keep Reading Literature?* (2004). She is also the editor of *The Critic's Spirit in the Sibiu Literary Circle* (2009) and has collaborated on a number of anthologies and lexicographical studies, including *Kindlers Literatur Lexikon* (2009).

CARLA BARICZ was born and grew up in Suceava, Romania, and earned a BA from Columbia University in English and comparative literature. She currently resides in New Haven, Connecticut, where she is pursuing a dual PhD in English literature and in Renaissance studies at Yale University.

RALUCA MANEA grew up in Bucharest, where her family still lives. A 2005 graduate of Harvard College, she currently resides in New York City, where she is pursuing a doctorate in French literature at New York University. Her research interests include contemporary French and American poetry, the poetics of place, and critical theory.